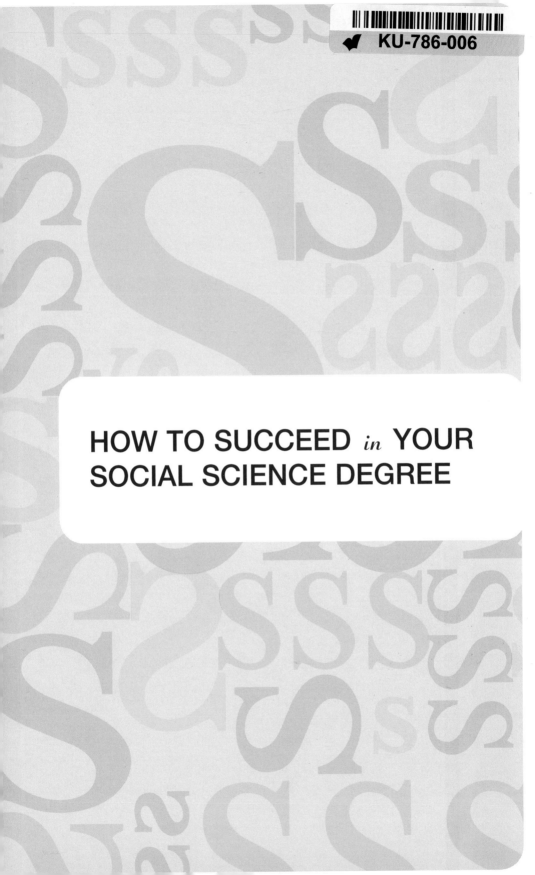

HOW TO SUCCEED *in* YOUR SOCIAL SCIENCE DEGREE

5405 0000 390799
21/11/12

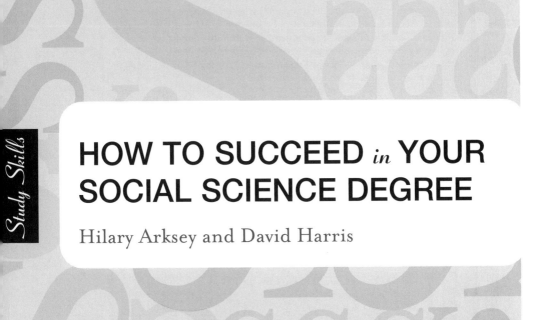

HOW TO SUCCEED *in* YOUR SOCIAL SCIENCE DEGREE

Hilary Arksey and David Harris

Study Skills

SAGE Publications

Los Angeles • London • New Delhi • Singapore

First published 2007

SAGE Publications Ltd
1 Oliver's Yard
55 City Road
London EC1Y 1SP

SAGE Publications Inc.
2455 Teller Road
Thousand Oaks, California 91320

SAGE Publications India Pvt Ltd
B 1/I 1 Mohan Cooperative Industrial Area
Mathura Road, New Delhi 110 044
India

SAGE Publications Asia-Pacific Pte Ltd
33 Pekin Street #02-01
Far East Square
Singapore 048763

Library of Congress Control Number: 2006932711

British Library Cataloguing in Publication data

A catalogue record for this book is available
from the British Library

ISBN 978-1-4129-0225-0
ISBN 978-1-4129-0226-7 (pbk)

Typeset by C&M Digitals (P) Ltd., Chennai, India
Printed and bound in Great Britain by The Cromwell Press, Trowbridge, Wiltshire
Printed on paper from sustainable resources

Dedication

This book is a salute to our respective missing or absent heroes, people who touched our lives and who would champion efforts like this intended to help future rising stars learn the trade while manoeuvring the thrills and spills of the academic roller coaster.

Contents

About the Authors

Hilary Arksey is a Senior Research Fellow in the Social Policy Research Unit at the University of York. Her research interests lie in the areas of informal care, employment and disability, and qualitative research methods. Hilary co-authored *Interviewing for Social Scientists: An Introductory Resource with Examples* with Peter Knight.

David Harris has been teaching undergraduates and postgraduates since 1973. He has taught courses in Education, Leisure Studies, Media Studies and Sociology. Publications include *Teaching Yourself Social Theory* (Sage, 2003), and *Key Concepts in Leisure Studies* (Sage, 2005). He has made recent contributions to various journals and to international collections, including handbooks in Distance Education, Leisure Studies and Sociology. His research interests include sociological approaches to electronic learning and distance education. Further details are available from his personal website at http://www.arasite.org/

Acknowledgements

We are grateful to colleagues who shared with us their ideas and sources of information about both study skills and research skills. We would also like to acknowledge the support we received from those students who completed the questionnaire survey; their responses form the basis of Chapter 2. Our families and friends have helped in the usual innumerable ways. We would like to thank particularly the support staff and librarians at the College of St Mark and St John. Janette Colclough, Sue Grace, Christine Skinner and Janice Simpson from the University of York provided Hilary with very valuable advice. Our special thanks go to Sally Pulleyn for her excellent secretarial support.

Many thanks to the Sage team, especially Chris Rojek, Mila Steele, Susan Dunsmore and Katherine Haw.

Introduction

Why another book on study skills? This one takes a different approach, based more on research in, and experience of, higher education. It offers students of social sciences a chance to use social science itself to understand the university, increasing competence in both areas.

Conventional Study Skills

You will have probably encountered some of these in taking your entry qualifications at school or college. We think that study skills are often presented as rather abstract approaches to a range of basic general activities involved in learning. Activities include being able to read effectively, take notes from a variety of sources, memorize sufficient material and prepare mentally for examinations. Important as these skills may be, they leave out a good deal of background understanding, and they often seem to generalize from secondary education and the requirements of unseen national examinations. Advice on how to write effective assignments on university courses specifically come nearer to what we take to be more important matters. Here students are introduced to some of the rather specialized requirements of university work, especially in the social sciences – they are urged to attempt to write or present a seminar in a 'balanced' manner, to be 'objective' or 'critical', to focus on the evidence.

You should set out to become more familiar with terms like these and learn to apply them to your own work. You can rapidly gain a working understanding of terms like 'balanced argument' by remembering that it is important to consider a range of alternative approaches and arguments. Being 'objective' is not too far from the usual notion of trying to step back from personal feelings to see the problem rather more technically. Being 'critical' does not mean just disagreeing with an approach or a piece of work, and this term can carry 'ordinary' unhelpful meanings of being aggressive and hostile. In academic life, it means something more technical again, something more like 'seeing both strengths and weaknesses'. These are brief definitions, and you will need to think about these terms in more depth and in the context of actual assignments. It is clear that if you can understand them, you can begin to meet the criteria without having to think out the specifics on each occasion: with practise, they will become almost like second nature.

Conventional 'skills' cannot be guaranteed to work for everyone in every situation. It is particularly misleading to think of them as magical formulae, or as 'technical fixes' that will overcome the problems of studying at university just on their own. You will need high levels of motivation to do well at university, and a fair bit of stamina. You will not get much time to find your feet or to develop commitment gradually, since assessment requirements appear early on. You need to perform at higher and more demanding levels as the course proceeds. The good news is that the majority of students do survive and do gain a degree at the end, and generally find themselves satisfied with their experiences overall. We have met many students who did not feel very confident that they would succeed at all in the beginning, but who still made that short trip across the stage at the Graduation ceremony to receive their degree at the end of their three or four years of studies.

Beyond Conventional Study Skills

This book sets out to help you to 'work smarter', to learn to cope as quickly as possible, to do as well as you can, and to have time to enjoy the other things that university life can offer. Gaining the maximum benefit, both academically and socially, is what supports and increases motivation and commitment. Feeling secure about the requirements and how to meet them is the initial goal.

It is this 'practical' focus that new students often seem to lack. It is quite understandable, given the powerful emotions that can be attached to university entrance and that we have sketched above. It is hard to be technical and dispassionate if you feel that you have a lot to prove. Nevertheless, we think that developing such a focus may well be the key to university success.

One way of putting this is to draw upon some of the classic approaches of doing sociological research itself. There is a technique called 'ethnography' which you will soon encounter if you have not done so already. What happens is that the researcher goes off to attempt to understand the culture and the way of life of a particular social group as the members themselves see it. In the early days, this group would often be members of another society remote from Britain or even Europe. Anthropologists would go off to spend time living with groups of people in Africa, Australia or Polynesia. These days, ethnographers also study social groups that they are likely to encounter in their own societies – bikers, drug-takers, musicians, homosexuals, street traders, professional sportsmen, even students.

Doing ethnography requires the researcher to try to investigate and understand the values, beliefs and behaviours of the group in question, without immediately condemning them. It is necessary to keep your own beliefs in the background, so to speak. Anthropologists rapidly encountered activities that a British academic would possibly find distasteful or immoral, for example. The way animals, enemies, or outsiders were treated in non-industrial societies can still seem shocking today when you read those early accounts. Nevertheless, the point was to try to understand the behaviour even if we do not approve of cock-fighting, animal sacrifice, cannibalism or the killing of surplus old folk. It is worth saying that early anthropologists sometimes did not manage this dispassionate approach very well in practice – it does require some thought and some self-reflection.

Similarly, modern ethnographers often join groups in order to try and understand them from within. This technique is usually called 'participant observation', and the idea is that you can understand people better if you attempt to see their world as they see it. Of course, the risk is that you will simply become another member of the group and forget about research – this used to be called 'going native', and there are still stories circulating about sociology students who joined packs of bikers and enjoyed it so much that they never came back to university. Ethnographers have therefore experimented with some form of limited participation – participating enough to understand, but also preserving a critical stance.

To take one classic case, Humphreys undertook to investigate the behaviour of men who would visit public toilets in the USA in order to enjoy sexual contacts with other men. Humphreys was not himself interested in actually engaging in these activities, and so his first problem was arranging to observe the activities without having to actually participate. The book (Humphreys, 1970) contains some explicit descriptions of what the men did to each other, but there is no moral comment. Humphreys' personal feelings are not prominent, even though we know they probably have affected his research to some extent. The same calm description and reflection are found in other famous studies too – Becker et al. ([1968] 1995) on students bending the rules on assessment, Wacquant (1995) on the world of the professional boxer, or Bourdieu (2000) on Algerian responses to modernization.

Reading classic ethnographic studies like this will, we hope, encourage you to apply the same procedures to your university experience. You may have strong feelings about universities and academic life. They are not always very positive feelings, as we have indicated, and even the most enthusiastic and committed can still experience anxiety and confusion. The solution, we think, is to become an ethnographer, both participating and observing, not jumping to conclusions, not letting stereotypes take the place of understanding. Wolcott (1999: 39) calls it 'deep hanging out'. Ethnographers play their way in, they set out to learn, they manage their own initial feelings of confusion and doubt in order to find out what is going on, not only in university settings, but on placement as well. Students of social science have a great advantage here because you will actually be discussing research techniques, including ethnography, and you can then become expert in understanding your own immediate surroundings as well.

Ethnographic approaches involve an intention to understand. In other words, they are educational in their own right. Sometimes we want to understand others just in order to perform better ourselves, and get what we want. This is the kind of thing advocated in Williams et al. (2006) who suggest that applicants for prestige jobs spend time researching the organizations to which they are applying in order to maximize their performance at interview or at the Assessment Centre. Sometimes this leads to feelings that applicants then have to 'play a game' and present some kind of false impression of themselves at interview. This can make applicants rather uncomfortable – 'purists' feel they are misrepresenting themselves and will never really feel happy in the job even if they get it, while 'players' are never quite sure how much to embroider their CVs without getting caught.

At the earlier stage of going to university, things are less complex ethically and personally, perhaps. You do not have to commit yourself too early. You can explore different possibilities and different ways of behaving or acting, and observe others and learn from them. This is not just an exercise in learning how to pose as something you are not: it is educational in its own right. It is about exploring the lives of others. It is what social scientists do. It is valuable and it is also interesting.

We have written this book to try to encourage an ethnographic approach to academic life and to study. Much of our focus is on the business of tackling assignments and coping with assessment because we know this is a major initial concern. The usual approach in 'study skills' material is to give you a list of techniques and rules to pursue. This can help, but it would be exactly like giving an ethnographer a short tourist guide: deeper understanding is really required. Conventional study skills material provides only a limited understanding. It often tells you the most immediate and obvious things to do, and these are unlikely to fit your exact circumstances anyway. It would be absurd to think of there being short and quick 'right answers' to educational problems – and even if we provided you with some, they would soon become well known and stale. Far better, we think, is to get you to understand the culture of academic life, to understand why things happen in the way that they do, and to understand your own reactions. Once more, social science students have an advantage because they are being encouraged to 'look beneath the surface' of social and cultural life almost everywhere else – why not do it with universities too?

To get in the mood, why not ask yourself what Wolcott insists is the key question for intending ethnographers: 'Where … do you think you are going?' You could even list what you expect universities to actually be like:

- **What will the other people be like? Will they be cleverer than me?**

- **What will the work be like? Will it be all lectures? How much reading will I have to do each week? What is a seminar exactly? How often will I be tested – every week?**

- **What worries me most? Coping with the work? Managing on a loan or grant? Coping with family demands?**

- **Who can I turn to for support? Will I make new friends easily? What does a personal tutor do?**

- **What will be the best things about it?**

- **What will it feel like to graduate?**

Returning to the issues of guilt and anxiety we began with, perhaps you should also ask yourself: 'Where have I come from?':

- **Do I really have anything to worry about and, if so, what is it exactly? Did I worry about earlier stages and was the worry justified?**

- **Have I shown I am adaptable and able to learn?**

- **What do I have of value to offer?**

- **What can people like me get from university?**

- **What can people like me contribute to university?**

As you go through the book you will see that our advice is entirely optimistic about any of these problems you may worry about. We have seen generations of students turn up feeling insecure and uncertain, and we have seen those very same students flourish and succeed.

The people might well be different from the ones you know already, but they will not usually be aiming to make you feel inferior. There might be some initial jockeying for status and approval, and you might be unlucky enough to encounter a few people who will try to use others as a foil to make themselves look and feel superior. You can assert yourself against this sort of tactic, and we suggest some techniques in the section on verbal skills especially. More importantly, you will meet people who could well be friends for the rest of your life, people who will extend your horizons and help you round out as a person.

The work will be challenging, but not impossible. You will have to learn to manage it, and deal with deadlines and difficulties – but also develop some of the pleasures of doing academic work at an adult level, finding your own interests and learning how to use academic resources to develop academic arguments. We will be offering a range of advice on managing academic work, but suggesting above all that you try to understand the underlying principles of work in social sciences rather than just use the usual 'study skills' techniques you have probably encountered already. If you establish what is actually required first, it makes it easier to plan your work and use the time available to best effect. Down time, away from academic study, is an important activity too, necessary for pleasurable learning and for maintaining motivation and commitment. The even better news is that leisure activities (broadly defined) can even be useful in the search for jobs at the end of your university career.

You will need a *support network*, and it is a mistake to think you need to cope strictly on your own. The network of family and friends you have already needs to be maintained, and you will also find support from fellow-students. You will also find that tutors and academic staff also want to help. You might have a personal tutor allocated to you, with a role that includes looking after your welfare and helping you cope with non-academic concerns (housing, finance, careers, or course choice, for example). Even academic staff want to help, and not pose entirely as assessors of your worth and morals. New students might not realize, for example, that lectures and seminars are intended to help cover a topic and show how to discuss it critically, often in a technical sense as we suggested above. Academic skills are being demonstrated, and you can learn much from seeing this actually done in detail. Assessment items often assume that students will have taken full advantage of such demonstrations: you are seldom expected to go away and cope with an essay or exam all on your own. The advice available from staff is often substantially under-used – new students feel embarrassed or otherwise unable to ask for help, although something like an essay plan discussed with your tutor can make a real difference to your efforts.

You will enjoy your university or college career. We cite many examples of this in what follows. Your enjoyment does not have to be at the expense of academic work, and may even combine with it. When you graduate, you will feel marvellous, everyone will be proud of you, you will have gained a valuable qualification that will help you get a good job, and you will miss your university or college afterwards.

We hope you will enjoy reading the discussion that follows in this book. We have tried to make it a discussion because we do not want just to hector you to work harder. We want you to think of building on the skills you have already, identifying any shortfalls at an early stage so you can get help if necessary and practise any new skills you might need. Our approach involves you trying to research the university, to find out what it values. There may well be an initial stage where the aim is to survive and cope with the novelty of it all. Then you might want to maximize your efforts to do more than just survive, but to do as well as you can. Finally, you will be thinking about operating as an independent

Honours level student. Although it might seem impossibly distant at the moment, everyone will tell you that that final year arrives very rapidly.

The main points to bear in mind now can be quickly summarized here:

1 Begin your quest for a good job as soon as possible. Think about constructing a better and fuller CV or résumé from the very beginning. You need to think of making the most of what you are doing at university, both academically and socially. So undertaking a short survey might not count much towards your actual assessment profile, but it is a valuable skill to offer employers. Taking an active part in leisure activities can also be turned into evidence of some employable qualities, as we suggest.

2 Try to adopt the stance of an ethnographer towards your new surroundings. You will be encouraged to take this stance if you do work placements, of course – you need to find out how to behave normally and effectively in a placement school, community or hospital. However, you can take the same stance to academic work too. Try to establish what is actually required in assessment terms, for example, what are the official criteria, but, even more importantly, how are they applied in practice? What is going on in lectures and seminars and what do they tell us about mysterious but valued practices like 'developing an argument'? You will not be starting completely afresh, but you do need to explore the specifics of your university or college too.

3 Finally, try to deepen your insight and expertise. There is little point in trying to memorize specific regulations, for example, although you may need a definitive copy to consult at times. Far better, much research suggests, is trying to get a general idea of how to do things which you can make your own and then apply to new and different situations. In particular, there is much to be gained from thinking about academic argument and how to understand and then do it. If you grasp that, much of the more specific advice – about referencing, meeting criteria in assessment, making effective notes from books or lectures, finding yourself able to participate in seminars – falls into place.

Part 1

University Life and Employability

1 Starting Off

CHAPTER OVERVIEW

- Building on (conventional) study skills.
- Adjusting to a new environment – adopting a research stance.
- Developing basic competence in academic work.
- Dealing with problems of social adjustment.
- Students from 'unconventional' backgrounds.
- Mature students.

We are focusing on requirements that depend not just on skills but on an understanding of the culture, values, and beliefs of higher education teaching. Luckily, if you are studying social sciences, you will be given some useful theoretical tools and perspectives which are designed to help you understand other organizations and other ways of life, but which can also be applied to university life too. We discuss later a few suggestions based on the work of Bourdieu or Goffman, for example, to help understand universities and social distinction, and social interaction respectively. You might well have encountered these writers already in your preparatory courses, but a quick summary might help you recall their work (Box 1.1).

Box 1.1   Some Sociological Insights

Pierre Bourdieu (1930–2002) was a French social theorist whose writings have been influential in a number of fields, including the sociology of

(Continued)

(Continued)

education (for example, in M. Young, 1971), the sociology of culture and leisure (1984), and research methods (1984, 2000). His work helps us realize that universities have a long history in preserving the powers and privileges of elite groups, for example. This history gets embodied in the very style ('aesthetic') of university life, its practices, the judgements used to evaluate people, and its assessment practices. These aspects of university life are held unconsciously and thus uncritically, and are often thought to be simply the only way to do things. It should be easy to see what follows – those from elite backgrounds will adapt straightaway to university life and find it 'natural'. By contrast, if you are not from an elite background, you will find aspects of academic life rather strange at first. We assume, in fact, that many readers of this book will indeed come from non-elite backgrounds, benefiting from the great expansion of university education in the UK and other countries which has produced a much more diverse student body than before.

Erving Goffman (1922–82) was an acute observer of social interactions, and he published some fascinating material on social exchanges between people in a variety of everyday settings (for example, 1963, 1969, 1975). Although his work is rather dated, and is mostly based on American social life, it can help you grasp what is going on in seminars as much as in any other kind of interaction – people will be doing impression management, playing roles of various kinds, trying to manipulate various props and settings, and so on. They might also be trying to gain a social advantage or diminish the efforts of others, behaviour which newcomers to university seminars can come to fear. Goffman sometimes analyses extreme cases of processes such as 'stigmatization' to help draw attention to much more routine and 'normal' interaction. Although it is very unlikely that you will encounter any particularly unpleasant stigmatization, understanding such behaviour is one way to help overcome more common versions, we want to argue.

Higher Education as Initiation

It is possible to borrow initial ideas like these from work in social sciences to begin to grasp what is actually involved culturally and socially in attending higher education. You will need to understand what is going on as quickly as possible so that you can live your life effectively as a member of 'the

University', and, later, as a member of an organization in which you work. This may involve some initial puzzlement as your existing conceptions of university or academic life are stretched to fit the new circumstances. Much will depend on the sort of institution you have been attending before, of course. In some ways, universities will be quite similar to the colleges and schools you will have just left. However, there will be new practices and new social relationships as well, and you will not necessarily want to just reproduce your old ways of coping, nor the assumptions which underpin them.

The stages involved are rather similar to those followed by researchers who go out to study unusual social groups, or communities in other countries. As recent anthropological writing indicates, the first stage is to manage leaving home. You may be physically leaving home to go and live in another city, or you may be 'leaving home' in the sense of developing a new independence. This can be difficult and involve challenges which can make you feel insecure. There are a number of ways to overcome this initial insecurity (Box 1.2).

Box 1.2   Anticipatory Problems

What do you think will be the main problems you face at university?
What would be the worst that could happen?
How would you overcome these problems? Compare your answers with our views as we go through.
Keep a record of these views and look at them again once you have settled in.

Entering the Field

You will want to leave home in the senses described above, but also to remember who you were in the first place. It seems that many students, especially from non-elite backgrounds, are afraid they will lose their culture and identity once they go to university. They are afraid they will have to give up everything they believed in, turn their back on their family and friends, and change their lives, their manners of speech, even their leisure pursuits and tastes. (We are not condemning these views as part of a rant about 'students these days', of course.) They will often still need support from home, however. It is fair to say that this might have proved quite a challenge for a working-class student entering an elite university in the 1960s, but it is not necessary to fear a total break with the past these days.

Higher education has become much more a part of normal life than it used to be, with far more people attending university, and you are likely to meet a range of people at university now, many of whom will be like you. The 'absented-minded professor' or other-worldly 'Don' of popular imagery is a vanishing species (Box 1.3). Having said that, some differences will remain, of course, including those of a generational kind. Universities are far more aware of their obligations to tolerate or even celebrate the social diversity of their student intake, and to try to encourage everyone to achieve to the best of their ability. It is important for students to do this too, though.

Box 1.3   What Is a Typical Lecturer?

Describe a typical university lecturer. What is this description based upon exactly?
Dave has asked student groups to say what they expected 'Dr Harris' would be like. Answers included:

1   an elderly schoolteacher wearing a gown and riding a woman's bike;
2   a man in his thirties trying to be 'down with the kids' wearing clothes that were fashionable five years ago and using equally outdated street slang;
3   someone who looked like a student revolutionary of the 1960s, complete with Afro hair, tanktop and sandals;
4   an accountant, wearing a suit and carrying a new briefcase.

The usual advice on encountering any strange social group is to see it as a challenge. Like all challenges, there will be a mixture of adventure and insecurity. All students face similar problems of managing credit and debts, and balancing academic and other commitments. These are important to a sense of well-being and will need to be tackled early. There are more specific challenges too. If you are a young person, you will want to push on and explore new aspects of your life – new friends, new leisure pursuits, and become relatively independent financially. Mature students may well face different challenges – returning to education, mixing with young people to whom they are not related, but who are similar to their own kin, encountering a wider range of reading material, and so on. In both cases, it is a matter of finding the optimal level of challenge, of course, resisting experiences that are too challenging and that cause insecurity at first.

You will find you are able to face more and more challenges as your confidence grows, but you might at first want to identify some sources of security as well. Obviously, you will still have friends and family from your old lives, and you will have to find a way to relate to them. Some students prefer a clean break, at least initially, while others visit their old haunts pretty frequently in the early days. Clearly, one factor will be whether you have far to travel to return home.

You will soon acquire new friends and acquaintances in the new situation, and they will be able to act as a source of esteem and support. Nearly all universities make a substantial effort to encourage feeling at home in the first few weeks and you will have a range of activities on offer for Freshers' Week. Students need to select their activities, of course, but shrewd ones may already be thinking of building their CVs as well as their immediate interests in joining clubs, teams and societies.

Surviving the First Challenges

Like all newcomers, you will want to feel that you can survive first of all. There are important matters such as housing and finance to arrange, and you should be thinking of these as soon as you accept a place. There are many guides available to help you and to warn against the usual pitfalls, especially for younger students, such as running up large bills on credit cards in your first few months, perhaps because you have not arranged an adequate overdraft or other borrowing facilities, or because you have not yet settled down as a consumer. These problems also face those who are moving away to get their first job, of course. A good relationship with parents or guardians, one where you can get free advice on finance or housing, is invaluable. Student Unions also usually provide good advice, together with the banks on the campus.

You will have to think about tackling some assignments pretty early on as well, and it is important not to get off on the wrong foot. This may be unlike your experience before, but it is essential to avoid the major academic crime – plagiarism. Plagiarism, which we can define broadly as copying other people's work and passing it off as your own, can get you immediately punished, stigmatized, and possibly even expelled from the university. Many first-year students can blunder into a series of demoralizing experiences by getting this wrong before they have really even begun.

Our job is not to join in the strong moral outcry against plagiarism, which we discuss at considerable length later on, but simply to explain that the tough reaction involves one of those strong beliefs and values found at university. It is not a set of beliefs and values of which many people outside university are particularly aware. Nevertheless, the rules have to be understood, explored and followed, much as a visitor to another country would rapidly have to learn the rules about behaviour in public. While you are at university, the need to avoid plagiarism will involve important conventions which you will have to learn and apply in almost everything you do for assessment purposes.

Developing Greater Competence

If all goes well, you will have survived your transition, and realized that universities are places where you can live and work reasonably comfortably. The next step is to begin to do more than just survive – to learn to cope, and eventually to do well. You will know when you achieved this first stage – no longer will you have to ask for directions, you will have your timetable sorted out, you will have learned a few names of people in your tutorial, and your domestic life will have settled down into something like a new routine. And, if you are a recent arrival in the city, you will know the shops, bars and restaurants where you get best value for money.

It can be interesting to meet newcomers to universities and to realize just how much the old hands take for granted. It is not immediately obvious, for example, that lectures are attended by everyone, but that students will have only one seminar group assigned to them which they are expected to attend. Similarly, timetables usually just indicate 'contact time' – occasions when students will be meeting tutors and each other. We have met newcomers who assume that they have no academic work to do during the rest of the time. Some have even complained that they 'are only in for two days a week'! Of course, much of the rest of the time is expected to be spent in the library, preparing academic work, meeting tutors and preparing for the contact time: the standards expected often simply assume this sort of steady background working.

Coping well involves you in balancing a number of demands on your time. The usual ones can be classified as social, economic and academic demands. Academic work has to be balanced and limited if you are to cope. It is not only that you may need to earn a living, or run a family, or have a good time socially in order to stay happy. Academic work, especially in social sciences, has no boundaries of its own to help to regulate your efforts. There are always more books to read, more articles to collect, more ideas to explore. Every interesting argument you read will reference a dozen or so additional readings, and when you track those down, they will refer you to still more readings, and so on. You can easily feel swamped.

There will be a syllabus for each course, but academic work in social science as a whole is vast and unmanageable. You may be disconcerted to find that the social science courses you have taken before are often quite different from university ones. We have met students who have either tried desperately to cling to what they know, or unrealistically attempted to learn it all, and have then realized it is impossible to do so. Your task, realistically speaking, is not to fully master the topic, the works of an author, or an entire argument, but to achieve a good working level of competence – not a total competence. This will mean that many arguments, references, and research findings have to be left unexamined for now and postponed until later. A lot of ambiguity will have to be tolerated. This will not mean that you are not a 'proper' student – it is part of the culture of being an academic, accepting that there will always be new areas to explore, new work appearing, new research findings, realizing that nothing is ever easily closed off, and that certainties are rare.

The situation can be more complicated if you are being taught on a number of courses, perhaps on a modular programme. Here, you will encounter enthusiasts who will encourage you to become an expert in one specialism, only to move on to your next module to meet a similar demand. On a typical social sciences course, you will meet experts in research methodology, theory, policy and practice. You will be expected to perform well across a wide variety of assessment tasks, ranging from writing thoughtful and critical essays on theoretical topics to demonstrating effective job skills on a work placement. It is rare indeed to feel you have mastered everything, especially in the first few months. The direction of your studies will become clearer as you progress, though, and you will be able to specialize a bit.

If you judge yourself entirely by an ability to fully grasp academic work in social sciences immediately, you are likely to be disappointed. The feeling is made worse if you come to university worried that you will be the only one in the group who does not understand the work. This feeling has been researched and discussed, in fact, and it seems to haunt particular categories of students such as mature female working-class ones. Perhaps we need to say again that we are not reproachful of such students or singling them out as offering 'problems', but simply trying to understand and sympathize. Part of the transition we discussed above, leaving home, involves trying to come to terms with any feelings of inferiority that past experience may have prompted.

To cope in university, you may need to set out to find what is required in academic work, and to deliver that first. If there is time available, without sacrificing other crucial areas like socializing and leisure as well as paid work or unpaid work in families, you can explore more deeply. Deep satisfactions and pleasures are available to the successful academic, and finding out what is required can lead to those pleasures. It is not always a matter of having to conform to the requirements of others, having to suppress your personal opinions, and having to reproduce other people's views all the time, as we shall see.

How do you know what is required to cope? How do ethnographers know how to cope in strange societies? A research orientation, explored further in Chapter 8, is helpful. Just as you would do on fieldwork, you spend time at first observing, listening and watching how other people act and behave. You try to be objective about the situation. You check out your own initial ideas, on tackling seminars, say, by looking at how other people perform, especially those who seem to perform successfully. You will be observing a range of other students, other friends, tutors and lecturers themselves. You are trying to find out 'how things are done around here'. Do not feel isolated or defensive if you encounter unusual ways of doing things, but be prepared to play your way in. Reserve your judgement at first, and avoid jumping to immediate conclusions about yourself, other people or situations. These are, of course, exactly the skills you need to be an effective social scientist or professional in the social services.

If you remain unsure, get help. As tutors, we are still surprised how little students come to ask us for help. We can advise about study plans for essays, study skills of various kinds, additional reading for the enthusiastic, basic reading for the so far uncommitted. We do not denounce people who do not share our values. We (or our specialist librarian colleagues) have endless patience in explaining how to use libraries and electronic search engines when trying to trace books or journal articles on particular topic areas. We write helpful and informative comments on student essays (but are often surprised to find how few students read them through). Naturally, there are familiar social barriers between students and ourselves – we are usually older, supposedly more expert, and not subject to formal assessment. Perhaps students think we will be fond of scolding them, expressing low opinions of modern youth or working women, or interested in seducing the more attractive ones? We are not sure where these strange expectations of tutors come from, but they can get in the way.

You may encounter different sorts of tutors in fact, and be assigned to a 'personal tutor', someone with a particular responsibility for 'pastoral' matters. These include offering advice and help if there is a need to claim extenuating circumstances in assessment, referring students to specialist medical, legal, careers or counselling services, or just generally listening to how things are going. Personal tutors can often represent you if you wish, in a range of areas such as claiming extenuating circumstances for late submission of work, or solving problems with missing library cards. Student unions also may have specialist officers to help.

Our advice is not to let stereotypes get in the way of contacting tutors – if actual experience leads to an unhelpful encounter, try another tutor until you find a more compatible one. For the more confident student, contact with tutors can have the additional benefit of making sure that they understand constraints you may be facing in the short term. If you have written a disappointing piece of work, for example, you will want to make sure that your tutor realizes that there were adverse circumstances responsible in this particular case, and that you want to do better next time. Some students may wish to do this entirely cynically, but most of them would simply wish to explain the context. Tutors try very hard not to leap to conclusions about you, and you can help us by explaining the circumstances.

Performing Competently in Assessed Work

You will see from the discussions that follow that we urge you to take a professional stance towards assessed work, finding out what is required, and knowing how best to deliver it. You might start by finding out about the grading schemes in operation. These can be found in student handbooks or course materials. Depending on your experience, you might find the vocabulary a little strange. In universities in England and Wales, for example, degree awards are classified into the categories of first, upper second (or 2:1), lower second (2:2), third, pass and fail. In the future, further classifications might be added – there is some support at the moment for offering some kind of 'starred first', for example. These can rapidly acquire an informal social standing, so that getting a 2:2 is something to be dreaded and seen as akin to failure, although in practice they are still considered to be 'good' degrees, and their value to employers is still acceptable, as we shall see.

More important, we think, is that students understand how these classifications are defined and explained, what the grading criteria are which lead to one rather than another. Again, we discuss this in more detail below, but it might be helpful to begin to think of different types of competencies being required (Box 1.4).

Box 1.4   Basic Requirements

1   Basic competencies and requirements are usually specified as being able to express yourself adequately, and avoid plagiarism.
2   More advanced competencies include covering (summarizing) the arguments in the background reading adequately, showing a good knowledge of methodology or deploying suitable concepts.
3   Advanced competencies turn on offering critical analysis, theoretically informed reflection, new insights, a wide range of alternative perspectives.

We have suggested a simplified version of these requirements in terms of making sure you offer competent coverage and summary, with some suitable additional academic comment, as you will see. The main point though is to find out about the criteria your institution uses, and become familiar with them, so that you can deliver assignments that show how you have complied with the requirements. As your confidence grows, you might feel able to explore a little more widely.

Social Acceptance

It could be argued that tutors in social science subjects should be particularly able to understand the problems and cultures of the students they teach. Of all specialists, they should best know about problems relating to low esteem and low confidence; they should best understand the cultural and social barriers that block effective communication; and they should subscribe to the old principle that 'to understand all is to forgive all'.

Let us air a matter that often lies behind student anxiety and ineffective performance. Both elitism and snobbery used to be quite common in universities, and you may still encounter them these days as well. Social divisions can also take the forms of current tensions in youth culture, where social esteem is based upon looking good or having the right tastes in music or leisure activities. Our argument is that if you understand what is going on, as a researcher might, you are less likely to be adversely affected personally.

Perhaps the first problem is being able to determine whether you have encountered a genuine 'put down' or whether you are just experiencing an alternative way of behaving that you have not come across before. If you have done any social science before, you will know that it is not always easy to judge people's intentions from observing their actions. People just do behave differently, and, in particular, they can act a part, sometimes ironically, perhaps when they are feeling insecure themselves. Acting ironically is well described as an aspect of popular culture, seen best, perhaps, in the deliberate use of 'bad taste' items. People like going to dreadful films (sentimental camp musicals, or low-budget horrors), or wearing *Top Gun* t-shirts (no offence intended if you are a fan, of course). The pleasures are rather complex in these cases, and can be aggressive, but they are familiar enough.

In more routine social interactions, people can pretend to be snobbish, sexist or racist, deliberately, as a kind of self-parody, showing they know that people expect them to behave like that. In a recent meeting, a male colleague loudly, patronizingly and entirely ironically congratulated the women for being the first to tidy up the room afterwards, for example.

However, what is often called 'elitism' can be a serious issue, and may still operate in some universities. We might try to be reasonably objective about it by considering the practice as a form of social discrimination. We have already argued that this could be a legacy from the time when universities in the UK were colonized by the (often male and white) offspring of middle-class families, and most academics were themselves middle class, with one or two admirable exceptions. The style in which they did things, and the values they held themselves, deeply influenced academic work itself. The best example, perhaps, concerns the central issue of objectivity and detachment, which we discuss later. To cut a very long story short, only those with financial and cultural security were really able to pursue objectivity and detachment, while only those with sufficient leisure time were able to pursue a deep and abiding interest in books, art, languages, or any 'pure' academic subject. The way in which social background influences academic work itself is still misunderstood, even by academics, who think they are dealing with abstract and universal skills and interests. Your task, which will be greatly assisted by reading the work of Bourdieu, as suggested, is to try to separate out what really is universal in academic life, as opposed to that which happens to express the values of (once) dominant groups. You need to sort out substance from style, to put it another way.

Perhaps the most obvious and immediate way in which you might encounter social discrimination is in group discussions, such as seminars and presentations. These may be relatively less popular activities for many students from unconventional backgrounds, perhaps because they involve judgements being made publicly and people being put 'on the spot'. We discuss this in Chapter 6 which is about verbal skills. Of course, academic judgements about the work itself are not only inevitable but can even be informative and helpful, as we will argue. What is really at the heart of the worry, perhaps, is that social judgements are also frequently made in group discussions. Students from unconventional backgrounds can come to feel as if they are not using the right language, are labelled as having an inferior accent, are made to feel self-conscious about their appearance, and so on.

This may indeed be the result of elitism or snobbery, although it is always worth trying to find out if this is the case, rather than assuming it must be. We will be suggesting some ways to manage discussions and presentations in later chapters, but at this initial level, we need to point out that university seminars and presentations are social occasions, and should be explicable by some approaches found in social sciences more generally. To start, let us explore the common social process of 'distanciation' or 'distinction'.

Basically, this involves a process whereby individuals form groups and draw invisible boundaries around those groups. The next stage is to try to establish some notion of social distance between groups, to claim superiority for the groups to which you belong. There are many ways in which this can happen, and some of the most commonly used distinguishing characteristics have already been mentioned – accent, language, personal appearance. Social distanciation can be seen as a source of social support if you happen to belong to the dominant groups, but it can lead to a feeling of exclusion if you do not. One social solution is to form a group of your own, often with the opposite characteristics of the dominant one ('inversion'). The classic sociological work here involves the formation of anti-school subcultures: briefly, those who feel excluded from the official values of the school invert them, and form groups centred on oppositional values instead – being tough rather than courteous, rebellious rather than conformist, rejecting school, playing truant, and adopting other deviant interests.

It is occasionally possible to see this sort of thing happening with university students as well. Many people will find support by joining sporting subcultures, another theme in the classic sociological work, gaining status as well as pleasure in being able to play football, surf, do athletics or extreme sports. A minority will seek support and companionship in groups specializing in semi-deviant leisure – drug-taking, drinking, and minor criminal activities associated with those pursuits. The problem arises when students begin to divide themselves into exclusive and mutually hostile groups with no friendly social ties between members – like 'jocks' and 'boffs' (to risk using some current terminology).

The sociological literature attempts to understand this search for alternative status, but also points to one major challenge. These alternative activities can effectively discourage students from participating in the mainstream of university life. They can find themselves accepting that academic life is not really for them, but best left to the elite. You can end up consoling yourself with sport and leisure, while others go on to gain the highest qualifications, work on their social contacts, and set themselves up for the best jobs.

At the risk of repetition, you will need to keep a foot in both camps, to remain flexible, and not allow your university identity to become too rigid and stereotyped. Again, the trick is to stay objective, curious and yet critical, willing to try things to find out just what suits you and not just reproduce conventional identities. Here, we return to the themes with which we began – 'leaving home', and leaving behind old stereotypes.

Discrimination and Self-esteem

In the unlikely event that you do meet some form of serious discrimination at university, based on your social background, ethnic origin, sexual preferences, age, or religious beliefs, there are ways to challenge it, using the complaints procedure either directly or through representatives like the ones we mentioned earlier. There is just no need to put up with discrimination, but you will need to think the situation through first. We have known students who reacted badly to what they perceived as discrimination and who have abruptly left university altogether. We have also known the occasional student who has perceived some practices of their university as personally discriminating or as personally wounding in some way, and who simply may have been mistaken.

Let us deal with that sort of case first. We have met students who have responded negatively to receiving a low grade for their first assignments, for example. In the case of some research that one of us did, some mature students had made a lot of sacrifices to get to university, but had received lower grades than they had expected for their first essays. Some of them assumed that this meant they were not as suitable for university as they had believed. In one memorable case, a student broke down during the interview and confessed that she had always seen herself as a bright and intelligent person who had just been unlucky in the past, but was now beginning to question that view of herself and was on the verge of dropping out altogether.

As part of the 'action research' (discussed in Chapter 8) we were undertaking, we persuaded her to have a discussion with us and several other current students. Some had struggled in a similar way. Others had come with similar characteristics, but had actually done well. The idea was to let the unsuccessful students compare their approach to that of the successful ones.

To summarize the results very briefly, the successful students had a rather more detached and 'professional' approach to their assignments. They had used their course materials and teaching to try to work out exactly what was required in the assignment. They pursued a rather 'instrumental' approach, making sure that they worked to the requirements of the task, even if this meant holding back on their own personal views for a while. Some successful students had made sure they contacted the tutor and got as much advice as possible.

Some of the struggling students were simply astonished by these approaches. Some thought they were vaguely immoral and insincere – there is a group, known as 'moral drop-outs', who take this view, and cannot bring themselves to do anything other than write an entirely sincere and personal assignment. This may be admirable behaviour, but of course there is a cost – if that assignment then receives a poor grade, the inference is inescapable. If the assignment expresses personal views and carefully gathered personal experience, low marks may be perceived as a personal failure.

Taking a Step Back from Personal Engagement

When we have encountered students of this kind, we have even found ourselves persuading them to be more instrumental, at least at first, as a temporary identity, a working stance. This is rather ironic, since the instrumental student is commonly seen as a problem, missing out on the higher pleasures of academic argument. In the real world, it might be a matter of choosing between two pretty undesirable options, however – if people drop out, and leave with feelings of personal inadequacy, they will miss out on the higher pleasures of academic argument as well! Feeling secure after an initially instrumental phase can lead on to other kinds of commitment once the initial crisis is over.

An instrumental approach does offer some safeguards, since it is not 'you' personally who is simply writing the assignment, but a different version of 'you' – you the new student in new surroundings, not you the person with an identity to maintain. It involves a little role-playing. We are not denying the need to maintain integrity and sincerity, and strong beliefs, but we are suggesting that these need not be made central in everything you do. Indeed, as we shall see, one of the social and personal benefits of university life is supposed to be a capacity to reconsider your beliefs, learn about them, consider alternatives and then come back to them at some later stage in life.

A famous study of university student life in the USA (Becker et al., 1995) suggests that fellow-students play an important part in helping newcomers adjust to dilemmas of this kind. To simplify, students often come to university fully expecting to be able to read everything, work constantly at their studies, and commit themselves totally to academic life. Some sort of crisis often ensues. Fellow-students soon 'wise them up', according to Becker et al., introduce them to the need to compromise, and show them how to do so. An important aspect of student support is to minimize the initial guilt and insecurity that students feel on first contact with the reality of the situation. Sometimes this advice is harmful, it should be said, and students can rapidly learn to neglect whole chunks of their teaching and learning. As we say throughout the book, balance is required. However, lacking the strong student fraternities and sororities of the US system, UK students might take longer to learn how to achieve this balance.

This can mean not reacting particularly strongly to any poor grades received initially. Poor grades do not mean that you have been exposed as an imposter and you should leave. They should be seen instead as a warning that your approach needs adjusting in the new circumstances. They can be seen as positively useful information.

The strategy of disengaging a little from an institution until you learn the rules and find your feet is simply a sensible survival strategy. You would do exactly the same if you were the mythical ethnographer we have urged you to think about. You would certainly not spend your first afternoon in contact with a foreign society by insisting on acting exactly as you did back home. You would have to learn why people do the things they do, and attempt to understand them. You might still personally disapprove, or come to the conclusion that you were right all along, but it would be a mature opinion, of the kind that lecturers expect students to be developing. In fact, you might consider the same tactic when you take your first job after graduating. You might feel personally that casual dress indicates low moral standards, but you would not necessarily want to announce that loudly on your first day. You might think that you know how to do things better, but it is not tactful to go round telling everyone, at least until you get to know them.

We have used the cliché 'in real life' to indicate that compromises of this kind are essential to initial survival in a strange world. Lecturers, faced with all sorts of bureaucratic requirements from government which have to be dealt with, sometimes, despite strong reservations about them, know this as well as anybody. However, we are not simply advocating that you attempt to conceal your true selves, pretend to be something other than you are, and live a lie. To refer to the work of Goffman (1963) again, this tactic is known as 'passing'. It seems to solve a lot of initial problems, but it is difficult to sustain over time, unless you are prepared to constantly monitor your speech and behaviour, constantly to be on your guard in case your 'true' identity and opinions slip out.

Managing 'Stigma': 'Coming Out'

Goffman refers to a number of other ways that the 'stigmatized' cope with others. We have already noted that this work focuses on some unusual and extreme examples, but it can be helpful none the less. Without making any value judgements, it is possible to think of identities provided by the factors that we discussed – social background, age, sexual orientation and the rest – as providing a 'stigma' in the technical sense (an aspect of identity that can lead to social discrimination). There are ways in which such stigma can be dealt with in everyday interaction.

Goffman's study of American life suggests that the stigmatized are often capable of relating to others without trying to hide their stigma. They stop 'passing', and 'come out', to use a more contemporary term. They may need to adopt a gradual approach to relations with the non-stigmatized. On some occasions, it will make sense to avoid contact with 'normals' as much as possible, and to stay with your 'own kind'. You can sometimes see students doing this, avoiding seminars or discussions where they expect to be stigmatized, and trying to make sure that they stick with their friends when they are allocated to groups. Again this is fine at first, but it may not lead very far, especially if you accept our view that part of the reason for going to university is precisely to encounter members of other groups and learn to relate to them.

Goffman describes ways in which the stigmatized themselves take the initiative and manage them (Box 1.5).

Box 1.5   Disclosure Etiquette

[The stigmatized may adopt] a formula whereby the individual admits his [sic] own failing in a matter-of-fact way, supporting the assumption that those present are above such concerns while preventing them from trapping themselves into showing they are not. (Goffman, 1963: 124)

Being 'matter-of-fact' is the key here, although we might add that Britons like a little self-deprecation and irony too.

(Continued)

(*Continued*)

1   Note how others might be using this sort of technique, perhaps when they give presentations.
2   Try this technique out for yourselves, disclosing, in a flat 'matter-of-fact' way that you are a parent, overweight, that you have poor school grades, that you have struggled to understand the topic, that you feel you are an imposter, or whatever. Just assume it makes no difference and that everyone in the room would agree.
3   Assist anyone trying to do the same.

We know that humour and social openness are impossible to convey just in words, but here are some examples we have noted:

I am a sociologist, but I will speak English.
For anyone unable to understand my accent, this talk comes with subtitles.
Looking at you all, I suddenly feel quite old and responsible.
I am a normal housewife and mother – but we can still be friends.
I am not at all sure I have fully understood this topic and would welcome some help with it from anyone who does.
Please be gentle with me – I am doing my best (best delivered by tough athletic types).

There are many other sources of advice on managing social interaction, of course, but we have chosen Goffman because we want to make clear that the social science work you are reading can be applied to your own situation. Goffman happens to be especially good at examining the minute details of interaction between people, and he writes insightfully about how people 'present' a self, manipulate social settings to support it, preserve a 'backstage' area where they can act more 'naturally', occasionally show how they have mastered a role by deliberately revealing some of the performer's tricks to onlookers, and so on. This work can help you see what is going on in lectures, tutorials and seminars so you can maintain a certain detachment.

Resisting Labelling

We realize that we may be talking about rather extreme cases here. All the better, in a way, because milder forms of labelling and discrimination are easier to deal with. To draw upon another sociological research tradition – 'labelling theory', commonly discussed in sociologies of education or deviance – we know that labels often do 'stick'. In the worst cases, usually described in terms like 'stereotyping', there is almost nothing the victim can do to break the stereotype – to a confirmed racist, black people will always be inferior, and high-achieving ones are the 'exceptions that prove the rule', or sometimes 'not really black people'. However, a range of other labels may be more context-bound and not so deeply integrated. They can be resisted.

At the personal level, the authority of the labeller can be doubted, and so can the validity of the label – if you have had an unpleasant social encounter, you need to ask yourself first whether the combination you attracted was really deserved. Are you really not bright enough to be at university and is your accuser actually able to judge? Are you insensitive, coarse, ill-mannered or gauche, or could it be that your accuser is just too class-conscious, has led a sheltered life or is a social climber? Are you hopelessly 'mumsy', or have you been misunderstood? Are you a calm, patient and tolerant person, or a 'doormat'? As we all do, you may discover a grain of truth in the accusations and decide to change your behaviour, but you will probably also realize that you have been unfairly judged. If it matters to you, you might decide to address the matter, perhaps by employing some of the 'disclosure' tactics listed above. As we suggest later, seminars, tutors and presentations can offer good opportunities to do this and should be approached in a positive way.

Mature Students

It is worth devoting a final section specifically to mature students, whose numbers have grown dramatically in UK universities in the past decade. Although a significant minority in many universities, mature students have often not been addressed specifically by university practices or conventions. As a result, they may have a particular sense of feeling marginal to the whole enterprise, starting from Freshers' Week as suggested: going on nightly pub crawls might not be very appealing to parents who have children to care for in the morning, for example. In fact, mature students will have some advantages too – experience, more confidence, close family support.

Mature students bring many strengths to university life, and we are not the only tutors who are pleased to see them in our student groups. Mature students usually can handle group discussions, and are willing to say what they think. They are usually extremely well motivated, sometimes to the point of feeling excessive anxiety about how well they are doing (quite understandably, given the sacrifices they make). They often still need to learn how to work smart as well as working hard, however. They can suffer especially from the feeling that they do not really belong, or will be exposed as not knowing enough. The answer in both cases, as we shall argue in detail in the chapters that follow, is to take a thoroughly professional stance to academic work, finding out what is required, and setting out to acquire an adequate level of competence, especially in assessment terms.

Mature students may have all of the social difficulties mentioned above, and some additional ones. There are a number of books and articles which outline some of the problems you may face (see Arksey et al., 1994; Reay, 2002) and suggest some solutions. One of the most comforting things in reading the literature is that mature students realize they are not alone in facing the difficulties – and that a growing number of them overcome those difficulties and do succeed.

The problems mature students face may be exacerbated if they have a family to care for as well. We know that for many (married) people the demands of the family come first. This can result in having to reduce severely the amount of time available to spend on academic work (Morgan, 1993), together with the need to interrupt those studies if there is a family emergency. Many colleges and universities are starting to become aware of these problems, and are making increasing provision for them. Crèches and childcare facilities are far more common than once they were, for example. On the other hand, mature students still can find themselves omitted from a number of university regulations, notoriously those that cover the late submission of work or unauthorized absence from courses. Timetables can still assume an easy ability to make an early start or a late afternoon session. Personal tutors can testify that many of the regulations still seem to have in mind the classic 18–21-year-old student, who is likely to miss a deadline through carelessness, lack of planning, or perhaps a traumatic injury or illness, such as breaking a leg while playing sports. Cases where mature students have had to miss deadlines because they have been sorting out a recurrent family crisis are often not cited at all. Decisions then often depend on the reactions of tutors rather than a written list of rights and responsibilities.

Mature students have often made a particular sacrifice and effort to attend university (which is just what Hilary did – she quit a job as a full-time lecturer in a college of further education and spent six years living on a student grant and wondering what her unknown future would bring). Like Hilary, they have sometimes given up quite well-paid jobs, they have put on hold their own interests and ambitions for several years, they have put themselves through part-time or access routes. They can get particularly disappointed by what can seem like a rather casual organization of teaching and learning, with lectures cancelled at the last minute, poor attendance at seminars, or a tokenistic performance by jaded lecturing staff. A dominant culture of post-adolescent enjoyment in binge drinking, drugs and clubbing can also look both unappealing and self-indulgent. Universities should address some of these issues themselves, but again excessive grief can be caused by mature students not wanting to understand the culture of their new organizations, and by trying to apply their existing personal standards to them. It is a cultural and political matter to get the balance between asserting your rights to be considered and included, and looking like you have come to set the world to rights and insist that everyone behaves as responsibly as you do.

A certain amount of cultural research and evaluation can help mature students better perform their 'juggling' act, in other words. Expecting the university to be a particular kind of place, and then feeling disappointed when it does not conform to high personal standards of organization and conduct can only increase the sense that the sacrifice has not been rewarded. We know from other sociological studies that those who approach work with a well-developed 'sacrifice ethic' nearly always feel that their sacrifices are not being repaid sufficiently – how could they be? We also know that nothing causes resentment more than a feeling that other groups of people are 'getting away with it', receiving the same or better rewards without putting in the same effort. Mature students may find it difficult to rein in this resentment if they are not prepared to consider the possibility that their way of doing things is not the only way to succeed. This recognition is probably central to all successful forms of adaptation to strange cultures, it could be argued.

Concluding Thoughts

In this chapter, we have attempted to paint a realistic picture of both the benefits and the challenges of what you can expect when you embark on your university career. Many of you will already have the social and cultural skills you need to cope with everyday life in your new institution, while others may need to think about them. The rest of this book suggests you use research skills to find out about some of the more specialist and technical values which under-pin academic work too.

Some students do experience at least parts of their stay as challenging, and may have to develop coping skills for those occasions when the demands made on them increase temporarily – at examination times, for example. We are not advocating a permanent and cynical instrumentalism, but we do believe that confidence grows with success in assignment and assessment terms. We are fully committed to the higher pleasures of academic life, but believe, with Bourdieu, that cultural and financial security is required first before they can be enjoyed. It follows that full appreciation of what has been studied may even have to wait until some years after graduating. Students need time to find their feet, and lecturers and university administrators can fail to appreciate this in the haste to get started.

No quick and easy technical fixes are available, in the form of either pedagogic formulae or programmes of study skills. In any case, these are meaningless without an understanding of the context, we suggest. Your tutors are there to help and nothing beats having a tutor who is skilled and flexible enough to sug-gest how best to meet the many and varied challenges you may face. The like-lihood is that you will encounter many tutors like this, and your stay at university will be all the more valuable for that.

The Rest of the Book

In what follows, we are trying first to explain the occasionally strange world of the modern university as its main participants and stakeholders can see it. Part 1 contains chapters that discuss what students want from university life (Chapter 2), what tutors want (Chapter 3), and then what employers want (Chapter 4). You may not agree with these wants. You might find them contra-dictory. You will have to pursue the normal tactic of deciding whose views to prioritize if they contradict each other. Your priorities may change as you move from wanting to make friends to wanting to get good grades and then a good job. Whatever you decide to take from what we offer, we hope you will at least understand something about what the different wants and expectations are, and where they come from. We think this will help you understand the more specific requirements for 'fun', 'deep learning' or 'employability', none of which are quite as simple as they appear. If you are better informed, you will be better able to focus your efforts accordingly.

Later chapters in Part 2 concentrate on how best to maximize your performance at university. They provide more detail of the more specialist skills required in writing essays, reports and examinations (Chapter 5) or presenting in seminars (Chapter 6). The next three chapters focus on producing a dissertation, the most specialist and in some ways the most valuable academic skill you will learn at university, which is why we take such a detailed approach. Chapters 7 and 8 look at developing research questions and doing a literature review, and the range of research skills that can be used to undertake a small-scale project, respectively. Chapter 9 considers data analysis and writing up a dissertation. The final chapter, Chapter 10, draws together the main themes running throughout the book. It helps to know what academics might mean by 'effective writing' or 'coherent presentations' – you can learn some new ways to proceed and you will be able to decide how to balance your existing skills with the new ones.

Chapter Summary

1 Programmes of conventional study skills are limited as ways to understand what is required at university level specifically.
2 You will need a deeper understanding of the cultural and social requirements of living and fitting in.
3 You should begin to think of adopting a research orientation to university life to gain that understanding. You need to depersonalize things and try to reserve judgement at first.
4 Social science courses can themselves provide tools with which to understand university life.
5 Many students will face problems which need to be discussed frankly if they are to be tackled and overcome – some of these will turn on being accepted and avoiding social exclusion.

(Continued)

(Continued)

6 Academic work has its own conventions and requirements and these need to be approached professionally, with a measure of detachment and objectivity. Much can be clarified by understanding marking criteria, for example, or trying to form a good working relationship with your tutors.

7 You might wish to start thinking early on about preparing yourself for assignments and even for employability at the end of your course – building a good CV can start in week one. Really.

8 University life has many benefits, some of which will become more apparent as you live your life. You will meet friends and enjoy new activities and leisure pursuits. You will feel you are really sorting out and deepening some thoughts about the world.

9 If you work 'smart' and not just hard, you can both succeed and enjoy yourself and get more out of the whole experience of university.

2 How Students See It

CHAPTER OVERVIEW

- Experienced students' views on expectations, risks, challenges, trade-offs and work–life balance.
- Student views – mature students and younger students.
- 'Deep' learning styles.
- 'Cue-seeking'.
- Research on the hidden dimensions of student life – plagiarism, 'playing the game'.

In this chapter, we are trying to present some studies which have attempted to pin down student expectations of university life and how actual students have coped. This should be useful to newcomers, who will discover that current and former students have had similar problems and have devised ways to overcome them. It is nearly always a comfort for the slightly insecure to realize they are not alone. We are not suggesting that student strategies are always successful or appropriate, though, and we add some findings based on more systematic research to round out the picture. There are some obvious problems in doing this which we ought to discuss first.

The student body is very diverse and it is also pretty changeable, at least in the UK at the moment. It is very difficult to get anything like a representative sample of the student population (which we discuss in Chapter 8), and we know of no research that claims to have achieved one. Mostly, the samples are drawn from local students, and the aim is to illustrate some of the possibilities.

When you get to grips with research methods, you will be able to discuss the pros and cons of this technique – sometimes it is called 'convenience sampling'. We are interested in the student views that result, even if they are not representative in the strict statistical sense. A 'typical' student would probably be described in so general a set of terms as to be not very helpful when encountering real ones anyway – if you average the characteristics of 30 year olds and 18 year olds you could get a strange hybrid that represents neither group. You, the reader, might not be typical yourself either, of course.

In addition, trying to establish students' views runs into a problem which recurs in other chapters. If you just ask for them outright, you get immediate answers, often shaped by what respondents think they should be saying. This can contrast quite markedly from what they might be thinking, or actually doing. It is a familiar problem in social research, which arises from the fact that people are not just passive databases but can actively interpret the questions for themselves. We are proposing to take into account some social science research findings on students (and, later, on employers and lecturers). Some of this tries deliberately to look 'behind the scenes', and sometimes it uncovers behaviours that are surprising and not what one would expect, as we shall see. As students of social sciences, you might as well get used to this sort of finding, and it suits our purposes to draw upon some of the discipline-based approaches you will encounter on your actual courses. As we argue throughout, there are academic resources which can be used to understand academic life itself.

The main reason for discussing the studies of student views is that they illustrate approaches and opinions that should be of interest to lecturers and tutors, or anyone at the university interested in communication with actual students. We are not endorsing any of these views, of course, simply recording them in a detached and research-like manner. It is also often very helpful to realize that students' perceptions can be quite different to those of lecturers.

In many cases, actual student views may be more reasonable and understandable than some of the stereotypes that persist about them suggest, especially in matters such as plagiarism, as we shall see. We may have just spent too long in education to remember what it was like for a new student. We may be encountering students who are from social backgrounds that are very different from our own. In this case, although we do recognize a great deal in students' views that we have met in our experience, there is also an element of 'surprise', which is one classic justification for doing research. Willis (in Willis and Trondman, 2000) makes this case strongly, as you will probably soon learn.

For readers of this book, we think it is useful to illustrate some views, so you can compare your own views with them. You may find that some of your best hopes and also deepest private reservations have already been experienced by students before you. You may find that students have developed ways to overcome such anxieties, and have managed to do well academically, enjoy themselves socially and not get too deep into debt all at the same time. Some students will have experienced problems that you will not face, but you can still learn from them, of course: it is our experience that some students have managed to cope with successive serious issues in their personal lives, and yet have still achieved good academic outcomes in a way that we find positively inspiring.

Even where students are discussing approaches that would be a clear breach of the regulations, as in plagiarism, we intend to focus on trying to understand what underlies this behaviour. That is a luxury that we can afford as writers of a book. Of course, as practising lecturers we do have to deal with breaches of regulations in our everyday work lives as well, and this does involve making judgements about things like motives or the effects of actions.

Let us begin with our own recent work. We recruited a small convenience sample of lecturers and students in order to investigate the kind of study skills that might be useful for them. We are not claiming that our sample is large enough or representative enough to produce scientifically valid results, but we found the exercise useful both in writing this book and in developing some practice. We have also produced a paper for the 2005 British Sociology Association annual conference (Arksey and Harris, 2005) that discussed the findings, and a summary appears below.

Expectations of Academic Life

We asked students taking part in the survey about their expectations of academic life, and how realistic these were. The results showed that some had anticipated that university would be similar to school and an extension of the sixth form, but this view is open to question (see below). Others thought that they would be encouraged to be independent and take responsibility for their own learning. Yet others thought that university would be demanding and challenge them academically, and they anticipated struggling. One person remembered thinking: 'Oh, my God, what am I doing?' because they did not think they were clever enough to be at university.

Generally speaking, the reality was not borne out for those who thought the work would be demanding: students did not find themselves working all the time, they were not as busy studying as they had imagined they would be and on the whole they perceived they coped well. As one person said: 'It certainly wasn't as much of a painful transition from A levels as I had anticipated.' This sort of remark could have been mistaken, of course, and it would certainly be wrong to use it to imply that you can get away with doing little work at university. Students commonly think that actual contact time with lecturers is all they are required to do, and forget the working assumption on the part of staff that they will be spending a lot of time in private study as well. A-level standards will probably not carry you through to the second or third year of university.

Not surprisingly, students' expectations about their new social life at university tended to focus on positive aspects (with the exception of anxieties about getting into debt – see below). Opportunities for meeting new friends and having a good nightlife were emphasized, as was having an exciting time. These expectations were met for some, but not all, survey participants. One person who had to do some re-evaluating in the hard light of day was a student who had been looking forward to 'freedom' and being 'grown up' which in practice entailed socializing and spending time in the pub at the expense of completing course work. Unfortunately, this person's belief that they could leave things until just a few days before the examinations did not bear fruit and they failed two exams. While this was a hard lesson to learn, it encouraged the student to 'put my priorities straight'. This seems to us to be exactly the sort of constructive response to failure that we would want to encourage.

Specific Challenges

Respondents were asked to identify specific problems they encountered while at university. The analysis shows that generally these fell into one of two categories: different aspects of academic work, and managing money and staying out of debt.

As far as academic work was concerned, challenges identified included: reading widely; tackling difficult assignments; time management; presentations; doing well in examinations and managing different lecture styles. One student commented on the process of getting to grips with what was actually required in lectures, seminars and essays. For example, was it acceptable to speak your mind and/or to challenge lecturers? Or instead was it the case that speaking out too much risked coming across as being a 'smart arse'? This might look rather like low ambition or anxiety produced by an anti-educational peer group, but it could equally be seen as becoming aware of a rather important matter of balancing individual talent and team working. Williams et al. (2006: 86–7) refer to the difficult matter of wanting to appear as a 'star' but not as a 'razor' ('someone who is just too sharp for their own good').

Another student, who twice mentioned coming from a working-class background and clearly perceived this as a barrier to achieving a good degree (although it turned out not to be in the end), said:

> Generally, I didn't have the first idea what was the difference between a seminar and a lecture; had never been taught to write an essay and generally felt that everything seemed to be geared up to a type of education that was alien to me. Once again, I just felt like the working-class kid in the wrong place.

This student was able to establish a working identity as a person from a background that made him interesting and unusual rather than deficient in some sense.

Maintaining high levels of motivation when attending lectures on only two days a week, or not being forced to do academic work, was also viewed as a problem. With the benefit of hindsight, one student compared school and university as follows:

> It is a world of difference from school where you are made to do work. If you don't do it at uni nobody cares; you just get kicked off the course. It is difficult to get things done when you have to leave notes for lecturers all the time and make appointments, so I didn't! I pretty much winged my whole degree – awesome!

We have to be careful here to distinguish bravado from actual behaviour, of course. People do not want to appear as what Williams et al. (2006) call a 'geek', obsessed with academic work with no life outside, and it can be much better to appear as some kind of heroic adventurer, defying fate.

Making judgements about who is responsible for 'enforcing' acceptable student behaviour and performance is difficult. The view of one person highlighted tensions between personal responsibility and institutional responsibility:

> You are allowed to do everything you want; your presence isn't even required as long as you get your results. Even then, when your marks aren't good they won't look at you except when it's time to leave, because of your bad grades or when you haven't paid!

This remark, like some of the others above, could be a classic case of misunderstanding. What lecturers think of as encouraging independence could be seen as neglect, lack of supervision and lack of interest.

Other perceived difficulties that were more obviously the responsibility of the institution and not under the control of individual students related to poor course organization and new courses still to bed down properly. Even so, students still had to manage them as best they could.

Having enough money to live on and managing money was a huge challenge. Indeed, one person went so far as to say: '[Managing] Debt is a requirement of going to university these days.'

Minimizing the Risks of Failure

How did students rise to the challenge of achieving a good degree? Were there any particular strategies or techniques that they employed to neutralize the risks of failure? The questionnaire responses showed that many students actively sought out help and advice from lecturers. This could range from discussing ideas and concerns to help with structuring an essay. As one person said:

> I can't express just how useful this was, and how important a factor it was in getting good grades … I mean, there's no point in second guessing what needs to be done, or diving in with doubts that could easily be addressed beforehand, is there?

Respondents also asked for help from their peer group, house mates, family and friends. Asking someone to read through a piece of written work, and/or proofreading it, was common. Some people rehearsed presentations; others worked in study groups. However, who belonged to your group was clearly important and one person reported that it was essential to avoid group work with 'slackers' and instead 'get in with the "swots"!!!'. This same respondent also emphasized the need to be strategic and choose what to study as it did not seem vital to know about everything in each module.

While conventional study skills courses were not that popular, those who had taken advantage of them had found the specific techniques they learned helpful – such as mind mapping and directed reading.

Other tactics to minimize risk included: good time management, not falling behind and finishing assessed work in good time; working out just what essay questions meant; practising past examination questions; reflecting on, and learning from, previously assessed work; drawing on a wide range of resources including books, journal articles and the Internet; using the assessment criteria.

These active help-seeking techniques suggest that students deliberately try to minimize failure in a way that is acceptable in terms of academic conventions and standards. However, that was not always the case. One person was exceptional in that they admitted voluntarily to committing plagiarism and pretending someone else's work was their own:

> I had a very close class, everybody helped each other. There was always someone that knew people in other classes, so I could copy their graded assignments and just hand it in. I knew in advance if the assignment was available from someone. If not, I would have enough time to work on it.

We will discuss plagiarism like this on several occasions in this book. Here it is important to note that this statement could be the result of bravado too.

As far as staying out of debt was concerned, some people worked either part- or full-time throughout their degree course to avoid getting into money difficulties. Those who were able to get a job with some degree of flexibility tended to work part-time and then increase their hours temporarily when they were less busy with academic work.

Balancing Studying, Social Life and Staying Out of Debt

Respondents held polarized views about whether or not there was any conflict between completing the work required of them, enjoying a good social life and staying out of debt. Those who believed there was a conflict gave clues as to how they tried to delay or minimize tensions, for instance, by getting help with assignments from other students, living at home, accepting financial support from parents, 'training' themselves to stay in and work, taking out a student loan, and undertaking full- or part-time work. One person explained how cutting down on their social life was doubly advantageous in that there was more time for academic work and it relieved the pressure of debt. Another had also scaled down their social life temporarily, and gave an insight into the sort of financial economies that current-day students may be making by reporting that drinking was too expensive so they were taking Ecstasy instead! We are sure we do not need to enter the usual caution and qualifications here!

Making Trade-offs

On the whole, people were clear about the importance of a good social life while at university. This period in their lives was seen as one for making friends and enjoying the 'good times' as they would be with them for the rest of their lives. However, this approach was not pursued at the risk of failing to obtain a good degree. Common advice included indulging in social activities for the first (and possibly second) year, but then really focusing on work thereafter. Given that the majority of respondents were in their first or second years, this recommendation may be more of a hope than an actual practice! One student who said they were constantly trying to balance their social life with their academic life went on to say: 'I eventually realized that I wasn't going to get a first but could feasibly get a 2:1 and maintain some form of outside interests.' This is the kind of 'informed choice' that we would want to encourage more generally. Academic achievement comes at a price, and students might well want to pay a high price to achieve the best grades. But not all will want to do this and they are entitled to pursue a different path as well. It is your choice in the end.

This summary gives a good idea of the sort of information or data we acquired from the survey. The findings helped us to understand our students and to sympathize with their views, although, again, it is necessary to point out that we do not always agree with them, and would not condone consuming illegal drugs, sexual promiscuity or attempting to 'wing' a degree course. The study sample contained a mixture of both mature and young students, (Boxes 2.1 and 2.2), and it might be appropriate to include a bit more detail from the responses of both groups. In each case, ask yourself how many of these views you share:

Box 2.1 Mature Students

I thought that being 'mature' might be a problem, not realizing how many others there were. Part of me thought that being 29 would somehow be frowned upon by others. I did think that this might be a benefit in terms of 'pleasures' though :-) [as it turned out, it was!] ... academic confidence was an issue to begin with. I didn't really know if I could learn particularly well, or what goal I should be setting. (Student 1)

Invest a bit of time in learning how to learn *effectively* ... it'll save so much time and pay dividends ... and don't be embarrassed by the fact that it's not a skill you're born with. Don't worry if you're a bit older ... nobody cares, as long as you're not patronizing and can make a bit of an effort to be friendly. Be adventurous and let your mind wander – what do you think. You don't have to just agree with things just because they're published. Be as social as you can, get involved, join clubs – that's what it's all about! ... but ... practise safe sex ... there's nothing like a dodgy night to put you off your work! (Student 2)

The prospectus was, of course, no help in preparing me ... the words used seemed almost foreign ... I really did take it one week at a time. I never expected to get my degree but I just kept plugging away and before I knew it I was in my final year and doing pretty well! (Student 3)

University was a real escape for me. I had just recovered from testicular cancer and been made redundant from a crap job and also come out of a very painful relationship with the mother of my child ... oh, and had my house repossessed – not bad eh? (Student 4)

I imagined highbrow discussions over coffee with some very intellectual sorts who were bound to discover my lack of knowledge very quickly. I also worried about mixing with lots of students who were far younger than me and had more right to be there – it would be awful to be on the outside looking in. Also, what if I failed – what if all that knowledge I thought I had was lost or irrelevant or too pulped by several years of looking after my young daughters at home? (Student 5)

I just gradually picked things up and my anxieties were eased when I saw some of the other younger students from the 'right' families obviously surviving, even though they didn't seem to have been blessed with much common sense. (Student 6)

Some useful insights into the world of mature students can also be gained from Arksey et al. (1994) and Tolmie (2000). A good comparison with a previous era when universities were far less welcoming to students from working-class backgrounds can be made by looking at some recent studies. For example, Plummer (2000: 40–1) reports students finding that:

> [After revealing her father's occupation as a steelworker] From that moment on I was totally excluded from the conversation ... It was the first time in my life that I'd felt I was unacceptable – not me particularly but my background.

> My encounter with university 'knowledge' brought the discovery that working-class people were not 'there' within the academy as participants or subjects but as 'others' and 'ordinary people' to be studied and observed.

There is also an excellent series of recent articles on the problems encountered by current mature students from unconventional backgrounds. Archer et al. (2001), for example, found that for some UK working-class men contemplating university entry, higher education was seen as incompatible with working-class masculinity. University students were seen as 'Other', as rich white middle-class men, or as 'boffins' or 'bods', as 'socially inadequate men who enjoy study' (p. 435). Study involved too high a price in giving up your social life and living on a low income. Reay's study of mature students on access courses found that 'issues around belonging, fitting in and feelings of authenticity are a key to understanding working-class experiences of the move into higher education' (2002: 399), and that the women faced worries about belonging, both to the past and to the new university.

We think these findings are important, even if they might appear gloomy at first, and would point out that many of these persons studied (especially those in Plummer's book) went on not only to thrive at university, but to gain considerable insights into their lives and themselves. Dr Plummer herself is an excellent example!

Younger students had different interests and issues.

Box 2.2   Younger Students

I thought I would find it difficult to adjust to living away from home, but found that was no problem at all. [I experienced] ... Freedom, fun, ability to select modules of interest which was different from school. (Student 1)

(Continued)

(Continued)

Debt is always going to be a problem for students, I accept that. There are some conflicts though as I work four nights a week in order to survive! So don't spend as much time studying as maybe I should. (Student 2)

University is not just about learning a subject, it's about learning to live life, i.e. learning to make new friends, deal with new/different pressures, meet deadlines, learn how to pay bills and generally look after yourself and your money. (Student 3)

Meeting new friends, having new experiences. It's been a blast! (Student 4)

You go from being a big fish in a small pond to competing with all the other people who are academic in the same area as you. (Student 5)

I went to college in the next town from where I lived so didn't really get into the whole college party culture as I either had to drive or was dependent on being picked up by my parents and therefore wary of getting very drunk. (Student 6)

Make sure you find out what's on offer from all angles – don't just accept what is being 'sold' as there is far more going on at Uni than you realize. Don't be afraid to ask for guidance with assignments as your tutor wants the best for you too! (Student 7)

I knew I would meet people that would help change my life, some have for the better and a few for the worse ... do your work to the best of your ability but don't miss out on the good times, they will be with you forever. (Student 8)

Other Research on Student Views

Instrumentalism and 'Cue-seeking'

Of course, there are several rather more rigorous studies of student views and perceptions as well. We are not writing an academic text as such, but we think it important to just summarize the findings of some of the more influential ones. Here, we are going beyond immediate views, as we indicated in the opening paragraphs, and exploring some findings gained from using various social science research techniques. You can also see these as examples of the sort of work we discuss in Chapter 8. As you will see, academics need to step back from their own public values and positions a little as well.

Perhaps the most famous early study was undertaken by Becker et al. ([1968] 1995) at Kansas University, USA. The study remains as an excellent example of the use of ethnographic technique, and has also been linked with studies of deviance. Becker and his associates intended to study the tensions of student collective life, and they did so by listening to, observing, and discussing matters with students. Some interesting findings became apparent. Basically, students saw university life in their own unofficial terms. In their particular perspective, maintaining a good 'grade point average' came to dominate their activities, and they shaped their whole approach accordingly. A wide range of 'instrumental' behaviour was the result – students chose courses on the basis that they would lead to a good grade; they 'selectively neglected' parts of their courses which were not being assessed; they tackled assignments with their minds firmly on their average grade; they got help from their fellow-students to approach the problem collectively; they even attempted to work out some of the personal characteristics of their tutors. If you look back over our student responses above, you can see traces of this sort of behaviour in current student stances as well, and it might be what lies beneath 'working the system' in works such as Arksey (1992) and Tolmie (2000).

A later study of students at a Scottish university by Miller and Parlett (summarized in Hammersley and Woods, 1976) also uncovered some interesting behaviour. Here, students had different ways of tackling the problems presented by an unseen examination. To be brief, some students realized that examinations were not quite as 'unseen' as might be thought, and that some lecturers were offering clues (the actual term is 'cues') about what sort of questions might come up and how to answer them. Following the strange conventions of university life, these cues were floated before students in various indirect ways – no one was explicitly told what to revise, but some topics were emphasized. In fact, this aspect of tutor behaviour remains relatively unresearched, and Miller and Parlett focused instead on student reactions. Some students seem to realize what was going on and began to actively search for cues in what their tutors told them in various formats ('cue-seekers'). Other students were aware that cues were around but did not actively seek them out ('cue-conscious'). The third group was apparently unaware that cues were being provided, and did not shape their revision strategies accordingly ('cue-deaf').

Curiously, 'cue-seeking' is covered rather lightly in study skills books. This may be because the topic arouses distaste or anxiety among professionals. However, our mission is to cite research like this to make you aware of some of the dimensions of practice: our suspicion is that elite students always knew about these grey areas of practice and did not need research findings to clarify them.

Once more, we are not suggesting you simply turn into a cue-seeker, even if you managed to overcome any reservations of your own. Although there was an overall pattern showing that cue-seeking was associated with gaining good grades, Miller and Parlett recognize that this does not necessarily mean that cue-seeking will invariably help anyway – indeed, one of their 'cue-deaf' students also did very well. We think that the research might better be understood more positively as suggesting that students who listen carefully to lectures and tutorials can penetrate academic discourse effectively, and begin to see the principles on which it is based – and we advocate that you do this.

For example, although tutors often try not to hint about the contents of unseen examinations, for obvious professional reasons, they often want to help students prepare for them. This can produce one of those grey areas of professional practice where an ear for ambiguity can sometimes help. Try to work out what might be happening in the following conversation (based on a real and recent example) (Box 2.3).

Box 2.3   Possible Cues (?)

Student: I am revising these two topics for the examination, do you think I will be OK?

Tutor: Revising just two topics is a real gamble, and a sensible student will want to cover more topics just to be safe.

Student: Yes, but I am only interested in these two topics. … Will I be OK in the exam, do you think?

Tutor: It is up to you in the end, but I would think about preparing quite thoroughly – you will find it pays off in the end.

Student: Well, I will stick with these two then and hope they come up.

Tutor: You must do what you think is best, but make sure you feel comfortable with your revision.

Action Research on 'Deep' Learning

On the same topic of student 'instrumentalism', some of the most famous research on student learning styles also discovered its importance but in another context. We discuss the work on 'deep' learning in Chapter 6, but it has certainly been influential. Students were researched in a number of ways, including making close observations of their behaviour when they tried to do some learning. Again, there are some interesting methodological arguments here, which you may encounter if you take a methods course. Very briefly, students seemed to fall into two general groups when it came to approaching the task of learning something. The 'deep' learners tried to respond to the challenge of the task, tried to link it with material that they already knew, focused on the underlying principles and did not get too bogged down in the detail. On the whole, 'deep' learners gained better grades and also found academic life more enjoyable and satisfying.

Some of the best work employing this notion of deep learning is rather obscurely published, unfortunately. The Study Methods Group at the UK Open University undertook a number of fascinating 'action research' projects working closely with students to see how they did approach their tasks, and tried to encourage a 'deeper' approach. Hints of the highly skilful diagnosis and subsequent tutoring can be found in Morgan (1993).

As an example of the work, Taylor et al. (1981) decided to investigate student understandings of the important concept of social class before and after they took an introductory social science course. Understandings before taking the course involved seeing social class as defined by a person's job, the amount of money they possessed, the educational training they had taken, their accent or appearance or other personal characteristics, the family background, their attitudes and values, or the social value placed upon a particular job as in 'esteem'. Students typically mentioned one or two of these characteristics rather than the whole list, and when asked for further clarification described some further social implications of class rather than attempting to define the term or placing it in any theoretical context. Many students were clearly puzzled by the term, and many said it was now a redundant concept.

Even after taking the social science course, fewer than half the sample showed any change in their understanding of social class! Some had developed new conceptions, such as suggesting that social class was now a historical classification, once useful but no longer important because there was no longer a working class. Some coupled it with a discussion of social mobility or power. Taylor et al. (1981) argue that these were close to social science discussions and terms, but people were still not really able to explain the term or to separate it from other concepts such as 'status' or 'role' (the discussion here refers to the way in which these concepts were dealt with as separate on this particular course). Implications were drawn for course design, but the team also supported a more general focused discussion, actually a 'negotiation', between students and tutors which specifically highlighted these differences of interpretation.

The team were also aware that learning, in this powerful sense of changing basic conceptions of the social world, takes place over time, that it takes courage, that students' initial positions need to be discovered and explored, and student approaches can vary (more or less along the lines of the work on surface and deep learning). In a later piece, Taylor (in Henderson and Nathenson, 1984) suggests that we focus on encouraging students to analyse and question their own approaches as well as attempting to grasp the concept that they are meeting in their courses. Much will depend on their motivation to do so.

We cannot know what your own views of social class are, of course, but we commonly find it is a difficult concept for many students. The difficulties show one of the classic problems of teaching social science, that it uses terms and concepts that look identical to words used in everyday discussion. Students clearly do find it difficult to switch on to the more technical senses of the term. To get in the mood, you might want to try an initial exercise (Box 2.4). Record your answers now and look back at them later to see if anything has changed. No one is going to inspect these answers, so be frank and try it out.

Box 2.4   Social Class – Test Your Understanding

Write down some thoughts on the following:
What do you understand by the concept of social class?
What does it mean to say you belong to 'the middle class'?
What other aspects are involved (check with the list above)?
What sort of evidence or experiences are your views based on?
Is the concept of social class an outdated one?
What evidence is there to support the view that class is no longer relevant?
What sort of evidence would you need to be certain it is irrelevant?
How do you think social scientists might define 'social class'?
How could the topic be researched?
What evidence of the relevance of social class might be found in social science?

One major issue turns on whether or not a 'deep' approach can be taught to all students. Certainly, many lecturers have realized some of the implications of the work, and changed their teaching to try and incorporate 'deeper' tasks and less 'busywork' (time-consuming but trivial tasks such as copying lists or maps). However, the main issue that we want to pursue here came from the realization that when students actually approach assignments they can develop another approach, specifically geared towards gaining the best grades. This 'strategic' approach may or may not be adopted cynically, as in the work by Becker et al. The approach seems to involve some quite skilled analysis of the task and its underlying principles, rather as in the 'deep' approach. At the same time, Entwistle and his colleagues seem to have also discovered that students can simulate a 'deep' approach as a strategy (Entwistle, 2000). Whether cynical, 'deep' or simulated, a strategic approach seems to offer a way of coping with the demands of assessment: we even suggest that students might consider adopting it, certainly if the only alternative is one of the less productive tactics such as plagiarism or dropping out.

Cheating and Plagiarism

There is also some recent work on outright cheating and plagiarism. We urge students to avoid plagiarism, as being far too risky and time-consuming as well as unethical, in several sections in this book, just in case a casual reader might miss it. However, some forms of semi-deviant activity which approach some of the broader definitions of plagiarism and academic malpractice seem quite common in UK universities, according to Franklyn-Stoakes and Newstead:

> These data suggest that over half the students sampled ... are involved in a range of cheating behaviours including: allowing coursework to be copied (72%); paraphrasing without acknowledgement (66%); altering and inventing data (66% and 60% respectively); increasing marks when students mark each other's work (65%); copying another's work (64%); fabricating references (54%); and plagiarism from a text (54%). (1995: 169)
>
> ... the findings reported here have considerable generality ... there were no significant differences between male and female respondents ... mature students perceived cheating as less frequent and more serious than their younger counterparts ... but their self-reported frequency of occurrence was the same ...
>
> [The main reasons given are] time pressure and desire to increase the mark ... time pressure may be due to increased amounts of contributory coursework ... having to take paid work ... juggling home and university commitments.

At least in the short term it would seem wiser to concentrate on informing students as to what behaviour is deemed to be acceptable, rather than introducing draconian sanctions … staff may well be … naïve about the extent and nature of cheating … students are ill-informed about correct practice … it may be the case that increases in the amount and importance of coursework are actually encouraging students to cheat. (pp. 169–70)

Norton et al. (2001) have also researched what they call the 'rules of the game' as perceived by students. Following these rules is also a widespread practice. Rules include the following (Box 2.5).

Box 2.5   What Students See as 'Rules of the Game'.

1   Choose the easiest title to give you the best chance of getting a high mark.
2   Play the role of a good student.
3   Use big words/technical terms/jargon to impress your tutor.
4   Present a false bibliography.
5   Try to reflect your tutor's opinions/views/style as closely as possible.
6   Make essays visually exciting.
7   Avoid criticizing tutors' views and/or research in the essay.
8   Avoid simple/basic textbooks in the bibliography even though you have used them.
9   Put a theorist's name against your own point … to make it look good.
10   Find out who would mark the essays so you could choose the title set by the easiest marker.
11   Invent studies/research/articles to include in the essay.
12   Get to know lecturers socially in order to favourably influence them.

Perhaps you might like to clarify your own thoughts about practices like these (Box 2.6). We are inviting you to make an informed choice. As we explained earlier, this is the only conceivable way to proceed. Simple moral hectoring is probably ineffective given the circumstances in which students seem to adopt this behaviour. As tutors ourselves, we could not allow such behaviour to go unnoticed, of course.

Box 2.6   'Rules of the Game' – Your Views

In which circumstances might you be tempted to follow these rules?

What might be the risks of following them?

How naïve do you think your tutors might be these days, in terms of knowing that students think there are rules like this?

How would you feel about students who got good grades after following these rules?

If you followed these rules and get a good grade for your work, how would you feel about yourself?

Finally, we are not implying that student life is completely dominated by cynical tactics designed to get good grades on the cheap. A recent project takes up Becker et al. and a number of other classic sociological studies in an attempt to find out 'what is really learned at university?' these days (Brennan and Jary, 2004). Interestingly, the authors find less support for a fully cynical instrumental approach in current British universities, and much more student support for what might be seen as the official aims of the university. Jary and Lebeau (2006: 24), in a follow-up to this important longitudinal study, say that Sociology students generally agree that they did find the work interesting and useful, for example, and that students report high levels of 'endorsement of Subject Benchmarks (official descriptions of the undergraduate curriculum) … generally positive self-identities, and strong self-development'.

Concluding Thoughts

It is important to note that we have been describing findings about student behaviour here and certainly not just recommending that you do likewise. Some of these activities will be considered as deviant if not illegal. In addition, Norton et al. (2001) showed that following these rules is not actually strongly associated with success, despite what students think. Students seem to have embraced some myths, rather than trying to establish matters for themselves. You may encounter these myths too, and it is wise to remain sceptical. We would be especially concerned if you were to think that 'playing the game' was some kind of default approach, the 'real' way to cope. Or that you thought the only alternative was some 'purist' stance involving literally working to do everything that seemed to be required. Your choice of approach to student life will be a personal and a social one, but there is no need for you to operate inside rigid limits.

You will certainly be offered advice about how to study by your fellow-students, and you will meet behaviour ranging from endless labour to down-right cheating. As always, we suggest the need to understand first before coming to any decisions.

There is one more aspect to making informed choices. You may now need to move on to read the sections (in Chapter 5 especially) on such matters as referencing and citing sources properly so that you do not appear to be cheating even if that is not your intention. Students with whom we have discussed the work on cheating or playing the game have sometimes been surprised by the definitions of cheating involved, for example. Universities have very strict and unusually well-defined notions of malpractice and a competent student will want to find out exactly what these are as soon as possible.

Chapter Summary

1 Many students these days are not in a position to simply devote their lives to academic work. Their normal lives outside university provide sources of both tension and support, and many students report the need to develop a suitable balance between social and academic life. The same problem may arise at work too, of course, one reason why the UK Government began its 'work–life balance' campaign in 2000.

2 There is a certain cheerful lack of respect for academic institutions and personnel, especially among the younger students. Again, this can be both 'good' and 'bad'. As long as it is based on a reasonable understanding of academic life, there is no problem with taking a somewhat 'strategic', detached or disengaged stance, as long as this does not stray into actual malpractice, of course. Indeed, such a stance can help develop a kind of critical insight and objective detachment. We advocate detachment throughout the book, urging students to attempt to understand the conventions of academic life more fully, and not just to adopt a kind of counter-cultural rejection of it, or avoid thought by embracing stereotypes or myths.

(Continued)

(Continued)

3   We want to warn you about some of the more risky strategies that you will hear about on the grapevine. We leave it to your own good sense to resist the temptations of the dubious if not illegal 'quick fix' offered by cheating or its near-equivalent.

4   The view that university is about having a good social life and meeting friends is not so misguided as it might seem either, given the importance these days of networking and teamworking for later employment. Some academics might not agree with this view, but there is some sense in it, as we shall see when we discuss what employers want in Chapter 4.

5   It seems clear from the views of several students that pursuing conventional study skills is not seen as very useful at the moment. It is hard to say if this is an accurate perception or not – it would be interesting to see what sort of degree classifications these students actually receive (we happen to know that the self-styled 'winger' in our own research got a 2:2). However, we felt that there was enough in this view to rethink what we mean by study skills as well. As you will see as you go through the book, we are more interested in the principles that underline study skills rather than rehearsing you in specific techniques as such.

6   You do not have to be fully committed to academic life as a kind of monastic calling to do well at university, although you may need to be tactful about expressing doubts.

3 What Do Tutors Want?

CHAPTER OVERVIEW

- Finding out what tutors want.
- Professional detachment.
- Grading assignments – criteria and learning outcomes.
- Notions of academic development, progression and 'graduateness'.
- Preferred learning styles.
- Avoiding plagiarism.
- A brief insight into the professional worlds of the academic.

It might seem obvious, but what tutors actually want could be a key concern for those students wishing to work to gain maximum returns in assignments. We are not suggesting that you simply try to find out what tutors want and then give it to them – that would produce rather dull and conformist essays, even if you could be sure you knew what was wanted in that much detail. As we shall see, many tutors in social science subjects reward independent thinkers who can argue, and do not simply expect to find the same material they have taught parroted back in essays or dissertations. Nevertheless, tutors do have an important role in defining what counts as good academic performance in practice. They have to decide whether a specific argument in an actual essay is sound or flawed, valuable or mistaken.

They also have to decide what is worth teaching and assessing, how to offer material at a suitable level of difficulty, what counts as an appropriate workload, and what counts as a reasonable expectation of student effort. In other words, they set standards in the broadest sense, and will be judging you against them. Sensible students will realize this and try at the very least to avoid demonstrating what counts as really unacceptable behaviour. At the other end of the scale, they might want to be more positive and try to explore the world of the tutor in order to learn something about how a professional social scientist sees the world, if only to test tutor perceptions against their own to see how they are doing. We have already suggested that this ability to see the world as others see it is a crucial part of learning and development: it is educational in the broad sense.

The topic has to be researched again. To begin with, you should try to avoid jumping to conclusions about what your tutors want. Lecturers often feel an obligation to represent views that are not necessarily their own, for example, in order to generate some debate and independent thinking. This is almost the opposite of everyday life argument, where you argue your personal case strongly and with as much conviction as you can, while minimizing the merits of any alternatives. In British Sociology in particular, there is a convention that students must be offered a range of different perspectives in the interests of 'balance'. Sometimes, it falls to one individual to present contrasting views. We know how ingenious an audience can be in trying to establish what the speaker 'really' believes, but this should constantly be tested and cannot be assumed.

Spot the Marxist?

It is not unknown for students to leap to conclusions about the political views of tutors, for example. Some excitement can be produced by having someone offer a lecture on Marxism, to take an obvious case. Marxism is an essential part of the Sociology repertoire, and you will be introduced to Marxist ideas pretty soon in your courses. It can be tempting to assume that the lecturer who is introducing the topic is a Marxist in the sense of having a personal political commitment to Marxist politics. Even if this were to be true, there would be no reason for alarm, unless the lecturer were presenting an unfair or one-sided discussion, with no opportunity to disagree. In practice, we know that a lecturer can be perfectly well informed and enthusiastic about Marxism in a lecture while thinking at the same time that the whole thing is badly flawed. In sum, lecturers feel obliged to represent the range of views and to argue for each of them effectively.

In the same vein, it would be a mistake to assume that female tutors are all feminists, that all male tutors are hostile to feminism, or that only black lecturers would want to embrace black political activist perspectives. In fact, if you go to enough lectures, you can sometimes find the same lecturers embracing quite different approaches in later sessions. This can cause confusion too for students who want to pigeonhole or label their tutors. More generally still, there are tendencies to assume that tutors who run sessions outlining views with which you might agree personally are supporting your views – students have assumed that Dave is in favour of a range of policies from renationalizing the railways to privatizing the NHS, from legalizing recreational drugs to supporting arguments for sport as a major route to social inclusion, from outlining the case to allow people to engage in fox-hunting to arguing for animal rights. Students can sometimes feel quite hurt if they notice any contradictions or find tutors arguing precisely the opposite in later sessions. They are still seeing the matter in personal terms. They have not understood what tutors want and are trying to do.

Students can sometimes feel disillusioned with what can look like glibness or hypocrisy, and come to see social science as a kind of cynical game, 'academic' in the worst sense. This can take the form of asserting that social science is 'irrelevant' compared to 'real' problems such as working with actual people. By contrast, we think that it is a matter of emphasis: social science does not always lead to practical and immediate solutions, but takes the process of research, critical analysis and debate as important background features of effective policy. These considerations can be seen as necessary preliminaries for entry into an actual profession: you certainly will not get much time for debate when you are actually in the front line.

Lecturers may appear to students impatient to enter the world of work to be chronically indecisive, always sitting on the fence, unable to offer any practical advice and thus socially useless – but they might simply have a different set of values about what teaching social science at university should be trying to do to contribute to professional practice. The lecture theatre or seminar room may be seen as the wrong place to push particular practical policies or solutions, at least until the problems are fully ventilated first.

We have met students who have commented at the end of their course that they are glad to be leaving behind abstract theory where there is never an answer to anything. We are used to being accused of living in 'ivory towers', especially by busy professionals who have to deal with immediate concrete face-to-face problems and are less interested in theoretical ones. However, your realizing that there are never (easy) answers to anything when you finally come to enter the vexed world of practice is probably a sign that we have been quietly successful at our stage of your career.

The 'Scientific' Stance

The difference between academic stances in social science and more 'common-sense' stances has been much discussed in more formal terms. One approach that seems to put it rather well is provided by the social theorist Alfred Schutz (1971). Basically, Schutz suggests that most people normally place themselves at the centre of their social world, and organize it around the 'here and now'. The people in that social world are divided according to how intimately we know them, with personal partners, friends and relatives at one extreme, and highly anonymous models ('ideal types' to be precise), like the postal worker who brings the mail, at the other. The 'scientific' stance is quite different by contrast, with a far more abstract starting point, and far more abstract interests.

We mean 'abstract' in the technical sense here of involving ideas and perspectives that are not grounded in personal experience but in the collective experience of social science itself. There is a strange but important 'virtual' 'community of social scientists' which guides the processes of theorizing and research. We do not mean that social science stays on the 'abstract' level of concepts and theories and never considers real effects on people – that is the easy stereotype, not the reality. That stereotype is usually buttressed by a view that academics and 'ordinary people' are still deeply segregated socially, that academics still live a life somehow remote from the realities, as they once did in the Middle Ages, and that 'ordinary people' have never done anything like a Sociology course. Actual experience does not support this view, though. (Box 3.1).

Box 3.1   An Example of 'Applied' Social Science

In discussing a practical problem like reducing street crime, sociologists do not deploy their own experience of street crime (if any) but draw on the

(Continued)

(Continued)

findings of others. These are not based on 'what everyone knows' (which is often what the popular media claim to know), but on some prior evaluation of what counts as good evidence. We know of cases where police and urban planners have applied sociological studies of the effects of urban environments on crime to guide their practice, or where they have examined their own procedures after reading some research on how policing itself can seem to increase crime and the fear of crime. This applied work in area policing derives not from the personal views of sociologists, nor from just asking the police or planners what they think, to reiterate the point, but from an initially detached perspective looking at the whole problem in a fresh and relatively disinterested (not uninterested) way.

What Do Tutors Want from Assignments?

We have argued throughout that it is important to feel confident and successful with student assessment, because that then permits some of the higher pleasures of academic life to be experienced from a more secure base. So, what do lecturers actually look for when they assess their students?

Asking tutors what they want from students is by no means a straightforward task. They may not have clarified their thoughts enough to be able to answer simple questions, but tend to let some notion of 'good practice' guide their actions. They may be tempted to give 'official' or polite answers thinking that that is what is expected. There may be a number of unconscious elements involved, as we shall see.

Certainly, our own attempts to ask colleagues to say what they expect in a good assignment, using a questionnaire, produced rather disappointing results. There was a low response rate. There were some colleagues who gave official answers and referred us to the published marking criteria. There were some who gave some indication about how they actually used the marking criteria, however.

They all valued clear expression and an attempt to answer the actual question, for example. Considerable importance was often given to the presentation of the assignment. Students tended to lose marks if they displayed irrelevance and lack of focus ('padding' and 'waffle'), and, above all, plagiarism. Colleagues also confess that they look less kindly on assignments that contain too many spelling or grammatical errors, even though students sometimes resent having these errors pointed out, and some complain that the essay is 'not a spelling test'. Given today's word processing packages, other tutors expected high standards of typing and layout. You might be surprised to find that these views are possibly even helpful – it is often argued that good presentation skills are also valuable in writing CVs, in entering paid work and pursuing future careers. Williams et al. (2006: 66) suggest that business is far less tolerant:

> Graduate recruiters love mistakes. Nothing thrills them more than receiving an application that is filled with errors of inclusion, presentation, grammar, spelling, punctuation or capitalization. … They can just put it onto [*sic*] the reject pile, happy in the knowledge that they have just saved themselves and their organisation lots of valuable minutes.

This is a fairly uncontroversial introduction to the real world of tutoring and marking, so far, so let us explore a bit further. Ideally, we are always and entirely fair and objective, and examine each answer clinically, using the published criteria. However, it is not too difficult to place yourselves in our position and realize that this can be hard to do in practice. For example, working to tight marking deadlines can add pressure which can affect our judgement. We hope you will not be shocked by this disclosure that we are sometimes less than perfect. Most working professionals know full well that this is a problem and instead of pretending it does not exist, they try to develop procedures to cope with any unfairness. On our side, second marking and moderation procedures (where whole lists of marks are discussed) are very useful, and help maintain equitable standards, as do published criteria. One implication for you to think about is that students can help us by making their work as easy for us to read and grade as possible.

Assessment Criteria

Let us develop our argument by examining those assessment criteria. They are usually published in student handbooks, and it is obvious that students need to look at them before and during their studies. We have met students who are unaware of any published assessment criteria, or who do not see their significance. We have even met students who prefer the informal criteria of their friends or family. Presumably, tutors were thought to mark work simply on an impressionistic basis and not to have understood the merits of the person involved, or, at least, not as well as their family. The real issue at stake was a more technical and less personal matter – how did the work measure up to the published criteria?

We like to encourage our own students to look carefully at the assessment criteria, and use them to assess their own work. We have welcomed students who have come back with their graded work and have asked to go through it with us, using the published criteria. It can be very helpful to provide a student with a highlighter pen, and invite them to indicate those sections that indicate 'critical analysis' or 'wide reading' or whatever the criteria specify (Boxes 3.2 and 3.3).

Box 3.2   Asssess Your Own Work

Play the role of the assessor for yourself.

Acquire your local assessment criteria and examine them.

Are there any problems, such as definitions of key terms, that are not clear?

How would you proceed as an assessor if you found any ambiguities?

Take one of your own assignments, or swap one with a (very good) friend, and mark it, using the criteria. Use a highlighter pen to mark crucial sections, as suggested above.

Focus in on 'critical analysis' (or your local equivalent). Where is it in the assignment? Is there enough of it for a good grade? Could there be more of it? Is the balance right between 'description' and 'analysis'.

Box 3.3   Make Your Own Assessments

Assess the following extracts from essay answers to a question on a Level 2 module. We have fictionalized these slightly, but they are still usefully close to actual examples.

Q: Is Britain a more 'open' society than it was 20 years ago?

Answer A

I think the character of Britain has changed and for the worse. I grew up in a respectable area in Liverpool, though that was before the arrival of loads

(Continued)

(Continued)

of asylum-seekers. I have got nothing against people from other countries, but this is a small island and we cannot keep taking more and more people. It is time that Britain was a lot less open in my view, and I feel that British people need to hang on to those traditions that made them great. Without keeping our distinctiveness, we will all end up in some large melting pot, all thinking, dressing, and acting in the same way. I can give many examples from my own experience of the problems faced by the native English in their own lands.

Answer B

The concept of 'openness' is usually seen in terms of the amount of social mobility apparent in British society. According to the early work by Glass (summarized by Goldthorpe et al., 1980), a 'closed' society would be one where there would be no social mobility between social classes, and no chance for anyone in the working class to rise and enter a middle-class occupation. A fully 'open' society, by contrast, would be one where parental social class was completely irrelevant in affecting the destinations of their children. These propositions and an examination of some of the work designed to test them will be examined first. The essay will conclude with a broader discussion of 'openness', moving away from social class to consider the effects of membership of other social ethnic and cultural groups.

- **Which one would get the higher grade from you?**
- **How relevant were factors like length of the extract, presentation or 'style' compared to the actual content in your decision?**
- **How relevant was your agreement or disagreement with the political views in the answers?**

For us, it would be the case that Answer A was much weaker, and, if it carried on like that, it would risk failing. But the main reasons for that would be technical. We might not agree with the politics at all, and we might prefer a much less ranting style, but the main problem is that it seems to contain almost no reference to any social science. It does not seem to want to discuss the concept, the research, or the arguments that have been covered (no doubt) on the course itself. It presents the sort of opinion that might be found among people who have never done any social science. It is difficult to find anything to assess against the criteria. That is not to say that Student A would not be welcome to make his or her point in seminars or other discussions, although it would be challenged like all such views.

We have also experimented by trying to reveal how we would have produced assignments ourselves so students can see how we actually operate. What follows is one example of some teaching material (drawn from rather earlier essay questions, not actual current ones) (Box 3.4). We based this exercise on the sort of marking scheme that we actually used in practice to guide our assessment of student answers. Our local criteria are probably different from yours, but you should be able to get some general ideas of what we were after (NB: specific assessment criteria are cited in bold type).

Box 3.4   A Marking Exercise

ESSAY TITLE: How useful is the term 'postfordism' in explaining recent developments in production? Illustrate with examples from the leisure industries.

The core of this essay is obviously a good critical account of postfordism. You will need to consult the literature on the reading list, or perhaps have a quick look at the file on the website, in order to **construct and communicate a coherent argument**, isolating central concepts and principles, and adding some examples.

At some stage you will want to suggest that there is a disagreement about the usefulness of the concept in explaining recent economic changes. Different terms are available to describe these changes instead, including 'flexible specialization'. Amin's *Introduction* also discusses a number of other terms, including Japanization. You can find a link to some notes on Amin's *Introduction* on the website too and you can then read the book itself. You will want to briefly discuss these alternatives in order to make some criticisms about postfordism. In the process, you will be able to **critically compare and contrast a range of academic approaches**. Try to identify the key issues and debates here, and not get too bogged down in detail.

We can then move to the part of the essay which invites you to illustrate the debates about usefulness with examples from the leisure industries. You can take as a guide the piece provided on the handout discussing flexible specialization in the film industry, but an excellent student will want to supply their own examples as well. There are many such examples – in the seminars we mentioned McDonaldization (which Ritzer thinks is still

(Continued)

(Continued)

fordist), and the local surfboard industry. If you can think of others and do a little research on them, you may be on the way to demonstrating a **mature ability to go beyond the given parameters of studied material**. In your illustrations, you will probably want to show how complex real-life examples actually are, that they show postfordist and flexible specialist elements, for example. You will try to demonstrate an **excellent use of relevant evidence** in the process. Your discussion will almost certainly make reference to other themes raised in this module or in others – what about some of the leisure businesses we discuss later on in the course? Do you know of any examples from Tourism Studies, or from Sports Studies, or from any of the other modules you study? Apart from the other good qualities, you will be indicating **an embracing understanding of a range of concepts and principles developed through the course of study**, and perhaps **an acute capacity for critical self-reflection**.

In your masterly summing up, you may want to stay nice and open and complex, good and balanced (although you can come to firmer conclusions if you wish, whichever way round you choose, as long as they seem justified). You might say that any general approaches are pretty hard to test against concrete evidence, that more research is needed on a wider range of industries, or that only time will tell which of the models is appropriate. You might want to consider whether 'Third World' countries might be exempt – we discussed Dubai in the seminar. You might want to say that management of the leisure industry simply does not fall into these simple categories any more, or that a proper history of the film industry would show different conclusions (especially if you have studied Management or History). In general, you will be demonstrating **a significant understanding of the criteria by which facts, principles and opinions are to be tested and judged,** or even **a recognition of the multi-disciplinary character of Leisure and/or Tourism Studies coupled with an ability to mobilize analyses for a range of the disciplines**.

All you then have to do is demonstrate a **fluent and concise style of writing** (do work on this and re-read before you hand in your essay), and a **thorough application of the Harvard system of referencing**.

If you have tried any similar exercises, you will also realize that assessment criteria have to be applied, and they have to be weighted. In other words, we first of all have to recognize in the work qualities such as 'coherent argument', and then to weigh up the different qualities in order to provide an overall mark. Sometimes this is quite difficult, since an essay can be strong in one quality yet weak in another, presented coherently and attractively but not showing much sign of wide reading, for example. Some marking schemes include precise weightings (such as the percentage of points to be awarded for each specified quality), but no scheme can avoid judgement and interpretation in individual cases, no matter how detailed. It follows that there can be no simple formula to draw on.

Going Behind the Assessment Criteria

From the student perspective, assessment criteria can provide only a limited insight. It is no good realizing that you have to inject 'critical analysis' into your work if you are not yet clear what 'critical analysis' actually means, or how to indicate that you have done one. Lists of definitions of some of these key terms, including rather good ones like those in Williams (2004), can only take you so far. What you need to know is what lies behind these words and criteria, what values they represent, and why academics consider them to be so important. We have to read published assessment criteria as clues, or as signs of a set of professional values. Displaying those values in your work is what gets good grades, rather than some literal attempt to learn definitions or follow popular recipes for success.

The same point can be made about learning outcomes (Box 3.5). These are commonly published as well, and some study skills advocates urge students to look at them and use them to guide their reading and research activities (such as McIlroy, 2003). Of course this can be useful, but our own experience suggests that writing learning outcomes can be more about bureaucracy and teaching audits than a considered and detailed account of what the course is all about.

Box 3.5   Learning Outcomes

Here is a set of learning outcomes from a first year module. The module will enable you to do the following:

(Continued)

(Continued)

- **Demonstrate your understanding of sociological research on education.**
- **Analyse familiar aspects of education sociologically.**
- **Distinguish between and critically evaluate sociological explanations.**
- **Exercise judgement in selection of and research into assessment tasks.**

You might wish to examine this set and ask:

- **Are you sure what the key words actually mean?**
- **Can you see why these outcomes might be important to the tutor concerned?**
- **Can you detect any hints of outcomes like these in the teaching materials and activities provided?**
- **How do these compare to the sort of outcomes you personally expect to achieve after taking such a module?**
- **How could you demonstrate you have achieved outcomes like these in an assignment?**

Academic Progression

Written objectives like these can contain important clues about the professional view of teaching, what tutors suppose about academic progression between one module and the next, and what tutors expect of students. It is common, for example, for learning outcomes to include a particular set of words, such as 'describe' ('demonstrate' in the case above?) for initial courses, and 'evaluate' for more advanced ones. Originally, words of this type were associated with some influential work undertaken by Benjamin Bloom in the 1960s in America. Bloom began by asking a number of important American academics to try to pin down the differences between elementary and advanced courses, and to specify the kind of intellectual operations that they were looking for. A brief account of the range of the work can be seen in Box 3.6.

Box 3.6   Educational Objectives

According to T. Allen (and others) (no date) [Bloom's] Taxonomy of Educational Objectives defines 'Cognitive domain' as:

(Continued)

(Continued)

1 Knowledge: recognize or recall information: 'define, recall, recognize, remember, who, what, where, when'.
2 Comprehension: 'describe, compare, contrast, rephrase, put in your own words, explain the main idea'.
3 Application: 'apply, classify, use, choose, employ, write an example, solve, how many, which, what is'.
4 Analysis: 'identify motives/causes, draw conclusions, determine evidence, support, analyze, why'.
5 Synthesis: 'predict, produce, write, design, develop, synthesize, construct, how can we improve, what would happen if, can you devise, how can we solve'.
6 Evaluation: 'does not have a single correct answer ... objective criteria or personal values must be applied. ... Some standard must be used ... differing standards are quite acceptable'.

Even today, these key words can be seen to represent the professional views of academics. This is how they see what they are trying to do, and this is how they define student progress, moving through the different stages from knowledge, through application and analysis to synthesis and evaluation. Bloom and his associates also went on to specify the key stages in other important 'domains' of academic life as well. The 'affective' domain refers to 'affect' in the technical way that term is used in psychology – that is, relating to opinions, values, emotional commitments, interests, and attitudes. Bloom and his associates thought that students could also make progress in this area, which is usually thought to be too difficult to define. The stages here range from passively receiving or noting emotions and interests, through responding and valuing them, to the final stages of realizing how they are connected together and might be used systematically to generate whole ways of living – maintaining 'balance between freedom and responsibility', accepting responsibility for your own behaviour, showing self-reliance, and so on (see Allen, no date).

Students undertaking social science courses that involve motor skills (such as in professions allied to medicine or in sport) might be particularly interested to see the work on the 'psychomotor domain' as well. Here, the focus is on performance, its development and control. There are stages of development in this domain too, ranging from mastering basic movements to the development of perceptual and physical abilities to permit 'complex adaptive skills' (Allen, no date). We are talking not only about obvious applications like physical skills here, but also about 'expressive and interpretive movement', music, performance and 'non-discursive communication' that can be found in many other areas.

It is possible to see from these classifications and lists that academics expect students to show some progress from basic to more advanced cognitive, affective, and psychomotor activities. Students might well consider these possibilities, use them as checklists to measure their own growing competence, and perhaps even try to demonstrate them clearly in their assignments, CVs and job applications.

Adult Development

Another piece of influential argument has affected thinking about curriculum design, especially in higher education. It is based on American practice again, but has become well known in the UK as well. It turns on the work of William Perry, who became famous as offering one of the few studies of adult (not child) cognitive and social development. Again, the point is not to assess this work as academic social psychology, but to read it as expressing a set of expectations and values. It can be read as a description of what academics expect to be happening to students as they go through their courses (Box 3.7). Perry's work has recently been usefully modified by Belenky et al. (1986).

Box 3.7   Perry on Development

'Journey along the nine "Perry" positions'

(as modified by Belenky et al.).

The nine positions, grouped into four categories, are:

A. Dualism/Received Knowledge:

There are right/wrong answers ... known to Authorities ... student's task is 'to learn the Right Solutions'.

B. Multiplicity/Subjective Knowledge:

There are conflicting answers; therefore, must trust one's 'inner voice', not external Authority ... everyone has a right to their own opinion or some problems are unsolvable. ... Student's task is to shoot the bull.

(Continued)

(Continued)

C. Relativism/Procedural Knowledge:

There are disciplinary reasoning methods ... [which may be] empathetic (what does this poem say to me?) [or] ... 'objective' (what techniques can I use to analyse this poem?). ... Student's task is to learn to 'evaluate solutions'.

D. Commitments/Constructed Knowledge:

Integration of knowledge learnt from others with personal experience and reflection. ... Student makes a commitment ... [or] ... Student explores issues of responsibility ... [or] ... Student realizes commitment is an ongoing, unfolding, involving activity.

Source: Rapaport (2004)

Box 3.7 shows the main points of the Perry scheme. Fuller details can be found on the website itself – http://www.cs.buffalo.edu/~rapaport/perry.positions.html (accessed 24 July 2005) (Rapaport, 2004). Perry also warns us about the emotional and social reactions that students can display as part of their development, including becoming temporarily alienated, avoiding courses that offer too much challenge, and sometimes dropping out of college altogether. This can be useful to remind lecturers of the possible personal impact of what they are trying to do.

For example, the idea that earlier certainties about the social world should be challenged by academic courses in social sciences seems a very widespread value position among academics. We have often experienced such challenge ourselves, sometimes in an uncompromising way. Dave's first encounter with Philosophy was memorable for the tutor explaining that his role was to get us to realize that nearly everything we thought was 'right' was in fact unfounded and poorly argued. This rather excessively frank and uncompromising challenge was overcome, but not before experiencing some anxiety.

However, we often forget the immediate discomfort of such a challenge for students. They have sometimes come to university unprepared to face a threat to many of the beliefs that they take as central to themselves, their identities, and their ways of life, which can still be involved. It can be seriously unsettling to come across arguments that question beliefs that have been taken for granted as obvious and valuable. Social science has this demanding quality, and it can easily spill over into everyday life – we are not challenging perceptions of molecules or galaxies, but perceptions about people from other communities, those with different genders, the political values that our parents or partners hold, the beliefs we might have grown up with. Perry's scheme suggests that there is a final harmonious stage, but it can be a struggle to reach it.

Developing a Learning Style

There is some work on learning styles which has also become very popular and well known, and will again provide us with some clues about what lecturers expect students to be doing when they learn. Box 3.8 provides the basic outline for the sake of clarity. It is fair to say that the work has been elaborated since, and is still proceeding. Later versions of it can be found in electronic format (Entwistle, 2000).

Box 3.8   Approaches to Learning

'Surface' and 'deep' approaches: an early definition.

Deep approach

An intention to understand. The student maintains the structure of the task:

- focus on 'what is signified' (e.g. the author's argument or the concepts applicable to solving the problem);
- relates previous knowledge to new knowledge;
- relates knowledge from different courses;
- relates theoretical ideas to everyday experience;
- relates and distinguishes evidence and argument;
- organises and structures content into a coherent whole.

Source: Ramsden (1992: Table 4.1)

An *internal* emphasis: 'A window through which aspects of reality become visible and more intelligible' (Marton et al., 1984).

Surface approach

An intention only to complete the task requirements. The student distorts the structure of the task:

(Continued)

(Continued)

- focuses on 'the signs' (for example, the words and sentences of the text, or, unthinkingly, on the formula needed to solve the problem);
- focus on unrelated parts of the text;
- memorises information for assessments;
- associates facts and concepts unreflexively;
- fails to distinguish principles from examples;
- treats the task as an external imposition.

An *external* emphasis: the demands of assessments, knowledge cut off from everyday reality.

The work is based on some extensive research, as are the other examples we have discussed in this chapter, and it has led to some insightful advice to students undertaking study at university specifically, which we review in a later chapter. However, for this chapter, it is convenient to see the work as again reflecting a set of values that tutors hold about what counts as worthwhile learning. Underneath the technical and neutral 'psychological' appearance of the scheme, it is possible to detect these values. Taking a 'deep' approach to assessment implies relishing the challenge of understanding reality differently, as opposed to the 'surface' approach which sees assessment as an 'external imposition'. This is exactly how tutors would like students to respond to assessment, of course. They would also like them to see the connections between arguments and existing knowledge, to be able to separate principles from examples, and generally to see the deeper purpose of higher education.

We have no doubt that these are perfectly acceptable values. We subscribe to them ourselves, as do most of our colleagues. We would tend to agree with the finding that a 'deep' approach delivers not only better grades but also far more security and enjoyment for students. We have met students who were so relieved once they realized that they did not need to memorize huge amounts of information in order to perform assessment tasks. One of the most remarkable examples was provided by a student who felt that he had to memorize 'all the dates' in a particular journal article – he meant the dates of publication of other articles referenced in the piece. You can imagine his feelings when he picked up an article with a dozen references in the first paragraph alone!

Perhaps you can also realize how relieved he was when he found he had misunderstood the whole point and had only made things impossible for himself.

Again, students might well consider locating themselves in this scheme of things. You can download the latest versions of the questionnaires used to classify students (via Entwistle, 2000), or try the simpler version in Ramsden (1992), for now, summarized in Box 3.9.

Box 3.9 Find Your Own Approach

Indicators of 'meaning orientation' (deep approach)

I try to relate ideas in one subject to those in others whenever possible.
I usually set out to understand thoroughly the meaning of what I am asked to read.
In trying to understand new ideas I often try to relate them to real-life situations.
When I'm tackling a new topic I often ask myself questions about it which the new information should answer.
In reading new material, I often find that I'm continually reminded of material I know already and see the latter in a new light.
I spend a lot of my free time finding out more about interesting topics which have been discussed in classes.

Indicators of 'reproducing orientation' (surface approach)

I find I have to concentrate on memorizing a good deal of what we have to learn.
I usually don't have time to think about the implications of what I have read.
Although I generally remember facts and details, I find it difficult to fit them together into an overall picture.
I find I tend to remember things best if I concentrate on the order in which the lecturer presented them.
I tend to choose those subjects with a lot of factual content rather than theoretical kinds of analysis.
I find it best to accept the statements and ideas of my lecturers and question them only under special circumstances.

Source: Ramsden (1992: Table 4.2).

The Social Values of Academic Life

We can now turn to some influential work by the French sociologist Pierre Bourdieu (1988) on the values of French academics. Despite its limitations – the study is based on France and is rather dated – there are some insights, especially on the value systems of academics. Bourdieu actually places some emphasis on unconscious elements of action and behaviour in his Sociology more generally. Very briefly, the idea is that we simply internalize values, set of judgements, classifications and ideas about what is valuable and how to behave, which we gain from our upbringing. We use these values and judgements all the time in our everyday life, without being aware of how they work or where they came from – it just seems 'natural' to us to behave in the way we do.

Academics are no exception, and when they come to perform their job, including assessment, they use these unconscious set of judgements and classifications in order to estimate the value of students' work. Students often suspect this, of course, but are not that systematic about finding out what these unconscious values are. Bourdieu has attempted to specify what some of them might look like and has noted 'disparate criteria, never clarified, hierarchized or systematized ... [but] ... including handwriting, appearance, style, general culture ... accent, elocution and diction ... and finally and above all the bodily *hexis* [which includes] manners and behaviour' (1988: 200). We might use the more popular term 'body language' to illustrate the notion of 'bodily hexis': Bourdieu talks of people who feel either at ease or awkward in their bodies.

It is clear from his own work recording grading operations that these judgements do affect the grades that students receive, and that it is not just a simple matter of identifying criteria or technical merits in a piece of work alone. Since these values tend to be shared and unconscious, they are not easily recognized or dealt with, despite the usual routines of blind double marking, although the increasing trend towards anonymous assignments might help. Again, we have no wish to alarm students or to seem to disrespect our colleagues by ventilating this work. The more we all know about the actual processes involved in assessment, not the idealized ones where everything is clear and objective, the more we can take suitable action.

Some students may feel angry or depressed that they are still being judged according to what might look like 'irrelevant' factors such as 'style', or body language. Others might realize that this gives them a chance to impress tutors by attempting to develop a suitable style or body language. Of course, given that elements of both of these are unconsciously held, and appear to be 'natural', simulating approved versions may not be easy, even if you decided you wanted to do so. Bourdieu suggests that those most likely to be able to match up to the judgements of tutors will be those students who come from the same sort of social background, and who have been brought up in a similar way. Such people just seem to know how to develop a suitable style in essays or in presentations. They seem to do so effortlessly and naturally, and always seem at ease with their bodies. For others, the choice seems to be either a complete refusal to change, or some attempt to approach the ideal, perhaps learning a bit about how to present in a seminar. At the extreme, some students might want to undergo a complete makeover, changing their accent and appearance to conform to the requirements of others.

A more realistic stance we suggest is to see the process of making social judgements and valuations – 'social distanciation' (in Chapter 1) – as offering social difficulties and challenges presented by universities, and, indeed, by work settings as well. The invaluable Williams et al. (2006) make it clear that unconscious judgements are being used to select graduates for elite management positions, and that the processes seem rather similar to the ones uncovered by Bourdieu. Basically, despite all the psychometric testing and interviewing, managers appoint applicants who look and act like a rather idealized and younger version of themselves. The justification is that only such people will 'fit in' and benefit the company.

These situations offer challenges which can be understood at least and thus dealt with. You may have to persuade your tutors (or interviewers) that your style and body language are acceptable, just different, not a challenge to them. Universities (and companies) are supposed to welcome diversity, after all. We suggest ways in which this might be done in presentations, for example. It helps a great deal if you can succeed clearly on the other official criteria as well. This can mean that you have to be prepared to be 'ten times better' than those from more favoured social backgrounds, or 'trade off' conventional success against unconventional appearances. We do not wish to overemphasize the point, and we do think that universities are generally very tolerant places, often much more ready to accept diversity than workplaces, it seems. It is also true that not all tutors come from privileged social backgrounds themselves, unlike the elite academics in Bourdieu's study. If you are from an unconventional background, you may well find yourself able to relate particularly well to such tutors, as we suggested in Chapter 1.

Bourdieu is also useful in arguing that change in past identities and social position is much easier if you feel financially and culturally secure. If anything, his work suggests that the financial security comes first. That mature phase in Perry, where everything finally slots into perspective, may be maximized for many students after they leave the university and start gaining financial stability.

Finally, Bourdieu has a useful phrase 'cultural capital' to describe the sort of resources that people use to manage different social situations. Like economic capital, cultural capital is held in far from equal amounts. It can be possible to increase your stock, however. Perhaps conventional study skills can be seen in this light, as one of us has suggested (Harris, 2005). Sometimes, students will deliberately set out to increase the stock of cultural capital in a broader sense as well, by expanding their cultural and social horizons, especially while they are at university. We have suggested that everyone should consider this, bearing in mind their individual circumstances, of course.

Apart from anything else, cultural capital is desirable when plumping your CV or approaching interviews for jobs as well, as we shall suggest. It is possible to cash in your cultural capital in a number of ways by appearing as a well-rounded, knowledgeable, cosmopolitan and civilized person with tastes and interests beyond the narrowly academic. A survey conducted by London Guildhall University (Wisdom, 1996) asked a number of university students to describe what they thought a graduate would be like. They mentioned factors such as having expertise and confidence; being able to achieve a balanced view, being open-minded, being able to debate; being well motivated and having initiative and drive; being able to grasp new ideas quickly and to 'multi-task'; and being able to communicate effectively. There is considerable overlap here with the whole notion of 'transferable skills', which we discuss in Chapter 4.

The UK Government itself has also researched this matter (Higher Education Quality Council, 1995). It has specified that there are likely to be three kinds of achievement:

1 *Field specific* – the possession of a body of knowledge and other qualities particular to the field (or fields) studied.

2 *Shared* – the possession of certain more general attributes some of which might be common to graduates from families of degrees.

3 *Generic* – the possession of yet more general attributes which might be common to all ... graduates.

After some rather bureaucratic ground clearing, the Council goes on to survey some of the work that has been done already in this field. The main characteristics include developing knowledge in the basics of the discipline, what might be seen as personal skills such as developing self-motivation and engagement, including engagement in research; developing a 'critical and analytical approach', and then the 'transferable or intellectual and practical skills' again. They also discuss competencies such as being able to work with others – including 'using logical and rational argument to persuade others; understanding and building/reflecting on how others perceive him/her; identifying the needs of others and building positive relationships'. You can begin to practise (and record) these competencies from the very beginning of your university career.

Achieving 'Graduateness'

Finally, some American research is useful, associated with the work of Boyer. The Boyer Report (Boyer Commission, 1998) , and the discussion it subsequently generated, were directed at university reform, an attempt to raise the status of teaching inside the prestigious research universities of the USA, but, again, we can reinterpret the arguments to indicate the kind of undergraduate education that many academics want and value. At first reading, Boyer does look rather idealistic, advocating that the university rediscover its role as a meeting place for different specialist interests, offering a chance for undergraduates to explore different options, and to meet people from diverse social backgrounds. Its most famous recommendation is that undergraduates be encouraged to undertake academic research, and be given some sense of the excitement and purpose of it. Reforms are suggested that would bring undergraduates into contact with the leading researchers, both on campus and elsewhere. The discussion of Boyer is riddled with phrases such as the 'excitement of discovery', and there is strong advocacy of a form of teaching that will not only focus on the transmission of knowledge alone, but also engage students in mutual exploration.

Boyer has been much admired in the UK as well, and his work has led to a number of discussions about linking research and teaching. From our point of view, the Report supports the sort of values we have been discussing – open-ended discussion, flexibility, pursuing multiple options and different opinions, developing what might be described as a 'research orientation'. Cynics might see these values as nothing more than a powerful occupational myth or ideology. However, they underlie what looks like some rather peculiar practices of the university. Trying deliberately to explore different options in seminars, keeping one's own views in the background, might be one, or holding judgement back on other people's views, trying to develop a calm and rational discussion of controversial items, trying to make sure that everyone has the chance to speak. In lectures, trying to expose some of the problems rather than offering accepted 'facts' might be an expression of Boyer values.

Whether you approve of these particular values or not, you probably need to be aware of them. You will have your favourite lecturers and lecturing methods. However, it would be a mistake to dismiss the others, and see them as simply offering inefficient teaching. They may be attempting to expose you to the real dilemmas and loose ends that a mature researcher knows are characteristic of the subject.

Academic Sins

The final area we are going to examine concerns plagiarism. This is an interesting area because it shows the strong values that inform academic life, and it is particularly important that you realize that this is what tutors definitely do *not* want! Most university regulations threaten plagiarists with the most severe forms of punishment, up to and including expulsion. Some of those expelled or punished in other ways will have their files or transcripts marked, so that the punishment remains as a permanent record. Be warned that plagiarists get no sympathy, and even otherwise calm and tolerant tutors seem to get angry about it: 'Do not plagiarize. It is unethical, immoral, unscholarly, cowardly and stupid' (Williams, 2004: 201).

Why does plagiarism evoke such an outcry? It does seem a strangely irrational concern in a way. The regulations and the punishments have been justified as preventing a kind of intellectual theft, for example, but cases of real theft of property do not usually attract the same level of reaction. The student plagiarist is portrayed as a threat to all the values that the university stands for, and is thus qualified for exemplary punishment. However, Franklyn-Stoakes and Newstead (1995) or Norton et al. (2001) reveal a rather different picture, as we shall see – most of those who plagiarize do so because they are simply badly organized, not deliberately subversive.

More promising, in our view, is to try to understand, by adopting the analysis offered by Levin (2004). He sees the widespread concern with plagiarism as a form of 'moral panic'. This term is commonly used in Sociology and Cultural Studies to describe the strong passionate reaction to some perceived moral challenge or defect – rising levels of street crime is the classic example. The term has also entered journalism and public life to some extent. It is easy to think that the term implies a value judgement as well – moral panics are exaggerated, distorted, blown out of all proportion, not based on the facts, and so on. We want to pursue a more detached account, while suspending moral judgements for now. A 'moral panic' has one particularly interesting technical feature in that it serves to combine a number of specific anxieties and worries into an overall feeling that there is some major crisis looming which threatens everything we hold dear.

We think that this notion of combination can be detected in the extensive concerns about plagiarism. A number of concerns can be focused – worry about increasing the intake of students and moving towards a mass university system; worry about the impact on standards of substantially increased publication, especially on the Net; worry about our own ability to keep up with the field or to assess students fairly. This helps to explain (not explain away) the considerable moral impetus behind campaigns against plagiarism. Unfortunately, this moral impetus can sometimes prevent adequate analysis of the reasons for the activity and adequate policies to prevent it. Rational considerations can be swept away in the urge to punish and to keep values intact: if you ever have to face an official charge of plagiarism, you will see how quickly an unforgiving and sometimes intolerant side of the university appears.

The main point here is to warn students about this very strongly held value position. We have suggested in the Introduction that your main task as a novice is to avoid any suspicion of being a plagiarist – you have a lot to lose as the following two examples demonstrate. One student was repeatedly warned about plagiarism and urged to seek help and advice, but she wrote her dissertation entirely without supervision nevertheless. It was judged as having been plagiarized, she received a mark of zero for it, she could not then qualify for an honours degree, and she left with a transcript that explained the zero grade as a result of plagiarism. Another student in a very similar position avoided a charge of plagiarism by pleading poor scholarship instead – he was awarded a bare pass grade for his dissertation, and his overall degree dropped a class band as a result. In both cases, these disasters could have been avoided simply by understanding the problem, and by employing an adequate referencing system to avoid it. We suggest how you might do this in Chapter 5.

Academic Loyalties

To round off this chapter, it is necessary to say that the values we have been describing are probably held in a much less explicit way. There is also probably far more disagreement about them in practice, with the possible exception of the strong condemnation of plagiarism. We suggest you think about these values, especially the ones expressed in official reports, as generalizations. They are helpful mostly in sensitizing you to the 'strange' occupation of college tutor or lecturer. Tutors may look like your parents or spouses, but they have been socialized into a professional culture with distinctive values and concerns.

Much of this occupation and its concerns remain concealed from the average student, we suspect. For example, it is not always obvious that the role of lecturer tends to include rather more than just teaching. There is quite a lot of administration and management these days, and many colleagues are under pressure to publish their research findings, and to get funding for research projects. This is not just the result of enthusiasm for the subject, since funding and publication are activities that are becoming increasingly crucial to pursuing an academic career. This is an important point when you get frustrated because you cannot contact a tutor when you want to do so. We still see notes and e-mails of the kind that say 'I tried to contact you all yesterday afternoon – where were you?' The answer usually is one of the following: (a) I was teaching on another course or module; (b) I was at a meeting; (c) I was in the library; (d) I am only on a part-time contract and I work somewhere else on Wednesdays.

Finally, there is a whole academic world of which students become aware only indirectly, and sometimes in rather mysterious ways. Lecturers have a number of allegiances and loyalties, to colleagues, sometimes colleagues in other institutions as well as their own, and to more abstract entities such as 'a research programme', or 'the discipline'. Some commentators have referred to the effects of these conflicting loyalties in terms of what Becher (1989) calls, rather ironically, 'tribalism'. We are not trying to demean our colleagues here (or to exempt ourselves), but simply trying to cast a little light so that students can understand us better.

The indirect ways in which you might become aware of this dimension is when you seem to provoke puzzling reactions in your assignments or discussions. For example, I have seen students using the phrase 'personality' in their essays, with tutor responses that refer to 'socially constructed selves' instead. To a beginner this can seem rather trivial, a quibble about words, but to us it is quite important in indicating which perspective is being developed. We have also heard students express puzzlement that 'the same topic' is taught on apparently separate programmes – 'popular culture' appears on History, Sociology and Media Studies modules, for example. They can sometimes become aware that the treatment of the topic is subtly different, but are usually unable to pin down exactly where these differences lie, and what makes them so important to lecturers. Students can draw quite the wrong conclusions here, and respond by completely compartmentalizing their work, never drawing parallels or comparisons between topics and their treatment on different modules or programmes. For our part, we may be simply trying to get you to see the characteristic differences between disciplines which are significant to us, but perhaps barely visible, as yet, to you. We suggest ways to handle differences and comparisons in later chapters.

Chapter Summary

1   It is important to try to understand what tutors actually want and expect, and how they see their roles. What you decide to do with this knowledge is a personal decision – you may find it useful to try and give tutors what they want, or you might just feel you can make a more informed decision about how to act to fit your own values and wants with theirs.

2   Although this can lead to some surprises, it is better to know than to guess.

3   We hope you will appreciate professional efforts to develop ways to overcome our imperfections – published criteria, double marking, open discussions and the rest.

4   The values and beliefs of university tutors are not easy to establish but examining assessment criteria, learning outcomes and course documents is one place to start.

5   Clues can also be derived from policy statements and background discussions about curriculum design. We want you to see these not only as technical matters but as expressing intentions and expectations – that there will be debate, open-mindedness, a noticeable development of views, progress towards more complex understandings.

6   Even the vexed issue of preferred 'styles' and preferences can be illuminated by using some sociological work.

7   There does seem to be consensus about the undesirability of plagiarism and cheating.

8   It can be helpful to get a glimpse into the professional world of your tutors and realize that they can face conflicting loyalties and demands on their time. This can help you fight any feelings of rejection if you cannot always meet when you wish, and it might encourage a more systematic approach to tutor contact.

9   We think that a professional and realistic working relationship with your tutors, based on mutual understanding and respect, is worth developing as soon as possible.

4 What Do Employers Want?

CHAPTER OVERVIEW

- What is 'employability'?
- Desirable skills and qualities sought by employers.
- Transferable skills and how to record them on your CV.
- Social and cultural capital and how to acquire more.
- Using social science to understand others.

The overall aim of this book is to give advice on how you can achieve a good degree in the social sciences. An associated aim is to promote employability to help you find suitable jobs in an increasingly competitive and diverse labour market.

Trying to establish what it is that employers actually want is a similar problem to the ones we discussed in the previous chapter. There are some sources of information that we can draw upon which will give us clues about what is required by employers in general, but such information can be incomplete or misleading. Individual employers may well vary in terms of what it is they are looking for, and, sometimes, there may be semi-conscious or unconscious preferences involved as well. These preferences can lie beneath the usual lists of 'skills' that are often produced by surveys of major employers.

The major implication that follows is that students should be prepared to research the wants and requirements of particular employers for particular jobs, sometimes in considerable detail. These will often be supplied in the form of job description and person description details that are provided with application forms. General knowledge of the company or body concerned is usually required too. It is a good idea to look at such application forms before you have got too far in your university career, because you may need to make sure that you can acquire relevant experience while you are at university. Williams et al. (2006) also urge students to attend recruiting fairs, not only to get specific information about jobs but also to research the values of the companies concerned. These values are often embodied clearly in the kinds of recruiters and employees that you will meet and get to talk to. You will want to present yourself as compatible with those existing employees, Williams et al. argue, so you might as well research carefully first.

Similarly, visiting the Careers Advice department should not really be left too late either. There is a range of material to help shape your ideas about careers, to make clear you know about the range of options, and to give you advice about building a useful CV, writing an application with impact, or performing effectively at interviews or subsequent assessments. You would certainly not want to be guided by stereotypes, folk knowledge and ideologies about 'suitable' careers – the research literature is full of examples about how talented women, for example, have been persuaded that particular occupations are best for them (classically teaching and nursing), simply because these occupations match ideological views about women and their traditional role in society. Williams et al. suggest that employers can even try to get applicants to disqualify themselves from even applying in order to make selection easier.

Thinking about Employability

Generally, there is a large amount of material on the Web which can help with a variety of activities from job-hunting to writing an efficient CV and preparing yourself for interviews and even psychometric tests. There is far too much to summarize here, but particularly good sites include the comprehensive ones run by Prospects for UK students (http://www. prospects.ac.uk/cms/) or Universitiesnet for US students (http://www. universitiesnet.com/careers.htm). We have frequently mentioned Williams et al., partly because the team claim to offer the only advice based on extensive (and originally academic) research done on employers as they actually select applicants.

It is perhaps easier to motivate yourself to do this if you have a particular career in mind, of course. The obvious example here is that students who are intending to be teachers often make sure they have arranged some experience in schools while they are taking their university courses. Similarly, those intending to have a military career typically make sure they are gaining experience with the Officer Training Corps, or the reservist forces. The same remarks clearly apply to a range of other intended professions, from the police to social work and the community and youth services (to list some currently popular choices). Students thinking of the increasing popular route of self-employment should also arrange suitable experience too, of course, and bear in mind the results of a recent survey (Tackey and Perryman, 1999) which noted that:

> Skills issues were important to the self-employed graduates. They relied extensively on their innovative and creative skills, which also they believed they had developed to a considerable extent at university. Other than this, there were significant gaps in acquiring and developing generic business skills such as accounting, book-keeping, product pricing, selling and, importantly, business planning. These skill deficiencies presented significant constraints to business start-up.

The emphasis on business skills raises an important point in that it is not enough to demonstrate a range of general skills or experiences without being able to show their relevance to your chosen occupation.

That still leaves a large area of relative uncertainty, however. You may be undecided about a future career, as many students are in particular subjects such as Leisure, Tourism and Recreation Studies. You may have decided that you will resume a career that you have begun before you came to university – sometimes, a degree opens the door to promotion or re-entry at a higher level. There may well be increasing numbers of students who do not have a particular vocational destination in mind at all. This is often forgotten in policy discussions, but some mature students are classically less interested in the vocational implications of their university courses. Perhaps they are living in an area with few occupational opportunities, and are unable to move in search of work because they have family commitments locally. Perhaps they have reached an age where occupational opportunities are more limited – 'occupational maturity' as it is sometimes politely called.

As usual, there will be a range of courses and other opportunities available for you to choose, and some will appear more 'vocational' than others. All students have to make choices between activities that will prepare them for a job, and activities that are simply interesting and appealing, without necessarily having any obvious vocational benefits – these include leisure activity such as clubbing, extreme sports, travelling, and so on. Some activities may present particular difficulties, like membership of an environmental protest group, for example. We would not advise people not to do these activities, of course, but there may well be a need to weigh up any possible disadvantages later in life.

As the last two examples indicate at least, however, it might be possible even to finesse leisure activities as vocationally relevant, as part of what Williams et al. (2006) call the task of constructing a suitable narrative about yourself. If playing sport has made you into a more mature, well-rounded, and confident person, able to demonstrate leadership or teamwork, then this is something that employers might well need to be informed about. There is some evidence from social mobility research that suggests that employers are looking for well-rounded people with a certain amount of 'cultural capital' (Aldridge, 2004) as well as those with particular skills. Similarly, there may well be leisure activities that you feel you should explain or soft-pedal. Much will depend on how you attempt to fit your experience to the requirements of particular employers when you construct a suitable application and CV. You may well want to consider your university stay as providing a range of experiences that can help you adjust to particular requirements. Williams et al. call this ability to tailor what you have done to the requirements of the post for which you are applying 'personal capital'. It involves writing about your qualities in such a way as to make it immediately obvious to the employer how you can demonstrate the competencies they require. Some basic advice follows but, first of all, what is known about what employers actually want in new graduates? There have been a variety of surveys, which quite often focus on the issue of 'skills'. The sort of data that they provide are shown below.

Employability – What Is It?

As a starting point, Hilary put the word 'employability' into the Google search engine, only to find there were 113,000 matches – even though she limited the search to UK and Ireland sites only! Her attempt to try to restrict the number of matches by entering 'definitions of employability' resulted in a mere 16,900 matches! Faced with this wealth of material, we decided to follow the definition of employability used by the Enhancing Student Employability Co-ordination Team (ESECT), a 30-month project completed in 2005 and run under the auspices of the (UK) Learning and Teaching Support Network (LSTN) Generic Centre (http://www.ltsn. ac.uk/genericcentre/index.asp?id=17641). In ESECT's view, employability is:

> a set of achievements – skills, understandings and personal attributes – that make individuals more likely to gain employment and be successful in their chosen occupations.

What are Employers Looking For in Graduate Recruits?

To what extent does the ESECT definition of employability match with what employers are seeking when they appoint individuals to fill their graduate vacancies? And is it possible to put flesh on the bones of this somewhat abstract description to help you know exactly what they are aiming for? A report by the Association of Graduate Recruiters (quoted in *Prospects Today*, 12 November 2003) highlighted the employability skills seen as most important by employers. The top five requirements were: motivation and enthusiasm; teamworking; oral communication; flexibility and adaptability; and initiative/proactivity. By the way, the Association of Graduate Recruiters has a useful website (http://graduate.monster.co.uk) that contains 'Career Hunting' tools, including a skills assessment test.

The student recruitment specialists Hobsons offer a careers service for graduates (www.get.hobsons.co.uk/service.jsp). Their annual directory of UK employers seeking to recruit graduates includes information about desirable skills and personal qualities required for over 120 job roles (CRAC, 2003). This comprehensive guide is supplied free to graduate job-seekers from universities' or colleges' careers services. Box 4.1 sets out those that appear most frequently, regardless of industrial sector and type of job. Here is further confirmation of the 'soft' skills or 'people' skills and personal qualities that businesses regard as important attributes that make students like you employable.

Box 4.1   Desirable Skills and Qualities Required by Employers

General skills

Oral communication skills, including giving presentations
Written communication skills and good command of English
Numeracy; practised ability to handle numerical data
Computer literacy (including word processing, e-mail and the Internet)
Ability to gather, assess and interpret data (including noting inconsistencies)
Accuracy and attention to detail
Creative thinking
Seeing the whole picture
'Juggling' and ability to meet deadlines
Managing own development
Problem-solving
Planning and prioritization
Organization
Influencing
Teamworking (including the ability to delegate, organize, lead and motivate)
Ability to work alone
Self-management skills

Specialist skills

Specific occupational skills and specialist knowledge (for example, languages; information technology; accounting; engineering)

Personal qualities

Motivation and enthusiasm
Interpersonal skills
Flexibility and adaptability
Initiative
Confidence
Tact and diplomacy
Sense of humour
Discretion
Leadership
Ability to get on with people at all levels

There are, of course, more idiosyncratic 'skills' required for particular jobs. For example, key skills for doctors, corporate bankers and cinema managers include the ability to work long hours (CRAC, 2003). Healthcare managers, on the other hand, need to be thick-skinned and emotionally tough, as well as sensitive to the political implications of decisions. Journalists need a 'nose' for a story.

What is not clear from the Directory is the importance of a student's discipline area. However, many employers take graduates of any discipline; they are as interested in your personal skills and experiences as in your degree subject. To this end, activities such as voluntary work, part-time work, working for the Students' Union, being editor of the university's newspaper, taking a gap year – these can all be seen as valuable learning opportunities to enhance potential recruits' range of skills.

It may be higher education's role to contribute to the development of graduates with the skills and qualities detailed in Box 4.1. For example, recent publications focus on 'employability-friendly' curriculum and assessment practices, and advise how these can be developed and implemented (Knight and Yorke, 2003, 2004). Specialist units such as the Centre for Research into Quality at the University of Central England in Birmingham are exploring the issues arising from enhancing employability and making closer links between education and the world of work (Harvey et al., 2002). Even if higher education is responding to the challenges of graduate employability, that is only one side of the equation. The onus is also on students themselves to first develop and, second, to refine to enhanced levels of complexity those skills and qualities viewed as highly desirable by employers. They then need to learn how to tell employers about these skills and qualities to maximum effect.

In the following pages, we present principles and techniques that have the potential to promote both good academic achievements as well as a range of interpersonal and transferable skills that can be adapted to changing labour market circumstances and organizational needs.

Transferable Skills

This list is one of many provided over the years by surveys of various kinds, and many universities now offer explicit advice, guidance, or even additional courses on acquiring transferable skills. This has affected even elite universities, with the University of Cambridge acknowledging 'its responsibility in the provision of opportunities to develop transferable skills, but [placing] the responsibility for doing so ... with students taking advantage of the opportunities provided'. Cambridge University (University of Cambridge Education Section, 2005) specifies that skills to be developed by all students include:

- **intellectual skills (for example, critical, analytical, synthesizing and problem-solving skills);**

- **communication skills (written and oral);**

- **organizational skills (for example, working independently, taking initiative, time management);**

- **interpersonal skills (for example, working with/motivating others, flexibility/ adaptability).**

Other skills, including research skills, numeracy, computer literacy, and foreign language skills are also available, but Cambridge University notes that 'Where the skills are not integral to the subject, the acquisition should be through activities such as voluntary study, extra-curricular activities or work experience.' These might be important to emphasize for any students failing to realize the possibilities offered by modern universities, and it is one answer to a misunderstanding which we have heard voiced more than once – that universities only require attendance for a few hours a week. This may be true for officially timetabled teaching – but there is nothing to stop anyone seeking out other opportunities to build up their skills portfolios in non-timetabled time.

There is an enormous amount of material including programmes and lists of skills found in electronic format, as a search of the Web will indicate. There seems to be quite considerable consensus among university providers about the nature and content of transferable skills, sometimes with slightly different emphases. For example, the University of Minnesota (University of Minnesota Duluth, 2002) has a very useful questionnaire that students can use to assess the extent of their transferable skills. The headings indicate the general categories:

- **Communication (the skilful expression, transmission and interpretation of knowledge and ideas);**

- **Research and Planning (the search for specific knowledge and the ability to conceptualize future needs and solutions for meeting those needs);**

- **Human Relations (the use of interpersonal skills for resolving conflict, relating to and helping people);**

- **Organization, Management and Leadership (the ability to supervise, direct and guide individuals and groups and the completion of tasks and fulfilment of goals).**

This site is also particularly helpful in adding a further section on 'Work Survival (the day-to-day skills which assist in promoting effective production and work satisfaction)'. This section carries people on into work and suggests that they need to develop skills to survive and become effective in the work situation. We discuss this important idea below. This section specifies skills such as 'implementing decisions; cooperating; enforcing policies; being punctual; managing time; attending to detail; meeting goals; enlisting help; accepting responsibility; setting deadlines; organizing; making decisions'.

You can see by looking at the boxes that university programmes and lists do seem to correspond pretty closely to those skills that employers have specified in their own lists of requirements. What this means is that universities themselves are well aware of the need to provide you with more than just academic knowledge. Indeed, as the University of Cambridge specifies, there is an expectation that you do more at university than just attend lectures and seminars, and produce assignments. The ideal student, it seems, would also rapidly identify possible gaps in their CV, and set out to remedy the situation by using their leisure time to acquire the transferable skills that they may lack. Many universities will offer courses outside the formal requirements, and these may include language skills and computer skills, for example. We know that some also offer students a chance to gain coaching qualifications.

Other Approaches to Discovering What Employers Want

In a very interesting survey of job advertisements (Jackson, 2001), there is a strong suggestion that employers are increasingly interested in what might be seen as informal skills. The paper is a sociological piece testing the extent to which Britain has become meritocratic, and it points out that despite all the general policies to widen access to higher education, and to make it more vocationally relevant, at the end of the day, it is individual employers themselves who decide what counts as 'merit'. Jackson set out to explore this by surveying a large number of job advertisements in a wide range of British newspapers. She found that formal qualifications were important most of all in the professions, but even there, other indications of 'merit' were important (Jackson, 2001: 22). These included:

- **cognitive abilities (such as being able to organize a workload);**

- **job commitment characteristics (including positive attitudes, reliability, flexibility, the ability to work under pressure);**

- **technical skills (including secretarial or numeracy skills); experience and track record;**

- **social skills (being a team player, working well with clients, and being able to communicate effectively).**

There were also other 'personal characteristics', including appearance and presentation, politeness, confidence, and having a good sense of humour.

Overall, Jackson thinks that her data indicate that these qualities are every bit as important as formal qualifications, except in the one occupational sector of service professionals. Overall, 'the role of education is now, if anything, becoming less important in the modern industrial society' (p. 19). This adds further to the point made above about employers' relative lack of interest in actual subjects studied at university.

We have heard many students and their parents say the same sort of thing. There is a widespread suspicion that 'everyone now has a degree', which is not actually the case, of course. Jackson's data add to this scepticism by pointing out that there is no automatic mechanism which guarantees graduates a job, and individual employers still have the right to decide who they want to employ and on what grounds. This is confirmed by Williams et al. (2006) as we have demonstrated earlier.

What implications follow for the new student? At the most extreme, we have known students who have abandoned university study, having gained some other route into employment, such as a place on a trainee management scheme. If your motivation is of the 'push' kind (where you feel driven to want to seek improvement on your current position), another route out of your existing situation may meet the requirement. At the other extreme, we have known students who have decided that since no jobs can be guaranteed from the possession of a degree, they might as well choose courses or universities that they will enjoy, regardless of their vocational relevance. This is the sort of 'pull' motivation (where the new destination attracts in its own right).

We have also heard views that the main purpose of going to university is not actually to study as hard as possible, but to make friends and contacts for future employment, to acquire not educational capital, but 'social capital', in Bourdieu's terms (see also Putnam, 2000). Social capital is gained from a number of sources, principally networking, which we have recommended before.

The concept of social capital has actually become an important one in recent government policy as well, in fact, where it is seen as a key to understanding how some people can survive and become socially included, and get themselves out of unemployment and poverty. Even the World Bank notes the importance of social capital in generating economic growth on a global scale (The World Bank Group, no date). The essence of social capital is well within the central concerns of social sciences in general – it depends on communication and developing trust between people, as we shall see below.

As the structure of this chapter indicates, many social scientists began thinking at first about employability for graduates in terms of providing vocational skills that employers would want to recognize and reward. The social sciences duly went through a substantial 'vocational turn' in the 1990s, focusing on the contribution of the disciplines involved to more specific courses in social work, youth and community, teaching, social administration and the like. Many of the courses that seemed to be particularly vocationally relevant thrived: they included research methods courses above all. Research methods courses are obvious ways to gain important skills of numeracy, ITC and communication skills, as well as offering a directly relevant expertise which can easily find its way into commercial market research, or policy evaluation. Our advice to students in those days would have been to make sure they signed on for such courses in particular.

However, there is now also a more general sense of thinking about preparing for the world of work. There seems to be a demand for more general skills as we have seen. We began advising students to rethink their university experiences in terms of transferable skills. For example, giving presentations to other students could be fairly unpopular (we discuss presentations in Chapter 6), but those who gave presentations could claim to have practised a transferable skill – being able to communicate to others in a group. Group project work could be seen in terms of developing the important skill of working with others. Many of our students discovered that their colleagues could be surprisingly challenging to work with, in fact, and would have very different ideas about the commitment required or the organization of the work. Some students avoided group project work as a result. We tried to encourage them not to do so, but to see the problems as providing essential experience in learning about working with others. Finally, dissertations could be time-consuming and demanding, but, apart from their other merits, they can also be seen as indicating important abilities like being able to solve problems and work on your own initiative. We return to the pros and cons of dissertations in more detail towards the end of the book (Chapters 7, 8 and 9).

This way of looking at academic work is still an essential part of the advice that students receive. Sometimes students are encouraged to note down the activities that they have undertaken, writing them up in terms of transferable skills, and recording the results on various portfolios or record cards. Schools often encourage this too, so that generations of students are accustomed to thinking of themselves as having 'records of attainment'. As tutors, we would often encourage students to list a wide range of things they had done, on various record forms, and to write them up in 'vocational' terms. These materials can become a useful archive in devising application forms or CVs.

To take some examples, we have persuaded students to share with us some of the activities they have undertaken as part of their normal workload, without seeing their possible vocational importance (Box 4.2).

Box 4.2   Examples of Transferable Skills

A Media Studies' student who became interested in editing and learned how to use some basic online editing software in her spare time.

A Sociology student who learned to use Microsoft Excel to display the data for his group project.

Leisure Studies' students who organized and carried out a survey of visitors to a local heritage site.

A Media Studies' student who became Fixtures Secretary of the ladies' football team.

Two Community Studies' students who attended a short course on writing CVs.

Education Studies' students who found some voluntary work working with children with learning difficulties.

Sports Studies' students who helped organize a school sports day.

A Sociology student who completed a local Certificate in Religious Education – she was not particularly religious herself but was interested in the 'spiritual' dimension to social life and was keen to explore the position of those who had definite faiths.

More recently, and partly inspired by some of the research we have just mentioned, we have started to see student leisure activities as having an important vocational dimension. We always saw them as important in personal terms, and as part of the pleasures of being relatively independent. Now, it seems, they are recognized as having quite an important role in preparing people for work as well. Leisure activities can also now usefully be recorded in terms of providing 'social skills', which is maybe what employers are increasingly looking for. There may well be an element of 'talking up' activities here, but there is a genuine benefit in reinterpreting for CV purposes collective leisure activities in terms of being able to cooperate with others, demonstrate responsibility and leadership, indicate motivation and enthusiasm, confidence, a sense of humour, and an ability to get on with people at all levels. It is certainly no longer

Table 4.1 Skills developed from interests

Interests	Skills developed
Climbing Snowdon (team orienteering task for Duke of Edinburgh award)	Leadership Problem-solving Risk-taking Cooperation
Music band (play regularly at local venues)	Commitment Entrepreneurial Organizational

Source: (GIEU, 1999).

enough just to mention these activities – you need to interpret them in the right ways (Table 4.1).

Try this for yourselves – what transferable social skills or competencies are involved in playing for the College sports teams? Acting as Secretary for a student club? Working as a lifeguard? NB: the website Prospects has an exercise which can offer a few clues. Box 4.3 can help you reassess your vocational activities.

Box 4.3   Identifying Transferable Skills

Try something even more ambitious. Rewrite in terms which show the transferable skills and competencies involved in:

- taking a gap year and travelling;
- campaigning for the abolition of vivisection;
- raising a 'blended' family;
- looking after an elderly parent.

Interesting implications follow, and some rather ironic ones. It may be that the seemingly least vocational courses, even the 'liberal arts' subjects at university, might actually help to develop the kind of social skills that now seem to be in substantial demand (Taylor, 2005). It may be that one of the more vocationally relevant activities you can do at university is to join the right sort of club or informal social group, and widen your experiences of life, although this assumes you will also have achieved a reasonable overall class of degree.

We suggest that you recalculate the balance between academic and social activities. Overall though, the implication cannot be shirked. In opposition to the usual advice given in study skills books, and just as a provocation to get you thinking, you might wish to focus on employability by placing social activities equally at the centre of your university life, at least, once you are sure you can complete the academic tasks!

This may not be quite the good news that it seems, of course. Jackson (2001) and others have pointed out that an emphasis on social skills for employment gives a great advantage to those who are brought up in elite backgrounds. As with 'cultural capital', qualities such as 'tact and diplomacy' or 'discretion' may have been well developed by particular kinds of family upbringing long before those privileged young people entered university. Indeed, those apparently simple 'skills', as listed above, might just be coded references to elite ways of behaving in the first place. We do not want to discourage anybody here, but it is true that an elite social background can provide ways of behaving and acting that offer a considerable advantage: as we saw with Bourdieu's work, these qualities seem to 'come naturally' to the elite.

However, we are not suggesting that you must come from an elite background to demonstrate qualities like 'tact and diplomacy', nor that people from elite backgrounds are paragons who always act with tact and diplomacy. The situation seems to require the research stance that we have been advocating throughout. You can learn a lot by watching people from various backgrounds who can demonstrate some of the desirable qualities employers seem to want. It is a matter of widening your horizons and learning what seems useful again. If this is a relevant orientation for you, it is something to look out for in seminars and in informal social gatherings (Box 4.4).

Box 4.4 What Can You Learn From 'People Watching'?

How do some students (or lecturers) always appear at ease in different groups?
How do they manage to disagree with others with tact and diplomacy?
What do they actually say? How do they behave?
How do they keep their sense of humour?

In fact, students of social sciences are at a particular advantage in the job market in this one respect. People often come equipped with social capital from their family backgrounds or the communities in which they live, we have suggested. Everyone belongs to such a group, and students should not let other groups devalue their own social expertise. This kind of social capital is what the UK Performance and Innovation Unit (2002) calls 'bonding social capital' – because it helps develop solidarity among members. However, equally important, if not more so, is 'bridging' and 'linking' social capital, enabling bonds of communication to be formed between ethnic groups and social classes respectively. This is where students from non-middle-class backgrounds can really score because they can use their time at university to build such bridges and links. Taking a social science course provides exactly the sort of theoretical and research skills to be able to do this and to talk convincingly about it afterwards (Box 4.5).

The new vocational emphasis of social science courses, one which is well worth stressing in your CV and job application forms, could help us understand others. To take a really recent example, some application forms for various UK police services around the country are asking students to address particular 'scenarios'. One of them is dealing with a person from another ethnic grouping who wants to argue strongly against your position. Personal experience in being able to take the viewpoint of another person as a detached research stance, and a grasp of the basics of the formation of ethnic identity will obviously help score points here.

Box 4.5   Self-assessing Your Value

To round off this chapter, why not conduct your own audit of your stocks of different sorts of capital? We hope you can add to your stocks after reading this book, of course. You can be absolutely honest in your answers here, since only you will be reading them.

What kind of *educational capital* do you have?

- knowledge related to the course you are going to take, gained from previous courses;
- knowledge of study skills and learning patterns.

What kind of *cultural capital* do you have?

- knowledge of current affairs, arts, ways of life in different countries, languages;
- knowledge of academic life and academic values.

What kind of *social capital* do you have?

- bonding – what sort of social groups do you feel at home with and feel you know well already?
- bridging – have you encountered any other social groups? How would you go about trying to relate to groups with different social backgrounds, religious beliefs, sexual orientations? What do you know about such groups already? Do you have strong views about them already, and if so, what are they based on exactly? How could you find out more about groups like this?

What kind of *personal capital* do you have?

- How can you interpret what you have done in a way that will persuade employers that you have exactly the sort of competencies and qualities for which they are looking? Can you tell a good story about yourself? Can you explain to others the value of what you have studied and what you have done while you have been at university? Can you demonstrate the vocational relevance of (a selection of) the activities you have recorded?

Chapter Summary

1   Students will want to consider the issue of employability early in their university careers.

2   It is not always easy to see what it is that employers actually want, but there is some information contained in employer surveys, application forms and details themselves, and some more in academic surveys.

3   What information there is suggests that additional personal and social skills and competencies are also valued, as well as academic qualifications as such.

4   Universities and other organizations often discuss these additional qualities as 'core' or 'transferable' skills, and most universities are aware of them and can provide opportunities to acquire them.

5   Careers services are particularly useful as sources of guidance and help in the acquisition and recording of transferable skills. They can also show you how to demonstrate your qualities to best effect in interviews or other kinds of assessment (including psychometric testing).

6   Personal, social, cultural and leisure activities can also be seen in terms of providing transferable skills, and it can pay to come to think of them in that way, and develop an archive for the purposes of building a CV. You will need to select from this personal archive in order to tailor your applications precisely.

7   The academic literature uses terms like 'social capital' to describe the importance of being able to work with others in the same social groups to which you belong, and to build bridges of understanding with members of other groups.

8   Social science students can be at a particular advantage in setting out to acquire social capital.

9   Many application procedures specifically require that you demonstrate these social skills and you can practise doing this to best effect.

Part 2

Maximizing Your Performance

5 Writing Skills

CHAPTER OVERVIEW

- Basic principles – plagiarism and referencing.
- Developing summary and comment – sources and types of comment.
- Polishing your academic writing – 'style'.
- Academic argument – developing good arguments.
- Reading academic argument.
- Writing examination answers.

It follows from what we have said before that you actually need to develop rather special writing skills for academic life, but, once you know where you are going, you can focus your efforts. The sort of writing you may have done so far might have been fairly limited anyway, given the increasing importance of texts and e-mail; fewer people write letters or diaries, perhaps. Yet universities often assume that the written form is still the most important way to communicate (and so too does business, so it is a good skill to acquire, in terms of future employment), and you will certainly have to do quite a bit of writing as a part of your assessment régime.

You will have begun this process already in the courses you took before coming to university. Of course, we are not implying that you are unable to communicate or that you 'can't write' (a view that is often expressed about young people these days). It is rather a matter of getting used to a particular type of writing, perhaps a particular technology (if your university insists on word-processed assignments). After practise, you should be able to feel able to express yourself fluently again, in the new media. You could even prepare by trying to get used to writing in the required way, perhaps with a diary or blog, or even a few trial essays on your thoughts so far (which you can throw away afterwards if you are not happy with them).

You will need to make sure that particularly long-lasting problems are not the result of any other problem such as any of the varieties of dyslexia or dissociated disorders: we know of quite a few students who had not been diagnosed until they arrived in higher education. Many found it a great relief to be diagnosed, but some still experience such a diagnosis as a stigma and do not wish to disclose their condition. You will have to decide what to do in your specific circumstances.

As usual, there are no fixed formulae to offer you here. You need to work out in detail what sort of writing gets the best results in your specific university, on your specific course, and with your specific tutors. We have already argued, for example in Chapter 2, that many tutors place a particular emphasis on presentation, on spelling, adequate grammar, and on the less easily specified matters such as style.

We are going to assume that you are able to take care of spelling and grammar for yourself. If it is a problem, you might need specialist help and practise in your actual institutions. Getting help could be slightly embarrassing but it is important to be able to write using a good standard of English. There are also some useful websites to help you if you need to work on this, such as Concordia University (http://cdev.concordia.ca/CnD/studentlearn/Help/Writing.html), the University of Toronto (http://www.utoronto.ca/writing/advise.html), or the Online Writing Lab (http://owl.english.purdue.edu/handouts/grammar/) at Purdue University. All these will use North American spelling, of course. A good basic UK site is provided by the Open University (http://www.open.ac.uk/study-strategies/index.htm).

We want to concentrate on structure and style here, and explore some of the things to pursue, and some to avoid, when trying to develop academic argument. Forms of assignment might well vary also between essays, portfolios, reports, and examination answers.

Basic Principles

Let us start with the most important points first. We have already argued that the major sin for many tutors and university administrators is plagiarism, and we have begun to discuss it from the lecturers' point of view (in Chapter 3). It is so important to avoid plagiarism that we want to discuss it again, this time in terms of developing basic writing techniques to ensure that you will not be accused of committing plagiarism.

Plagiarism

What actually is plagiarism? As we have indicated earlier, essentially it involves passing off someone else's work as your own. However, you will find different local definitions and variations which makes it difficult to give a precise description. To help, Box 5.1 gives examples of different practices that may be used in a piece of academic writing, and indicates how these relate to the risk of plagiarism. Later in the chapter, we tell you how to improve your practice so that you do not accidently arouse suspicions of scholarly misconduct.

Box 5.1　Basic Issues

Bad practices – things to avoid	Risk of plagiarism
Copying the sentences or paragraphs of the work of others and *not* using 'quotation marks' and referencing properly.	*This is Plagiarism!*
Copying and pasting material from the web directly into your essay.	This is *extremely risky* practice. It is all too easy to forget to add quotation marks and reference properly – in which case it would be plagiarism.

(Continued)

(Continued)

Copying sentences or paragraphs and just changing the odd word or two.	This is *extremely risky* practice and is highly likely to be considered as plagiarism.
Using too many quotes. A social science essay should contain your words to present evidence and critique or argument.	Low risk. *But only if* put in 'quotation marks' and referenced properly. This would also be considered a poor quality essay.
Forgetting to add page numbers in the reference in the text when using quotes and statistics.	Low risk – this is *sloppy practice* and should be avoided.
Using the references given in other people's work and presenting them in your own bibliography.	This is *incorrect* – it implies you have read this material when you have not.

Source: Skinner (2005)

In our view, the key to the kind of plagiarism that really stokes up anger and a desire to punish involves the deliberate attempt to copy out someone else's writing and pretend it is your own – in other words, the bad practice that is described in the top row in Box 5.1. You must simply avoid doing this at all costs. We are not going to offer a simple moral argument, which will work only if we have a strong principled standing for you, but to pursue our stance on 'informed choice' as always. We shall argue that:

1 **The effort involved in copying other people's work and then concealing the copying is increasing dramatically as techniques of detection get better.**

2 **It is almost impossible to be sure of getting away with it.**

3 **It is less work, and far more satisfying, to just write the assignment in the approved way.**

We have met one or two students who have clearly broken the rules. In one case, one student copied, virtually word-for-word, the essay of another. They both handed in their essays 'innocently', and seemed mildly surprised when we demanded an explanation. In cases like these, it is hard to think what students expected to happen. Could they seriously have imagined that the tutor would not have noticed that two essays were identical? We have heard students assert that tutors do not mark essays very carefully, that they skim, and even that they occasionally weigh them and do not actually read them at all – but it is amazing to think that students might actually believe this. Perhaps they imagined that two tutors would happen to mark the two essays separately? Again, this simply shows a lack of understanding of marking practices – we very commonly divide essays up according to topics, and tend to take away and mark all the essays on a particular topic. Maybe this particular pair of students had done something similar in the past and got away with it, but it still seemed to be very reckless to attempt to do the same again. They were caught quite easily, and punished.

One other issue occurred to us as we dealt with the case. We could hardly imagine anyone being unimaginative and uncreative enough to simply copy out the work of another. We could hardly imagine ourselves wanting to just copy without looking to make some small alterations, to rephrase things, to argue differently, and to come to different conclusions. Of course, electronic forms make literal copying much easier, but not bothering to read through a copy, even to correct any errors, seems careless, risky, and also an embarrassing sign of deep misunderstanding of what academic life is all about.

We have also met students who have clumsily copied sections of books, articles, or, more commonly these days, websites. In the worst cases, their essays have been nothing but someone else's sections, paragraphs, or sometimes whole pages, just pasted together. Once more, the perpetrators seemed completely unaware of the risks that they actually ran. When they were caught, it was clear that they had no real defence – those pieces could not have been put together by accident, and there were clear signs of a deliberate attempt to conceal the sources.

It happens to be often very easy to spot plagiarism of this crude kind, which explains our view that it just is not worth risking There are a number of telling signs, that researchers have called 'smoking guns', which classically raise strong suspicions in the mind of the experienced marker. Box 5.2 includes the more obvious ones.

Box 5.2   Smoking Guns

1 *Jekyll and Hyde writing.* Here, a fractured, fragmented, tortuous and badly expressed paragraph is followed by a fluent summary of something difficult.

2 *Obscure arguments and references,* or impossibly learned citations.

3 *Words written in or spelled in a foreign language*: values given in dollars, confident references to American legislation, technical terms left untranslated, such as *Zustammsreduktion*, the confident use of French, German or Spanish proverbs, Latin or Greek phrases.

4 *Well-written but mostly irrelevant or unjustified sections,* asides or implications. Sometimes these are accompanied by fresh introductions, even though they appear halfway through the essay.

5 *Inconsistent performance.* A student clearly has no idea at all about a topic in a seminar, and then produces an expert essay a week later. A student writes an essay about feminism (or whatever), and then seems unable to produce a feminist argument, indeed never seems to have heard of one, in an essay on something else.

6 *Inefficient editing.* Borrowed material is not searched for incriminating clues to its origin, so that a student essay sometimes contains references to 'my first university', or to 'experience I gained in the 1960s'. Headers and footers are not always edited in heavily borrowed material. Electronic information about the author of the piece or the date of last editing can sometimes be retrieved from both Microsoft Word documents and web pages.

7 *Phoney bibliography.* Massive, learned, multi-lingual bibliographies listing 10 or more lengthy and challenging texts that would take weeks to read – there is usually a true bibliography, one or two famous summaries or textbooks, concealed by these transparent attempts to bluff.

Clearly, the determined plagiarist will have to carefully read through their work to make sure there are no such 'smoking guns', or else the game is up. The work involved is likely to be substantial, and may take longer than just doing the essay 'straight', as we suggest. Some students might believe that there could still be ways to plagiarize and get away with it, however.

More Sophisticated Plagiarism

You can get someone else to write your assignment. You might be able to persuade a friend or former student to do this. This seems safe but you would need to be sure that your friends can write effectively themselves, that their own work is not on record somewhere, and that the work cannot be recognized. The risks mount up again, clearly.

Some commercial sites will write an essay for you, as long as you are prepared to pay. You have to be sure that they can meet the correct standard, and that they are not simply plagiarizing well-known material themselves. We have picked up some 'smoking guns' in material written by a third party (a tutor from a sixth-form college, it turned out), that our own students have failed to remove, which defeated the object of the exercise.

Just this year, we met a student who had used a lot of material from a website, and had given only the most general reference for the website. On that website were several hundred specific articles and essays. People logging on would pay a registration fee and then a further fee to download one of the articles or essays. Our own suspicion is that it is easy to download the 'wrong' essay and thus to require several others as well, so the costs can mount up. Of course, the whole tactic assumes that those articles have not been published somewhere else: in this particular case, many had been published somewhere else, and typing a few keywords into one of the search engines easily found them. There is also no guarantee of the quality of the work you get, of course.

There may be a temporary advantage offered to the plagiarist with such developments, but it is surprising how quickly the technology can catch up. Students may not be aware of this, but a UK Government-sponsored website is now available that has the latest word-matching electronic technology to detect plagiarism. Further developments, tracing syntactical structures, not just words, is not far behind. These structures are very hard to conceal, and it would require substantial rewriting in your own words to be sure. Rewriting in your own words, with proper referencing of sources, is quite close to what you would be doing if you tackled the essay properly in the first place.

Ultimately, a simple low-technology device can also be deployed. We could simply ask students to discuss their work. We could ask them why they have come to the conclusions that they have reached, exactly how they used the sources that they have cited, and why they have included some arguments and not others. We have employed this oral examination technique once or twice in our own institutions when we have had suspicions, and have easily detected copied material. On both occasions, students very sensibly decided to admit the offence early on. On another occasion, it must be said, a student managed to convince us not only that he had adequately used references, but that he had understood the material to a much greater depth than was apparent from his essay. He left the oral examination with a substantially increased grade!

Referencing

Overall, we hope you are now convinced that it will probably take so much effort to plagiarize with a reasonable chance of success that it is worth simply writing the essay or assignment in accordance with the conventions in the first place. It is really not that difficult to reference source material correctly. If you are copying a quotation, you need to indicate that clearly and give the source that you have copied it from. There are various particular styles and techniques of acknowledging sources, which may vary locally. It is reasonably common practice to use quotation marks around short quotes, but to indicate longer quotations, more than 40 words, say, by indenting the quotation, marking it out from the text with large margins around it. As for giving the source, there are a number of conventions again, some of them extremely detailed.

You will need to contact your local institutions and practise these conventions. Our advice is to learn the basic ones first – how to cite books, articles and websites – and then explore some of the other regulations for citing personal communications or newspaper articles, say. In essence, what you have to do is to identify the source in one of these conventional ways.

To take an immediate example, we have used the 'Harvard' referencing system in this book, which is the system commonly used in the social sciences. If we are referring to an author, the author's name is provided in brackets, together with the date of publication in the actual text (as in Brown, 2005). In the References section at the end of the book, all the books and articles cited are listed alphabetically with full details of the title, the title of journal, if appropriate, the place of publication and the publisher, if it is a book. If you turn to our own References section at the end of the book, you will also see how we reference material obtained from websites. These conventions are provided by our publisher and are fairly straightforward.

There are good examples of referencing rules and conventions on various websites too, including an excellent one at Bournemouth University (http://www.bournemouth.ac.uk/library/using/harvard_system.html). Alternatives to Harvard can also be used, of course, and you will need to check your local requirements. For example, some acceptable systems involve inserting numbers in the text so that the references do not interrupt the flow for the reader. The references are arranged numerically either at the bottom of each page (footnotes), or at the end of the manuscript (endnotes).

As with the other study advice we supply, we see it as important not to provide great detail, but to explain the principles. There is another good reason for not taking you through more detail on referencing conventions because we are not far away from having cheap and convenient software which will set out the sources for you, using any one of a number of preferred styles. Some academic writers already like the 'Nota Bene for Windows' software, for example, and you can currently try a version free (on https://www.notabene.com/nbdemo8.html).

The main point is to remember you will need a lot of detail to reference properly, and that you need to note down details of publications as you read the material. It is time-consuming to have to go back and look things up just for referencing. Websites can offer particular problems here in that the information required may be located on home pages rather than the specific pages you are examining. One of our local institutions provides a helpful service in that you can save the books you have found on the library catalogue in an archive and e-mail it to yourself: the e-mail arrives with all the relevant publication details like date and place of publication, publisher and the rest.

Even if you are paraphrasing, summarizing, or putting arguments in your own words, you still need to indicate if it is someone else's work that you are citing. This is sometimes called indirect quotation. You need to introduce your paraphrases by saying things like 'According to Harris (2005), Leisure Studies has become one of the most important social sciences ...' As long as you indicate the source of your ideas and views in one of these reliable ways (the ways in which your institution has suggested) you are not plagiarizing. Indeed, you are demonstrating that you have read widely and thus 'covered the material' or whatever your local assessment regulations say you should do.

We have again encountered student misunderstanding here. Some students fear that they will fail their assignments if they produce an essay which is merely a patchwork of other people's opinions. The first thing to remember is that it is better to declare the sources of your patches, and that being able to assemble a patchwork of relevant material is an important scholarly skill. You will get a reasonable grade for a properly referenced patchwork: it is a poorly referenced patchwork that should be avoided.

Of course, there is no need to simply offer a patchwork of other people's opinions anyway. You do have to show that you have examined some of the background literature, and summarized the main points made in that literature. You may wish to use direct or indirect quotations, with proper acknowledgement of the sources, to show that you have done this correctly and skilfully. It is not easy to arrange your summaries of different pieces of literature into a coherent and effective structure – which we discuss below – and again, you will gain credit if you can do so. However, you can then add additional comments of various kinds to add value to this summary.

Box 5.3 draws together some of the points made above and is a quick guide to good practice; if you adopt these behaviours, then you should avoid falling into accidental plagiarism. The most important thing is to be aware of the risk when you are collecting and recording material for essays or reports, and to make sure that you clearly distinguish between the ideas and thoughts derived from other people and your own.

Box 5.3   Good Practice – Things to Master

Always add 'quotation marks' and reference properly in the text when using the sentences or paragraphs of the work of others.

Take accurate essay notes. These should include the author, date of publication, title, place of publication and name of publisher. MOST IMPORTANTLY use 'quotation marks' and note the page number when you are copying words directly. This will remind you these are not your words or ideas.

Cut and paste material from the web into a separate 'essay notes' file and not directly into the essay itself.

Keep accurate details of web-based material – including the web address and the date accessed.

Use your own words and rephrase and summarize as much as possible when taking notes.

Be accurate and precise when referencing in the text and adding references into the bibliography.

Check that all references used in the text are reproduced in the bibliography.

Only include work that you have actually read in your references and bibliography.

Check with your supervisor or a tutor if you are unsure about referencing.

Source: Skinner (2005)

Adding Comments of Your Own

You may feel that as a beginner you cannot add anything of value to the considered and published works of the experts in the field, but this is not so. There is always something to add, even to the views of experts.

It is unlikely that published experts will have taken the precise modules, courses, or programmes that you are taking, nor will they be reviewing the very latest work. As a result, you will have an unusual (maybe 'original') combination of arguments to draw upon. If you can bring to bear arguments you have encountered on other topics, modules or courses, you are in a position to make an effective comment. To take an example from one of our own social science courses, there are expert summaries and published materials which attempt to account for the commercial success of leisure goods such as the Sony Walkman, and Nike trainers. One important book on the Walkman (du Gay et al., 1997) offers a general model to explain how the product managed to combine effective production, advertising, and knowledge of consumer culture. The equally central and important book on Nike trainers (Goldman and Papson, 1998) offers a different model to address the same issue. Any student that happens to take the particular module that offers both discussions is clearly in a position to use one source to make a comment on the other. If they are writing an essay on the Sony Walkman, they can summarize the model offered in du Gay et al., and then, by way of comment, refer to the different approach found in Goldman and Papson. Or vice versa. There is also newer material which neither classic book mentions, obviously.

It might be helpful to think of this sort of comment as offering 'external' criticism. No single book is perfect, and there are several different approaches, so one approach can be compared with a number of other external sources and arguments. Sometimes the essay title itself might invite an explicit comparison between two or more approaches of this kind. Even here, it is quite acceptable to make additional comparisons, point out similarities and differences, to note that some approaches are better at explaining some aspects of the issue than others, and so on. Comparisons of this kind help develop a particularly fruitful approach to understanding and argument which we discuss later in this chapter – using analogies.

Once you have gained a little confidence, you might want to attempt another kind of critical comment as well – what might be thought of as an 'internal' criticism. Here, you might notice some controversial issues for discussion, even in the most prestigious books and articles, as you work through and summarize them.

1   They might be out of date, for example. The essay on the Sony Walkman we mentioned above was written before the advent of the iPod, or, indeed, the more recent kinds of mobile phone. If we considered these

recent inventions, not developed by Sony but by rival companies, what would be the implications for duGay et al. and their argument?

2   Some arguments are well supported by evidence, and others less so. Should there be more evidence? What sort of evidence might be particularly important? In the case of du Gay et al., there is little evidence about how people actually use the goods. Sometimes, this lack of evidence becomes apparent if you think of your own experiences as consumers.

3   In other cases, you might be able to transfer into your essay some material from a research methods module that you happen to be taking at the same time, or that you took in an earlier year. The general issue of methods is always worth discussing, and it is always controversial, which means that you can always make a comment about it. What would be the best way to research consumers' use of their electronic goods?

4   There are many other sources of comment. Feminist work, for example, has been very successful in pointing to the ways in which much conventional work takes a male-centred point of view (defined in various ways). Ethnic and other minorities are also commonly sidelined. What would happen if we tried to introduce their specific interests and conditions into the debate? Was a recent Nike campaign really about empowering women by urging them to participate in consuming sporting culture or trying to exploit them? Were women customers able to turn the tables by using the goods for their own purposes once they had bought them?

5   There are always implications which you can draw from arguments. You might wish to consider how the project might be continued, with further research. You might think what kind of policy issues are involved – do consumer goods have a 'bad' side, and should they be regulated in some sense? Does the provision of flexible and pleasurable leisure technology offer a 'good' side to globalization?

These are only examples and it is the general issue that is important. The interesting thing about social sciences is that even beginners can make insightful comments about it. We often find it is the case that students lack the confidence to make these comments in their essays, even though they think of them. This is almost certainly because they have misunderstood what academic work is all about.

You might want to go back and look at Chapter 3 on what lecturers want. Here, and in several other places, we are trying to insist that academic work in social sciences is about debate and argument. It is about considered discussion. In other words, it involves both summary and comment as we have defined them. It does not matter who is involved or what the topic is. There is always discussion available. Looking at the assessment criteria commonly cited, we are confident that you will find that it is almost universal to require discussion, even though that is sometimes called analysis, synthesis, being critical, or whatever.

Academic Argument

Academic argument is central to academic approaches in social sciences. We have already argued that it takes a different shape from the sort of arguments you are likely to have in everyday life, because it operates from an unusual starting point and stance. We can now explore this in more detail when looking at written assignments. One major problem with student work is that it does not sufficiently display academic argument, even though it might contain 'arguments' in the ordinary sense. That single major problem is probably what lies behind many specific comments you are quite likely to receive on your written work. Problems with academic argument can also affect verbal presentations and discussions, as we shall see in the next chapter. The specific comments take the form of remarks such as: lacks critical analysis; too descriptive; you need to structure your argument more effectively; try to avoid repetition; you need to provide more evidence – and so on.

In fact, there is quite a lot of work on, and interest in, getting students to learn how to argue in a suitable way. Cioffi (2005) suggests that students simply misunderstand the constant requests made to them to engage in argument, because, for them, an argument means some sort of unpleasant confrontation or heated disagreement. As Bonnett (2001) adds, this means that we are often used to trying to avoid arguments in various ways, or, if we find ourselves in one, to see it as a kind of personal combat with only one winner.

What academics usually have in mind is something much more controlled and guided by conventions and rules, though. Of course emotions can be involved in both, but the main issue with the latter is to be able to deliver a good technical performance. If this is achieved, everyone can benefit, with no losers. This stance is likely to produce better results in assignments, but also to increase your sense of involvement and your academic pleasures, as Bonnett (2001: 1) suggests: 'The ability to engage in argument is what makes learning exciting … It transforms you from a passive and bored receptacle of another's wisdom into a participant.' This is real participation in higher education as opposed to the tokenist variety where you are invited to do little tasks of various kinds to keep you busy.

Some recent work tries to suggest that various kinds of computer programs might be used to help students engage in technical and constructive argument. Chryssafidou (2000), for example, has produced a flow chart specifying that students should undertake particular steps in order to produce an effective argument, and has devised a way to display these on a computer. You might want to try out the basic principles just with pen and paper.

1 **Define your own position on a topic – say, whether the National Health Service should charge patients for treatment.**

2 **Then anticipate a position opposite to your own – what would charging for treatment actually look like and how could it be done? Would it make a difference if insurance companies were charged, not individuals? Should all patients be subsidized – even those with injuries resulting from lifestyles?**

3 **Consider arguments and evidence for and against each stance. The difficulty might be in thinking of evidence to support your views, and rational arguments to support the alternative views.**

4 **Finish with the last step – considering counter-arguments and counter-evidence for each position. You have summarized your opponents' arguments and evidence in Step 3 above – which weak points are now apparent and what evidence would we need to resolve any problems? Then try what is perhaps the most difficult of all – how would you counter your own arguments?**

More generally, there is quite a bit of discussion of academic argument and how it actually works to persuade somebody. This can be rather technical, but you may well meet versions later on in social theory courses. Crow (2005) stresses the 'art of argument' in his introduction to classical social theory, for example. There is also a view that methods courses should also be recast to move away from learning surface techniques to grasping the deeper issue of argument.

It is worth pointing out that learning both how to do academic argument on your own, and how to understand the arguments of academics, takes practice and commitment. As you gain more experience, it tends to make more sense. No doubt, developing judgement and gaining confidence and security also help.

Let us confine ourselves here to a few basic problems that new students often display when they attempt to pursue an academic argument. There are a few types of argument, and a few features of argument that you probably need to learn to avoid as soon as possible. Bonnett's excellent text (2001) gives some useful examples of how to both develop and criticize arguments, including verbal argument (and we return to his ideas in the chapter on presentations). Rather than just summarize Bonnett's work here, we have selected a few characteristics of poor argument which we encounter quite frequently (Boxes 5.4, 5.5 and 5.6).

Box 5.4 *Ad Hominem* Argument

This is where the strength of an argument is reduced to the personal characteristics of the person making the argument. Common forms include:
The problem with Freud is that he is clearly obsessed by sex.
Marx was not afraid to sponge off Engels when he was writing his criticism of capitalism.
Butler is clearly one of those American feminists who hate men.
Ritzer obviously wants to show us that he is not as stupid as the rest of us.

This approach is not only offensive and impolite about major academics, but is a weak argument. Even if those personal characteristics were correct – and, of course, they are highly debatable – it still would not necessarily disqualify the argument made by the person concerned. You might be obsessed by sex, a hypocrite, a man-hater or an elitist, but still be right. Academic arguments are not just produced by some spontaneous outpouring of essential personal characteristics, but by research of various kinds as well.

Box 5.5   Excessive Generalization

Here, a student writer often expresses what represents 'what everybody knows', or 'what they say', as in:
Women feel safe in shopping malls.
Government policies never work.
Young people are naturally rebellious.
Obese people simply do not do enough exercise.
Television programmes glamorize crime.

Although this kind of argument might be suitable for general discussion on social occasions, social scientists tend to expect generalizations to be either qualified or supported by evidence. Citing the sources for these views, and evidence that might support or qualify them indicates a crucial readiness to discuss them.

Box 5.6   One-sided Argument (Sometimes Called Bias)

Here, a controversial view is defended in an essay without considering any criticisms or problems. To those who are enthusiastic, it might just seem obvious that more government money should be spent promoting a particular leisure pursuit, sport, or policy, for example, but all such views can be criticized carefully. We repeat that this can actually be helpful for all concerned, since no one wants to support a policy that is ineffective, even if it is well intentioned.

There are other characteristic forms of argument that can attract critical comment as well, but let us move on to consider other more general features of written assignments that can cause problems. It is common to find essays that offer a mere list of points rather than a well-structured argument. This is sometimes associated with a poor preparation strategy, where students have made notes from a number of sources, which are then simply copied and pasted end to end. As a result, a particular point can be made on page 2, and then revisited on page 4, and yet again on page 6. Introductory remarks can appear at intervals throughout. The conclusion to one section is ignored or contradicted by the conclusion to another one. This kind of random collection would be an extreme example of the lack of structure that we have discussed above. A good discussion of this and other problems is provided by Dunleavy's classic account of essay writing (1986) (especially his Chapter 4). Bonnett (2001) offers a number of useful techniques including developing claims, counter-claims and evidence in a flow chart, rather like the exercise derived from Chryssafidou (2000) we suggest above.

In academic discussion you do not just express a view and find evidence to support it. You address the topic from different angles, not just the one you are particularly interested in. Sometimes essay titles begin with a quote that expresses the sort of views that you encounter in popular discussion, but again, these are there to provoke academic discussion. An essay title that asks 'Does Nike exploit its workers?' is quite likely to be about the benefits and drawbacks of globalization, and probably it will require you to outline different approaches to globalization, and then organize discussion of the good and bad effects, before coming to some technical conclusion about whether more research is needed, or whatever. We have provided an example of a tutor's view of a particular question in Chapter 3. You should be able to see that 'deep' principles are involved rather than too much surface detail.

It is really straightforward once you put it all in context. What is the reason for setting academic essay titles at university? It is largely because we want to test whether we have managed to teach you anything successfully. In particular, we want to see whether any of the ideas we have been discussing on a course or module have been understood. We might want to see if your arguments are developing along the lines we expect and value. We are not particularly interested in hearing your specific views, based on your specific experiences in having your children pester you to buy Nike trainers, or whatever – not in essays, that is. Essays are formal exercises connected to assessment. It is a mistake to see them as a chance to put the world to rights, demonstrate what a long and interesting life you have led, or get back at us ivory-tower academics by explaining what the real world looks like when you are young and enthusiastic.

Some students misinterpret this sort of advice and go to the other extreme. They find no personal interest in any of the essays, and can approach them entirely cynically. Or they feel inhibited and unable to express any kind of opinion. We have met students who have told us that they have simply been forbidden to express an opinion in their essays. Our own view is that it is uninformed opinion that is unwelcome. Even 'unwelcome' is the wrong word, perhaps. What we mean is that uninformed opinion can be largely irrelevant to the task that the essay requires. It may be desperately relevant to students on a personal level. They may feel that their whole identity is involved in taking a stance on consumer goods for the under-fives, or the ways in which leisure seems to be encouraging social isolation, or whatever. Our views are simply that:

1 **Opinions are acceptable if they are based on informed understanding of the relevant literature.**

2 **Personal and unsubstantiated opinions based on personal experience cannot really be assessed, and so including them is not a very effective use of limited time and space in essays (and even less so in examinations).**

Let us briefly explore that last point. When we assess essays (we discussed assessment in Chapter 3), we have to try to work using agreed criteria covering all the essays in front of us. We cannot judge students' personal experiences using general criteria. You probably would not want us to do so anyway, in case we judged you adversely or unfairly. We are not uninterested in your opinions, and we may enjoy discussing matters with you – but there are better and safer ways to write essays, and better places and occasions to discuss your personal views.

Polishing Your Writing Skills

Once you have got the basic idea of what you have to do, you are well on the way to developing an effective essay style. You can still practise the tasks involved, especially the ability to express yourself effectively and clearly. There are some books which recommend particular kinds of academic style, and some local regulations which lay down some fairly tight prescriptions about it. We know of institutions where, for example, you are not permitted to use the first person singular – that is to refer to yourself as the originator of ideas, as in sentences such as 'I think the real reason for the popularity of labelling theory was ...'. It may be the case that some disciplines particularly prefer this impersonal mode of writing. You are supposed to replace those sentences with more anonymous and 'objective' forms – 'The real reason for the popularity of labelling theory was ...', 'It has been argued that the popularity of labelling theory grew because ...', 'One reason for the popularity of labelling theory was ...', and so on.

We take the view ourselves that occasionally it can be quite appropriate to confess to the authorship of an argument. Indeed, you may well encounter some arguments in debates about ethnographic methods, for example, which suggest that authorship should be openly acknowledged, that research should be 'autographed', to borrow terms from the debate, but some colleagues would argue that this should be practised by experienced writers only. As usual, you should always bear local conventions in mind. This particular one can lead to other problems with style, however, especially if people run out of ideas about how to write sentences anonymously and objectively. We have encountered clumsy formulations where students sound a bit like US Marine recruits and use phrases such as 'the student thinks that ...', or 'this researcher thinks that ...'.

You will sometimes encounter other forms of prescription. It seems to be increasingly common to tell students that they must not introduce new information into their conclusions, for example, especially in research reports (see Chapter 9). However, much depends on what you consider to be 'new information'. Clearly, you do not want suddenly to introduce a whole new debate or completely new data, but you will see that we have advised you to make comments, in conclusions and elsewhere, which do suggest that further research might be needed, new applications of approaches might be tested, or new comparisons made. Made as a series of fairly brief comments, these points seem perfectly acceptable in conclusions as indicating a way forward.

Certainly, as with all easy rules, it does not always pay to apply advice too literally and too specifically, and to remember that experienced and professional academics might be able to experiment successfully where a newcomer might not. On one of the courses we have taught, we have invited students to critically analyse a chosen piece of published academic work. To our surprise, some students have proceeded to rebuke well-established authors and famous arguments on the grounds that it is not good practice to introduce new information in the conclusions.

With those cautions in mind, let us refer you to some of the widely available advice on how to do academic writing (Box 5.7). Here is some work that we have used with our own students. A very useful site at Glasgow Caledonian University includes advice on academic writing (http://www.gcal.ac.uk/student/coursework/writing/index.html), writing essays (http://www.gcal.ac.uk/student/coursework/essays/index.html) and referencing (http://www.gcal.ac.uk/student/coursework/referencing/index.html).

Box 5.7   Academic Writing: Some Guidelines

The emphasis in academic writing is on facts and interpretation of the facts. These should be presented in a logical way using an *academic writing* style.

Use straightforward language

Take care with grammar and sentence construction. Avoid using a note-style of writing.

Try not to use pompous language

For example: use 'find out' rather than 'endeavour to ascertain' – try not to use jargon or clichés.

Provide definitions

Include explanations of technical or unusual terms, unless you can reasonably expect your reader to know them.

(Continued)

(Continued)

Use impersonal language

Essays and reports should be written in the third person singular. Avoid personal terms such as 'I' or 'We'; the word 'It' should be used instead. For example: 'I decided to interview the Tourism Planning Officer ...' should read 'It was decided to interview the Tourism Planning Officer ...'. The only exceptions to this convention may be where you are asked to link theory to your own professional practice.

Be precise

Avoid using terms that lack a precise meaning such as 'nice', 'good' or 'excellent'. One person's idea of what is meant by 'good' is not necessarily another's.

Be concise and to the point

Use 'Now' or 'Currently' instead of phrases like 'At the time of writing' or 'At this point in time'.

Use cautious language

This means that statements cannot easily be challenged: 'Cold calling **may** not produce results.'

Use appropriate verb tenses

Reports often use the present tense in the Introduction and the past tense when discussing findings. For example: Introduction: 'This report examines ...'; Findings: 'Results showed that ...'.

Be careful when using acronyms

The use of acronyms is allowed provided that the first time you write the letters you also write the words out in full. For example: Curriculum Vitae (CV).

Ensure you are linking points together

When using a lead sentence make sure that the points follow on and link to this.

There is a whole series of workshops on academic writing which have been undertaken by Queen Mary College, University of London, and which seem extremely sensible. They are written in the form of advice to lecturers wanting to assist their students in developing good interactive writing practices. There is no reason why you should wait for lecturers to suggest these, however. You can consult the relevant website (http://www.thinkingwriting.qmul.ac.uk/) for yourselves, but we have borrowed one of the exercises suggested (Box 5.8).

Box 5.8 Interactive Writing

Before the start of a lecture … write down the main points … [you] … learnt in the previous week and what … [you] … hope to learn today.

In the middle of the lecture … students … [should] write down what the main point is so far, or a question/confusion they have in their minds.

At the end … [try to] … summarize in a couple of sentences the concept … [the lecturer] … has been trying to put across. …

… make a progressive series of summaries: 200 words, 100 words, 50 words, a sentence, a phrase. …

… summarize the same piece for a couple of different audiences/purposes: for example, a younger sibling, a peer asking for ideas.

… write two summaries – one for someone who broadly supports the views expressed, one for someone who is seeking to argue against them. How can the 'neutral' language of summary be made to indicate a position?

… produce a 'negative summary' by tak[ing] a thick marker pen to a text and delet[ing] everything that is unnecessary. (The excuse could be that … [you] … are preparing the text to be read by someone who is far too busy to read the whole thing.)

… do the above on (a copy of) … [your] … own essay/report. Then … produce an abstract for the essay/report.

[Take] … a short article and … expand it (by adding in further evidence/examples or by developing the explanation/argument).

Reading Academic Writing

Note that the rationale for the last few examples is that reading the academic writing of others is the same sort of activity as writing in an academic way yourself. Students can probably only ever feel at home with academic writing when they have read enough of it for it to become familiar. Reading academic pieces can provide a considerable challenge, of course, and we have some exercises to help here too. You can try out these exercises and activities on a piece of academic writing of your choice, (Box 5.9).

Box 5.9   Play 'Buzzer'

When we give our students examples to work on, we also encourage them to do things like highlighting words or phrases that cause them difficulties. In group situations, they can press an imaginary buzzer (or actually make a buzzing sound if they are into drama). 'Jargon' is a notorious problem in reading social science texts, and you might wish to stop on terms like 'alienation' or '*geisteswissenschaft*', but 'educated' English can also provide problems (words like 'vicissitudes' or 'dichotomy').

The point, of course, is to discuss how to get over words like these and keep going. For example, perhaps the best thing to do is try to get the sense of the word from the context. This helps you keep reading and also develops your critical skills. If that fails, stop and look up words in dictionaries, including specialist dictionaries, or ask experts.

Another common problem is trying to get to the essence of the argument while avoiding a number of common distractions. These can include being sidetracked by a minor argument, or sometimes even an aside. Distractions can include mentioning names of other academics in passing, or using 'shorthand' terms used to reference a whole debate. We endorse the usual advice to look for summaries, conclusions, subheadings and abstracts in the text, but there is a broader task too (Box 5.10).

Box 5.10   Identifying the Audiences

Is an academic article or book simply written to communicate with new students? Who else is being addressed in the piece? Our answers would include the following audiences.

Other academics, including those who referee or peer review (explained in Chapter 7) the article or recommend the book for publication – these people have an important 'gate-keeping' role and have to be addressed.

Publishers, who often have a definite market niche in mind for the book and who have technical and commercial interests as well as academic ones (for example, they often want international audiences addressed as well as UK ones, or they like to see a book with broad coverage so as to widen its appeal to several academic disciplines).

(Continued)

(Continued)

Students at different levels of expertise, perhaps including postgraduate ones.

The same author(s) in earlier guises – writers change their minds, develop their ideas, respond to criticisms, re-think their earlier work.

Politicians and policy-makers.

Journalists and the media.

One reason for trying to note these different audiences, if not actually identify them, is that it can give you the confidence to read selectively. Do you need to track down the academic sources mentioned in the introductory sections, or are they there to convince other academics of the quality of the work? Are the policy recommendations relevant to you at this moment or can they be left for another reading at a later time? Do you need to grasp the full academic justifications for a point, or should you just try to get the main points for now?

Reports

It is conventional to think of reports as taking a specific form, and this form is well described by a number of writers and experts. Usually, for example, the content is expected to be 'factual', reporting research findings, policy statements, or government documents. The idea is to present information so that readers can feel informed, perhaps knowledgeable enough to make a decision. Of course, this implies that you have worked with similar audiences already and can anticipate what readers want to know in addition. In writing reports at work, you will often be given a rather tight brief, or be expected to be able to derive one from what the clients stipulate. Academic reports can be less well specified, but there is still a need to undertake research or at the very least to take account of and write up the work from a particular angle.

The actual structure can sometimes be specified quite tightly. The real problem is often structure in a different 'deeper' sense, not only summarizing, but making the report flow. Williams (2004) has a very useful section covering both issues. To borrow from his discussion, we might consider the typical structure of a report as featuring the usual stages (Box 5.11).

Box 5.11   Contents of a Report

Preliminaries (executive summary, background to the topic, introduction).
Main body (major findings, including the clear presentation of any data, major issues to be decided).
Endnotes (conclusions, recommendations, issues to think about or explore further, references, any relevant appendices).

Reports should flow in ways which help the audience to anticipate what is coming and thus get involved. Williams (2004: 78) suggests the following (Box 5.12).

Box 5.12   Making a Report Flow

[From] general [axioms, agreed truths, common perceptions, accepted knowledge] to particular [consequences or implications for action].
[From] particular [urgent problems or issues, recent findings or events] to general [conclusions about what the particulars mean or where they are pointing].
Spatial [where an area has to be mapped, machines logically explained, layouts of facilities analysed].
Historical or narrative [following chronological order, but not forgetting to address the main issues].
Familiar to unfamiliar.
Dialectic [rather a specialist philosophical procedure, often encountered in discussing the work of Marx. Williams gives the usual formula of 'thesis–antithesis–synthesis'. A good way to present a debate, giving opposing views then exploring resolutions, ways forward or common ground].

Further information about report writing is available on http://www.gcal.ac.uk/student/coursework/reports/index.html. We return to this topic in Chapter 9, where we provide more detailed information about how to write a research report or a dissertation.

Examination Answers

Writing an examination answer can actually be easier than writing an essay or a portfolio. This may sound odd to students who find examinations very stressful and whose minds go blank as soon as they enter the examination room. Conventional study skills books often recommend that such students engage in a number of relaxation techniques to reduce the stress, ranging from simple yoga-based breathing exercises to techniques which sportspersons might find familiar, like attempting to visualize the successful completion of an examination while controlling negative thoughts.

We want to break with convention a little, as we have done in other sections of this book, and argue that examination answers can sometimes involve a lot less stress if you know what to expect. You only have a limited time to write your answer, instead of having to decide what to do over a longer period of time. This should help you focus on the essential elements. The other advantage, which you may not know about, is that examination answers are probably marked slightly more leniently. We know that you will be under pressures of time. We will not usually expect lengthy quotes or tables of statistics. We even make an allowance for simple mistakes. There can be no suspicion of plagiarism, and specific forms of malpractice (like impersonation) are still rare, which is one of the reasons that unseen examinations may be making a comeback.

As usual, you have to adapt your writing to the conventions of the test. The basic structure we have discussed above – summary of debates followed by comments on them – still applies to examinations. Indeed, there is even more reason to focus on these core elements, because you do not have time for lengthy asides, preambles, rants, thinking aloud, or long descriptive sections. The task renders itself down to the real basics.

As with writing essays or longer coursework pieces, your strategy for preparing for examinations should bear in mind that you have to deliver an answer based on summary and comment. It follows that you prepare for examinations by being able to note and then remember (if it is an unseen exam) brief but accurate summaries of the main approaches and pieces of work. You can do that in a number of well-known ways. Study skills books often recommend that you produce memorable summaries by reducing your notes to key bullet points on file cards, for example, or that you visualize the debates and draw a spider diagram, flow chart or 'mind map'.

Some useful work picks up some of the points we made earlier about structuring arguments and offers 'scaffolding' to help students focus their efforts (for example, Nussbaum, 2002). Nussbaum suggests that students follow a template he has devised to help them. Basically, it consists of three sets of boxes, which invite students to summarize main points, note the evidence that supports the main points, and then focus on the relations between the points and the evidence. Some intriguing work on computer-mediated discussion (Hirsch et al., 2004) offers a set of options to guide argument. We can borrow their idea here and apply it to preparing revision materials for exams. Students might want to think of themselves as learning to use arguments of the following type (Box 5.13).

Box 5.13   Developing an Argument

I agree with [this] statement because …
[This] statement is not right because …
[This] statement can be substantiated by the fact that … or clarified by saying …
[This] statement is true to an extent but ignores the fact that …
In support of [this] statement, I give the following example …

Source: Hirsch et al. (2004: 75)

Note that there is a similar but briefer general statement that the Thinking Writing website (http://www.thinkingwriting.qmul.ac.uk/ and http://www.thinkingwriting.qmul.ac.uk/shortwrite2.htm) also suggests students might add to their lecture notes – 'Yes, but …'.

At the very least, what these particular techniques encourage you to do is to take notes with the need to argue economically in mind. You can then further reduce the notes by thinking about them, with or without the aid of further writing and mind-mapping. Some people like to think of a model of their memories where information is stored in the pre-conscious or sub-conscious mind. A few words on the file card can help to bring that information back into the conscious mind. A homely analogy that is often cited concerns being able to drive for several hundred miles. Drivers can rarely remember their journey in detail, but as they come to each section of the road, it reminds them of what to do next.

Working over notes, either by constant re-reading or by attempting to transform them in various ways to shorter or more visual versions, can often simply help students to feel at home in a debate. Confidence grows, or what is sometimes called 'ownership'. Indeed, we have met students who have only really felt they are on top of their subjects when they have prepared material for examinations. Paradoxically, this often comes at the end of the module or course. No doubt this is partly because information provided during the course gets recalled, as in the driving analogy. It may also be something to do with getting the right level of stress and motivation, perhaps even combined with a feeling of relief that the examination ordeal is nearly over.

What is often not realized is that you can also revise and prepare comments as well. Remember that you will need to provide all sorts of alert and intelligent argument and comment on the summaries that you are providing if you want to do well. To overcome the effects of stress, we have sometimes recommended a really simple structure which reminds students to provide comments. When you write down your six or seven sentences or bullet points in your examination answer plan, to remind you of the content of the debates, we have suggested that you also draw a box at the beginning and the end of this plan. You are going to fill the boxes with comment, and the most convenient and simple locations for comment are in boxes labelled 'Introduction' and 'Conclusion'. This simple structure may not suit you, and you may prefer to introduce comments as you go along, at the end of sections, or even intertwined with summary. However, if you are not a good examination candidate, it might be best to follow the simplest structure, at least until you find your own way.

You can obviously think of comments to make as you do your note-taking and revision, and you will want to record these comments so you can revise them as well. Of course, with any luck, the stress level of taking the examination will be exactly right, and will stimulate you to recall all kinds of additional links, comparisons, and critical comments of both the 'internal' and 'external' kind as we argued above. If you are a poor examination candidate, you will prefer to have at least a few comments ready-made, just in case.

What sort of comments will you be noting? The same kind of things you were noting in your essays, which we have listed above. It is impossible of course to specify detailed comments because they depend very much on the topic, but we have made some general suggestions that apply to examination answers as well – comments on alternative approaches and comparisons, on the methods used, on additional cases which have not been discussed, including recent developments, comments on the arguments involved, and what they both emphasize and ignore.

Where do you get comments like this from? Although you will be focusing on chosen topics for revision purposes, you may well get ideas for interesting comparisons from other topics discussed on your modules or courses, perhaps those that were discussed in the same section as the ones you have chosen to specialize in. If you have been to most or many lectures and taken notes, you can often get ideas for comparative comment. You will have almost certainly received some lecturers' comments on your written work, and they can clearly be borne in mind. We have certainly written comments ourselves that are specifically designed to provoke the sort of reflection that can be used to generate useful material for revision.

You can also get comments from seminars and presentations. If you have attended the seminars and presentations on adjacent topics, and listened skilfully, you may well have some comparisons to make. In fact, if you are really well prepared, as we suggest, you will even have asked about comparisons in presentations and seminars so that you will have some material already to hand. You can get material for comments from discussing topics with other students, perhaps when you revise together, or from tutorials, including special revision tutorials. Of course, you will have to remember to note down these comments and include them in your mind maps or file cards. To our continued surprise, many students never do note down interesting comments that have arisen in discussion, even if they take lots of notes in lectures.

You can get ideas for comment from other questions on the examination paper. If you are tackling a question on youth subcultures, and there is also a question on the difficulties of doing research, or one on policy developments to combat illegal drugs, or one on Marxist approaches to deviance, you should not be short of ideas for comments. Sometimes the actual question itself will remind you to comment. It may include a quotation which you have to 'critically discuss'. You may be invited to apply arguments to a specific example. There may be an additional part of the question that specifies that you should focus on methodology, current relevance, comparison with other approaches or whatever. You will gain marks if you take up the invitation to address the specific issues as you go through your summaries and comment. Students tend to get rather poorer grades if they simply reproduce a very general debate with no particular focus, as with essays. Worst of all is the answer that gives the impression that some set of notes, sometimes even an essay, has been memorized and is being regurgitated, regardless of the actual question.

Incidentally, some of the features of examination questions can sometimes puzzle or distract students. We have known students who have been 'put off' answering particular questions even though they have prepared the topic. Sometimes this is because a question is unnecessarily obscure, perhaps because it includes a piece of difficult jargon or some other kind of scholarly flourish. However, sometimes it is a simple misunderstanding on the part of the student. The specific cases we have in mind are questions that are deliberately designed to encourage a range of answers. If you remember our assessment task, it is to provide a test that will produce different sorts of answers, so that we can award different sorts of grade. To put a nice gloss on it, we want to design a question that will permit the really well-prepared, well-motivated, and well-read student to generate a first-class answer. At the same time, we want to allow a student who has made a reasonable effort to produce a reasonable answer.

One technique to produce this range of answers is to divide the examination question into two parts. The first part might require a reasonable survey of some of the literature, but the second part might require some additional demonstration of knowledge or commitment. The general form of the question might well ask students to first summarize a well-known debate, which they can find in the materials they encounter on the course, and then to apply it to a new area: here, they will not find ready-made answers in the materials but will have to demonstrate their own understanding. To take an obvious example, we could ask: 'What did Durkheim think were the main causes of suicide? How might this be applied to understanding recent suicide bombers?'

If you only have a reasonable knowledge, and can feel fully confident only with the first part, you might still wish to attempt questions like this, of course. If you have practised doing critical comment and argument, you could profitably apply these skills to the new area.

Turning to more detailed advice for the examination itself, one approach which sometimes works well is to devise a plan for all the required examination answers as soon as you are allowed to begin the examination. That helps students who worry that they will forget material for the later questions, or spend too much time on the first one. It can also serve as a calming ritual to get you started actually doing something. Having devised your plan, you include the boxes for comment, and sketch in any ideas you might have already. Then you begin to address the questions, thinking of summary and comment as before.

As with all the writing and presentation techniques we have discussed (and will discuss in later chapters), examination questions will require you to not only remember summaries of debates and make comments on them, but also to edit what you know as you go along.

Chapter Summary

1 Academic writing is specialized and has its own conventions, but these can be discovered and practised in order to improve returns.
2 Plagiarism can be a major problem and should be assiduously avoided. Systems of detection are now quite advanced. Clear and honest intentions, and using a scrupulously accurate referencing system, recommended by your local institution, should avoid any suspicions.
3 In essence, good academic writing requires you to perform the twin tasks of accurately summarizing the work of others, and then adding comments of various kinds of your own. Comment is always possible in social science.

(Continued)

(Continued)

4   The ability to develop academic argument is becoming a key issue, and you will need to abandon popular forms and develop more technical approaches instead.

5   Arguing in written forms can be practised and you should develop your knowledge of the conventions and the requirements – but avoid too literal an application of them.

6   Writing in an academic form is easier if you read academic material with confidence, focusing on essential points and with a sense of the different audiences being addressed.

7   Writing in examinations can help focus your efforts and should be approached positively. Effective revision involves revising comments as well as summaries.

6 Verbal Skills

CHAPTER OVERVIEW

- The importance of verbal communication in presentations and seminars.
- Types of seminars.
- Sources of student anxiety and some ideas to overcome them.
- Techniques to deliver competent performance.
- Encouraging dialogue and discussion, building confidence.

It is becoming increasingly common to expect students to take part in group discussions, and sometimes to lead them. This is thought to be a helpful exercise to get students engaged with academic material, and it also involves 'transferable skills' of the kind we discussed in Chapter 4, since giving a presentation is common in work situations too. As usual, you would expect to find the actual procedures to vary from one university to another and even from one course to another. Some of our own colleagues over the years have run student seminars in particular ways.

What is a Student Seminar?

1   An academic topic has been assigned to individual students, or sometimes pairs or groups of students. Students have to prepare to lead a discussion on their topic, usually following some form of the general

structure we have referred to earlier – they are asked to summarize some debates, and then to offer some sort of comment suggested by an actual topic.

2 A more general topic has been assigned, and students are expected to focus on elements of it. The example here might be to suggest the general topic of 'gender inequality in educational achievement', and let students focus upon particular aspects that they choose. One group might decide to discuss the classic work on the underachievement of girls in secondary schooling in the UK; another might pick a focus on the specific effects of the curriculum, or of popular culture and the media, or a focus on policies to remedy underachievement such as 'girl-friendly science', or 'women into science and engineering'. Other groups might pick other agendas, or other foci, perhaps choosing to look at higher education or to examine the work on boys' underachievement at school, or the problems faced by gay or lesbian minorities.

The actual procedures of the discussion can also vary. The topic can be introduced through a variety of means – students may read from their notes or from a paper they have written; students may be expected to produce a short summary of their discussion, and distribute it beforehand; students may be expected, or at least allowed, to use presentation software such as PowerPoint. The academic tutor can play a number of different roles too. He or she may chair the discussion, or expect students to do so. There may be a standard academic agenda to follow – debates are summarized and comments made, and then other members of the group are allowed to ask questions, discuss comparisons with other work, and pursue relevant applications, and so on. There may also be a more open-ended session, where any kind of relevant question may be permitted – we will discuss some of them below.

Seminars and student presentations are supported by academics for two major reasons. In the first place, they can encourage a more active kind of learning, where people can think things through and try to make sense of them in their own terms. Preparing a seminar or presentation definitely encourages personal involvement with the material, and this can be more vivid than listening to someone else talk about the topic in the lecture. Of course, an additional motivation for preparing a presentation or seminar is that you are responsible for finding enough material and for attempting to make it relevant and interesting for your fellow students. This is where you can demonstrate communication skills, thinking out matters such as optimal speed, duration, level and timing of your presentation, responding to different audiences, and cooperating with your fellow presenters. This is precisely the sort of thing you may be asked to do in your eventual job, or, indeed, at an interview for a job. However, this sort of skilled activity can sometimes cause anxiety, in each of those settings, as we shall see.

You may have had some relevant experience in public speaking already, of course. You may have spoken at student union meetings or on sporting occasions (especially if you have captained a team). Sometimes, students will have worked in a public medium such as hospital radio, pub quizzes, student helplines or phone-ins. Many students will have practised their verbal skills in various ways at their previous school or college, in ways ranging from appearing in amateur dramatic productions to practising academic presentations in study skill sessions or in dummy runs for job interviews. After all, we all communicate pretty effectively every day – it is a matter of bringing that competence to the new situation of academic work.

In the particular constraints of academic work, it can be a challenge to summarize complex information succinctly enough to provide a 20- or 30-minute presentation. There can be a problem in clarifying issues sufficiently for others to understand them, without trivializing the issues too much. It can be difficult to keep the attention of a group and to manage their involvement. You need to keep people interested but also keep them 'on task'. You may need to demonstrate that you can use presentation technology, such as PowerPoint or an electronic whiteboard, while keeping attention focused on your material (and coping if the equipment goes wrong). You should resist the temptation to cover any embarrassments by playing for laughs or by trying to bluff it out regardless – the two most common characteristics of poor presentations for Bonnett (2001).

Student Anxiety

We have certainly picked up student anxiety about these matters, even among those with some experience of public speaking, sometimes to our surprise. We are so accustomed to academic speaking ourselves that we can underestimate the feelings of newcomers. For example, one student said:

In my opinion, presentations are the worse forms of assessments, due to the stress they cause which begins weeks before the assessment takes place. In addition to this, there is the aspect that you are assessed straight away and in front of your peers. As soon as I hear I have to do a presentation I start to panic and frantically think of a topic to do the research on.

It seems that it might have been the stress of not only speaking in public but feeling that the performance was being publicly assessed in an academic way that caused the tension. This can be unlike anything that has been experienced before.

Some research carried out by our colleagues confirmed the same level of anxiety. It seems that the students they interviewed disliked seminars and presentations, and reported they were 'too challenging and unrewarded whilst other participants could be intimidated and unmotivated' (Casey et al., 2002). Students felt unsure about what was expected in seminars, and some expressed an initial 'shock' at the prospect of speaking in an academic situation.

Much can depend on how clearly the role of the presenter and of the seminar is explained, and exactly what is at stake in terms of assessment. Students face the challenge differently too. Some delay and fail to prepare adequately. We have seen students desperately trying to find something to download on the topic on the morning of their presentation. When they have succeeded, their 'presentation' has consisted of them simply reading out a page or two of material that they have barely laid their eyes on before. The results are usually obviously embarrassing to all participants. The students in the Casey et al. (2002) study have clearly experienced such poorly prepared sessions:

> All agreed that mumbled speech and poor preparation made for boring, futile presentations: 'some poor sod who is really desperately shy sits at the front and reads it (presentation) and you can't hear what they're saying and you feel sorry for them and yourself as well because [you] don't know what it is about, there is nothing to be gained from that – it's just a waste of time'. (Year 3)

Embarrassing silence in seminars can also be a problem: the students in the study above saw silences 'arising from their peers' laziness or, more likely, fear – 'they are scared of saying the wrong thing or something stupid' (Year 3) (Casey et al., 2002).

Possible Role-models

At this point, it might be worth turning to some advice commonly offered to new tutors on organizing effective student seminars. Students might like to think of comparing themselves with lecturers at this stage. When you have attended a few lectures, you can start to consider what is 'good' and 'bad' about particular examples. It is common for students to like lectures that are well informed, enthusiastic, mildly humorous or good-natured, conveying a sense of exploration, for example, while students dislike lectures that are long, boring, patronizing and too 'academic' (presumably meaning not well related to the needs of the audience, and assuming too much of them). We have also suggested that lectures are a performance, a technical matter of conveying arguments, not a personal form of disclosure or persuasion.

Indeed, there is a substantial literature on presenting effectively – lecturing effectively is the specific focus, but there are some general points of advice that apply to anyone having to introduce a discussion of an academic topic to an audience. For example, a particular guide to practice, supplied to lecturers taking a recent Open University (UK) course on teaching in higher education (Gibbs, 1998: 4) begins with some findings that will seem familiar to any student (and which we have discussed in Chapter 1):

> New teachers in higher education are characteristically anxious about their recently acquired status as academics ... Many subconsciously fear being exposed as an impostor at any moment ... [as a result] ... they tend to focus their attention on content ... gathering piles of notes which they then struggle to cram in to an hour's lecture. They also concentrate on not getting anything wrong. This is seldom a successful strategy.

Gibbs goes on to recommend following a clear structure, which includes student activities and a shrewd use of additional materials such as handouts. We shall discuss some of these as suitable advice for student presentations later in this chapter, but it is worth discussing his additional point that watching televised debates, documentaries and news programmes can also provide ideas. One of the exercises he recommends to new lecturers is to note down especially how those broadcast examples are introduced, structured and concluded. Any media students will have an advantage here, of course. It is also worth pointing out that some television programmes contain examples of unpleasant and sensationalized confrontation and aggression: *The Jerry Springer Show* is probably not a good model for seminars.

There is also some general advice suggested specifically by the Casey et al. research which we have mentioned above. It seems that students preferred workshops to seminars, and one difference was that in workshops they were given smaller and more specific tasks. This leads us to a point about teaching or presenting: it is always up to students to modify the tasks they are given. Even if the tutor does not suggest changing the tasks, they can always be reinterpreted by the students. In this particular case, there is no reason why students should not themselves reinterpret a seminar as a workshop, taking the general task or topic and splitting it down themselves into more specific and smaller tasks. In other words, they could easily have imposed their own agenda. Incidentally, if students find it embarrassing to have the grade for the session announced in front of their peers, the solution seems simply to ask for the grade in private afterwards – we are sure tutors mostly do not mean to make things personally difficult deliberately, and nor should they do so.

Useful Procedures

Certainly, the sort of agendas that we have already discussed in the previous chapter will do as well for seminars and presentations. Students can break down the topic under the usual headings, for example, and think of offering basic stages covering preliminaries, main body, and concluding remarks. Students might also pursue one of the suggestions to keep the flow going in report writing found in Williams (2004) to structure their presentations. Alternatively, students could rely on the basic general structure of an essay or an examination question, thinking of summarizing key debates and then adding comments to them. Given that a presentation normally is a fairly short exercise, the structure of the examination question seems particularly suitable here, with its list of main points topped and tailed by reminders to tackle introductions and conclusions. Exactly the same kind of introductory and concluding points that we suggested then can be used here – setting the scene, clarifying the agenda, particularly recommended by Gibbs (1998), making comparisons and links with other topics.

Finally, the most common versions of PowerPoint contain suggested structures for presentations of various kinds themselves (the now-redundant version of Word 97 used to offer them too, but not the latest versions packaged with Windows XP). Students can use these templates to guide their offerings, modifying them to suit the specific task that they are doing. As usual, once you have got a reasonable structure, and have broken down the task into manageable steps, everything looks slightly easier. Breaking the task down like this can also produce an effective group contribution, of course, because you can then allocate responsibility for different sections to different members.

Bonnett (2001: 85–6) has a range of suggestions for preparations including practising the actual talk with friends. He even suggests that students might like to record their rehearsals, on audio or video, and analyse their own performance afterwards, using a checklist. This covers matters such as 'Clarity of Argument … Use of Aids … Attention to Audience … Response to Questions'. We can certainly recommend this technique, although it can be quite disappointing to see oneself on video and we would not advise public analysis for particularly self-conscious students.

Pros and Cons

It might help to remind presenters of what can be achieved in presentations and seminars at this point. When they work well, they can produce feelings of real achievement and gain. Presenters feel they have understood something and so do the participants, often because they can feel sympathy with their fellows and can relate better to them. We have known students who have got involved and have carried on discussing the topic even after the session has finished. Some groups do generate feelings of high morale, a sense of purpose, and a sense of mutual exploration, and it is a pleasure to take part in them. Topics seem manageable and less remote, and discussion can be much more open and equal. We have run groups that have simply begun and ended discussions entirely by their own efforts. Even the most unpromising subject matter can be managed well, and we have heard seminars in a neighbouring room buzzing with excitement, animated discussion and good humour, with students spilling out on to the corridors afterwards still talking – and found, on enquiring, that they had been discussing Kierkegaard and the notion of 'sickness unto death'.

Perhaps the Casey research and our own experience of student anxiety are picking up characteristics which are specific to talking face-to-face in groups. There are many ways to reduce the anxiety, in fact, including facing the common worry that fellow-students will make adverse or personal comments. Much will depend on how the task is conceived, and how the group has been allowed to operate. The lecturers concerned clearly have a role to play here. They should be open to requests for further clarification from presenters, and they should chair or run the meeting in such a way that personal attacks are ruled out of order. If students chair their own meetings, this can still be accepted as a basic set of ground rules. Ground rules can be specified explicitly at the start, if necessary. It should be easy to gain consent for a rule that says no personal attacks are allowed, especially as all members of the group are expected to do a presentation, and so it does not make sense to launch a personal attack if you are likely to receive one back when it is your turn.

Some groups still seem determined to use the occasion of a group presentation as the chance to slip away from the task and do something far more entertaining, like trying to become the most popular member of the group, picking on some other members, or getting back at the tutor. We have run groups where some sort of consensus seems to have emerged that the whole point is to complain about the course and the university in some way. We have already mentioned examples of groups which have split into two polarized sub-groups who have spent the time cheerfully insulting each other and scoring points, sometimes in a very personal way. These groups are more difficult to manage, but the techniques remain the same – to rule out of order personal attack, and to insist that the academic purposes of the group discussion are the ones that should dominate. If necessary, 10 minutes or so can be set aside for hearing complaints about the administration of the assessment system, or whatever, but even here, participants should be reminded that there are channels for complaint, and that a student group presentation is not one of them.

Bonnett (2001) addresses the issue of aggressive audience responses, and points out that no one need tolerate actual abuse. You can deal with it by stating that you recognize it as abuse and thus refuse to respond to it. Bonnett's advice in answering audience questions is applicable to most situations:

> Where you think your challenger is right say so. Where they are wrong, tell them why. Where you don't know if they are right or wrong … [avoid] … stubborn and egocentric defiance. Indeed, if you are engaged in a debate you should expect to concede points. (2001: 81–2)

The same principles apply to electronic discussion in forums, bulletin boards or discussion boards. It is easier sometimes to just dash off a comment without really thinking about its relevance, and it is surprising to see the ease with which electronic discussion can go off task, even though the medium is supposed to be cold and unemotional. In fact, it is very hard to pick up the differences between anger and humour, or sarcasm for comic effect and aggression. It is common for universities to specify a code of conduct for these activities, usually known as 'netiquette', which forbids the most blatant kind of abusive words or inappropriate forms of speech. Nevertheless, some contributors attempt to start a 'flame war' rather than a discussion:

> I know I wasn't THRILLED to be asked to start at **9 o'clock** on a *MONDAY* and I know there were other students who felt the same way. I don't see why I should cycle in for AN HOUR just to have one session with you. Who are you anyway? Why didn't you run the seminar after the lecture like last year?

This sort of comment is pretty unlikely to receive a helpful response, of course. Indeed, it is hard to see what sort of response the sender was expecting – a grovelling general apology? A resignation?

Setting the Tone

You can help maintain a suitable tone in the group discussion yourself. If you are presenting, you need to make the session worthwhile and positive yourselves, and not start out to settle scores or exclude people. You will need suitably neutral and informative language, and you will need to be prepared to listen carefully to comments. If you do not feel personally threatened, no one can score personal points against you. Everything depends on the frame of mind with which you approach the topic. You might want to practise by tackling topics that are not close to your personal concerns at first – if you have strong feelings about animal cruelty, or social inequality, let someone else take that seminar until you have settled down and feel comfortable.

You can help to establish the right sort of neutral tone when others present too. You can exert a certain amount of discipline over yourself, and refrain from personal attack or deliberately annoying behaviour (yawning, fidgeting, chatting to your neighbours, texting, sorting through your notes) when someone else is speaking, for example. The form of questions you raise can make a difference, and you may notice from your reflection on lectures or TV programmes that there are different ways to ask questions or make comments. You need to find out for yourselves how to participate in a discussion without unnecessarily and unintentionally offending anybody. Sometimes this may require unusually polite forms of speech. Instead of simply asking 'Why do you believe something as obviously stupid as that?', you might find it more effective to say something instead like 'Could you give some of the evidence?', or even 'I can understand the point you are making, but I would like to think more about the evidence for it – what exactly was it that convinced you?' Similarly, questions can be about the issues rather than about the personalities (a move away from *ad hominem* arguments as we discussed in the previous chapter). Slightly more formal and polite speech of this kind can help depersonalize, even though it can sound mildly comical or pompous.

If a slightly more formal tone helps to depersonalize, so can a technical focus for the discussion. After all, the point of a seminar or student presentation should be to offer some material that shows you have learned something, and that it can help other students learn material related to the course they are studying. They are not really occasions to seek popularity, to fly flags of particular kinds, to try and impress people, or to score points. It does not matter if other students do not particularly like you as a presenter, and you should not spend more time rehearsing your jokes than you do preparing your academic material. You can even think of it as a role you need to play: you are presenting a viewpoint, not necessarily your viewpoint, and you are acting as a kind of tutor, not necessarily as your normal self. An avoidance of the first person can help a great deal to focus people on the issues. We have encouraged inexperienced students to play this role by suggesting they ask questions or make comments based on a 'typical' response, a 'Marxist' or a 'feminist' response, or the stance of a proponent or opponent, rather than necessarily giving their own views immediately.

Standard Questions

As we have indicated in earlier chapters, discussions also offer a chance to develop the kinds of comment on a topic that can help you write a better essay or examination question. We addressed the need to be able to form views on matters such as the overall importance of the topic, the place of the topic in the course as a whole, the way in which the discussion addresses general themes discussed in the course, such as research methodology, policy, or the comparisons that can be made between discussions on different topics. Group discussions are ideal places to hear the views of other students on these matters, and to begin to formulate and contribute your own. Pursuing these topics also provides fairly standard and technical ways to intervene in a discussion, to break that awkward silence that only gets worse the longer it goes on. Students are often advised to make a contribution early on, so that they do not fall into the role of silent participant ('lurkers' as they are known in electronic discussion formats). Here is the opportunity to ask a question that is not personally threatening, is of general relevance, and which might actually help you to gain a better grade. Again, you need to ask such questions in suitable language. It might be appropriate to ask the entire group rather than just the presenter, for example, and perhaps preface your remark with one of those matter-of-fact disclaimers that we mentioned in the Introduction (Box 6.1).

Box 6.1   Asking Low-risk Questions

Try something along these lines. Don't forget the 'matter-of-fact' or slightly self-deprecating style.

I am probably worrying too much already, but can anyone help to relate this discussion to essay five?

One thing that interests me is the methodology used in this discussion, but I am not sure how to describe it. What do people think?

Perhaps I am the only one here who hasn't got them straight but could we just go over the general issues?

I have to do a presentation next week on [another topic], and I was just wondering if there were any connections with this topic?

I haven't got too much time left this week, so what is the best single thing to read to get the gist?

How would the argument go if we extended it to (a more recent example)?

There are no scripts to learn, of course, and no need for them. It is an attempt to maintain this kind of tone that lies behind the more specific advice to presenters, which you often find in conventional study skills books, to bear the audience in mind. As we noted when discussing written assignments, it is not always easy to relate to an audience if you do not know anything at all about them, and this is perhaps the most daunting kind of presentation, especially if the audience is appraising you, as at a job interview. It is helpful to practise with student presentations, when you know more about your fellow-students and your lecturers. Keeping your eyes and ears open when other people give presentations can be very helpful. Setting yourself specific objectives, or outlining key concepts, can be a way to remind yourself that there is an audience, and the point of the presentation is to inform them about something. If you can get the confidence to do so, an effective technique is to constantly think of the audience's reactions as you proceed and try to 'read' them.

Focusing on the Audience

We have seen many presentations where elementary mistakes in the beginning are not rectified – the typing on the slides is too small (if that is so, read out the text), the pace is too fast (slow down, even if it means you do not get through all the material), the presentation is too long (stop when the time is up and say you have more material if anyone is interested, or refer to the later material in the discussion). The best presenters are able to edit on their feet, to repeat points if they have proved difficult to understand, to omit material if it is not helpful, to adjust the pace and level of their presentation as they go along. The worst ones soldier on grimly with what they have prepared, sticking to the script.

You can rehearse all these matters before you start, of course, as suggested earlier. It is sometimes difficult to know if you can be heard at the back of the room – you need to ask people at the back if they can hear and see, or station one of your friends at the back and get them to give you unobtrusive feedback. As lecturers, we have also benefited from training or from helpful encounters with our students who have reminded us to cater for a wider range of members of the audience: there may be people present who need to lip-read, so you need to make your face visible; some people have problems reading particular combinations of text and coloured background and prefer other combinations. All these are matters which are easy enough to change with PowerPoint, on the actual day, as long as you know the basics of how to alter the designs and formats.

The best way to keep in touch, of course, is to let the audience members contribute too – announce that you will be taking questions at the end, or pause and ask for them after a particularly challenging section, and throw open the discussion to the audience itself. You do have to convey a sense that you are being genuine here, that you are really interested in the question, and that you do not have a pat answer already, and you have to leave room for discussion.

As a presenter, you can make it easy for the audience to discuss your efforts by providing them with some hints to get them started. You might want to suggest the sort of technical or task-based questions mentioned above – a good way to signal that you are handing over at that point and that you are not just asking questions to which you alone have the answers. You can give the audience questions to think about in advance, or ask them to write some down before you begin your actual treatment. You can use some of the questions mentioned by the Thinking Writing website, which we summarized in the previous chapter, such as encouraging them to think of questions like 'Yes, but …'. You can suggest a structure for the argument that will follow your presentation – inviting comments on the main points, the evidence, and linking the two. You will not then be rattled by completely unexpected questions or comments and you may increase the general usefulness of the session. It can be good to remind the academic audience that they are not expected to be passive, and that they need to contribute to the effectiveness of the discussion as well as you do.

You can, perhaps with the consent of the tutor, organize different sorts of discussion. A famous approach has been advocated and tested by Northedge (1990) which involves discussion in stages – personal reflection for a few minutes, followed by discussion with the people next to you for another five minutes, and then a whole-group discussion. A variant is the small group and plenary structure – groups discuss topics and spokespersons report back to the larger gathering. Here, a certain helpful depersonalization can be introduced by having a spokesperson for each small group note and present the findings of the group, or the range of opinions within the group, while actual contributors remain nameless.

Expect the Unpredictable

Verbal discussion is almost inevitably unpredictable, since it can develop in so many ways. Theoretical analyses of the kind you may meet show so much possible ambiguity and misunderstanding that it is almost surprising that people manage to understand each other at all. Even the best of us constantly encounter occasions where misunderstandings have arisen. Here are some examples from our own experience (Box 6.2).

Box 6.2 Misunderstandings

Example 1

DH: So you can see from these data, which the British Government has collected, remember, that Roberts is suggesting that levels of taxation on the richest groups have clearly fallen over this period too.

KS: [Year 1 student] Are these figures right?

DH: [rather nervously] What do you mean? They are not foolproof, of course, they are based on assumptions …

KS: No. … Is it true that some people were paying over 80 per cent in tax? Really? That can't be right, surely? You work hard all day and then have to hand over 80 per cent of it to the government?

AH: [Year 1 student] [heatedly] Well, what if it's all been left to them?

KS: So you're saying that if their parents worked hard all their life and handed over their money, left their money, the State should get 80 per cent of it? How is that fair?

PH: [Year 1 student] [heatedly] Well, what about the Royal Family …

AW: [Year 1 student] [*sotto voce*] Oh no …

Example 2

DH: Apparently, mature students have additional problems which they … [Translation: I am about to tell you something about Hopper's research.]

AS: [Year 2 student] [rather heatedly] Excuse me … why is it always mature students? Lots of us have problems too, you know …
[Translation: I do not like the way you seem to favour mature students all the time. Don't let them dominate seminars so much! Make a bit of eye-contact with us!]

Example 3

DH: Just as a final word, let me point you back to the issue of methodology …
[Translation: Let me add some value to the discussion for you. The student presenters probably should have emphasized this a bit more, but I am not going to criticize them openly. I think this is the

(Continued)

(Continued)

main way you can connect this topic with the one we discussed last week. This is often a way to get a better grade on this topic.] Students begin to click files and put papers away in their bags. [Translation: We have got enough information for our assignment. We do not see the point of going on to discuss methodology as well. We are hungry and want to leave now. We will not be able to concentrate anyway if you force us to stay.]

These misunderstandings are routine and inevitable and they cannot be designed out of the interaction. When they occur, it does not mean that the session has failed or that the presentation has been ineffective. If you let people make contributions, they will often compound the misunderstanding as in the first example above, but if you do not let them speak at all, you may never know what they are thinking. No one is to blame, and the incidents cited were not ill-tempered, despite some initial heat. All you can do is be alert to misunderstandings and misperceptions and try to retrieve the situation. On those occasions, although not on all occasions, the dislocations were only temporary. It is quite hard to do repairs at the time, and it is common to puzzle out what was going on only afterwards – but it may not be impossible to rectify the situation in subsequent sessions. If all the participants are genuinely trying to understand each other or the topic, this sort of minor breakdown can even be insightful. For further advice on presentations, see Glasgow Caledonian University website at http://gcal.ac.uk/student/coursework/presentations/index.html.

Chapter Summary

1 Verbal presentations and group discussions are important components of university teaching and can also be occasions to practise important communication skills.
2 Students need to think about tailoring their existing communicative abilities to the specific constraints of academic discussions.

(Continued)

(Continued)

3 Presentations and discussions can lead to anxiety but there are several basic techniques to solve this problem and to maximize the considerable benefits.

4 Students might do well to examine professional communicators such as their tutors or television presenters, and think about what makes some effective and others less effective.

5 Students are encouraged to minimize anxiety in consultation with their tutors.

6 A technical and slightly depersonalized tone can help participants focus on the actual task.

7 Students should remember the advice often given to new lecturers: neither under- nor over-prepare, be prepared to structure their contributions, and permit the audience to make contributions too.

8 All human communication is open to misunderstanding and interpretation and there is no perfectly clear and transparent utterance. Misunderstandings can be informative and sometimes even amusing.

7 Starting Your Dissertation

CHAPTER OVERVIEW

- Introduction to writing a dissertation.
- Getting started on small-scale research.
- Selecting a topic area.
- Doing a literature search.

This is the first of a series of three chapters that take you through the process of producing a dissertation. A dissertation, usually undertaken towards the end of a degree course, is the furthest away from anything you are likely to have been involved in at school or college so from this point of view is probably the most advanced academic skill for undergraduate students. You could see it as the end of the journey through university.

So, what is a 'dissertation'? Essentially, it is a small-scale project or research study that focuses on a topic area of your own choice. It comprises a piece of original, personal research, and generally uses information or material that you have collected and analysed yourself to provide answers to the research questions you are addressing. It is a little bit like a long drawn-out essay or short book that you have written yourself which draws together and demonstrates your abilities as an academic (to find out more about writing a dissertation from a student's point of view, see Hampson, 1994).

Remember that research skills such as searching for information, learning to work either individually or with other people, using computers, seeing a piece of work through from beginning to end, time management and writing will be valuable when it comes to looking for a job. The hard work – which research undoubtedly is – will be worth it in the end. The satisfaction of doing a substantial piece of work, to all intents and purposes your own, can be a huge confidence booster, it will look good on your CV and the skills you have developed will be transferable into the workplace (see Chapter 4).

For examples of accounts of empirical research, i.e. research that involves the collection of new data, then look in your university library for academic books or journal articles that include reports of studies carried out by individual academics or a research team. Classic examples for sociology students include Willis's study (1977) of 12 working class boys, known as 'the lads', in a Midlands schools, Jack Young's research (1971) on drug-taking in the 1960s and Barker's investigation (1984) of the early years of the Moonie religious cult. Recent personal examples include work on 'raves' as 'moral panics' (Critcher, 2000). If these look a bit intimidating, then look on Dave's website (http://www.arasite.org/) and there you will find examples of dissertations written by past students. Take a look at one about the belief systems of 'New Age' travellers (Keller, no date).

The aim of this chapter is to get you started on the dissertation, which usually involves deciding on a topic area to research and doing a literature review so that you can contextualize your own original work within the relevant body of literature. The following chapter discusses research methods, sampling strategies and ethical issues, and Chapter 9 focuses on how to analyse, present and write up the material. In recent years, whole textbooks have been written on each of the topic areas that follow. However, time and space constraints mean that we can only provide key points or summary information, and we are leaving it up to you to follow up our signposting with a visit to your institution's library or some useful websites. To help, we have included references to valuable textbooks and websites where relevant in the text.

Preliminaries

By way of reassurance, the first point to make is that you are not expected to complete a piece of research or a dissertation without academic advice, guidance and support in the planning, conduct and writing up of the study. One of the lecturers will supervise your work; ideally, you will have the freedom to choose your own supervisor. At the risk of sounding naïve, it is important that the supervisor is someone you feel happy working with, and ideally the two of you will already have some past experience of a good working relationship. This is particularly the case if you are doing an individual rather than a group piece of work, as you will be supervised on a one-to-one basis. Other criteria that you need to consider include genuine shared interest in the topic area under investigation, academic expertise specific to the topic, enthusiasm and availability.

You might want to weigh up just how much direction you think you will want and/or get from a potential supervisor. Some students appreciate direction in how to proceed, whilst others prefer to have the freedom to explore the topic in their own way and dislike being over-directed by their supervisor. It is reasonable to liken a dissertation to an examination; it is a major piece of work that requires a range of skills and knowledge. Like an exam, you have one chance at the final version; having said that, your supervisor is there to steer you in the right direction.

When first thinking about a study, it is very easy to be over-ambitious. A research project can grow, which is why it is essential to draw up a timetable at the start and discuss this with your supervisor. They are the people who know first-hand just how time-consuming research that involves collecting new empirical data can be. Their realistic estimates of how long the different stages are likely to take, what hurdles you may come up against and where you need to allow extra time will help you rein in the proposed work to something that is manageable and can be completed within the time constraints. And remember – the dissertation will be just one of any number of demands on your time!

Whether or not you feel that the research and dissertation process constitute a good way of being assessed, our advice is to find out as much as you can about the marking process and assessment criteria (we discussed this earlier in Chapter 3 about what tutors want). Doing well in a dissertation is an important part of getting a good degree overall, and it is a piece of work where you can get lots of advice and help before you submit it. Dissertations will be marked by one or even two members of the teaching staff. Marking criteria will probably be set out in the student handbook for your department. Hilary has recently been looking at the student handbook for a BA in Educational Studies at the University of York. This contained over three pages of detailed information about what was required for different degree classes, and left students in no doubt as to what had to be demonstrated for the different levels of achievement.

It is also important to make sure that you fully understand the examiner's expectations. It goes without saying that they will expect the dissertation to be about the subject it says it is about; they do not want it to be over-long; they want tables to be correctly labelled, and accurate references for all the source material presented in the appropriate style (see Chapter 5) (Box 7.1). And as we have emphasized throughout, plagiarism is the great academic sin and is absolutely unacceptable: you will fail if you copy other people's material and pretend that it is your own.

Box 7.1   Assessing the Quality of Completed Dissertations

Ask your supervisor for examples of previous dissertations so you know what you are aiming for. Try to assess just how good you think each one is. What makes the difference between a good quality dissertation and a poor one?

Go and find other examples in your library, on the C-SAP website for sociology, anthropology and politics (http://www.c-sap.bham.ac.uk/) or on Dave's website (http://www.arasite.org/). Try to constructively criticize those as well.

These are good exercises to do in a small group, because your friends might have useful points to make that you had not thought of.

Selection and Scope of the Topic Area

We have already indicated that a dissertation requires a lot of time and effort, the equivalent usually to one or even two modules on modular schemes. To help sustain this, it is important that the topic area is one that interests you and will ensure your levels of motivation remain high even when you appear to be making fairly limited progress. An easy mistake to make is to be over-ambitious, but given practical consideration related to time, resources and access to data sources, then our advice would be to tackle a limited topic area thoroughly rather than tackle a huge area superficially.

You might have to select a topic from a given list supplied by your department, in which case you will have limited scope for choice. However, if you have the freedom to choose your own topic, then here is the ideal opportunity for you to develop your own academic, vocational or personal interests and growth. Whilst these might derive from past experiences, this might well be the time to look ahead and think about whether there is any merit in undertaking a piece of work that has the potential to enhance your future career prospects (Box 7.2). If you are considering work in the social care field, for example, you might want to choose a topic looking at welfare benefits and service provision for older people; research examining schooling and children's rights would be useful for someone wanting to get a job in the educational field.

Box 7.2   Choosing a Topic Area

Write down up to three topic areas that you are interested in researching which relate to:

1   academic subjects;
2   personal interests/growth;
3   future career prospects.

Which will hold your interest for up to six months, and why?
Which would be of interest to a potential supervisor?
Which would be of interest to your peers and others who might support you?
And, finally, which one would you choose for your dissertation?

Doing a Literature Review

Having selected the general area for your dissertation, the next step is to focus and develop specific research questions, or identify hypotheses that you want to test. These emerge through the process of undertaking a literature review, which is a foundational first stage and usually forms the second chapter of a dissertation (see Chapter 9). A literature review is a survey of academic articles, books, government reports, statistical surveys and other sources that have a bearing on the field of research you are interested in. The underlying principle is that all scientific inquiry involves an initial assessment of pre-existing knowledge. In order to persuade other experts in the field that an argument or theory or new research findings should be taken seriously, then mastery of the literature must be demonstrated.

A review of the available literature serves a number of essential functions for research (Denscombe, 2003). First, it shows that the researcher is aware of the existing body of knowledge in the area being studied, or at least its most important dimensions. As implied in earlier chapters, Sociology and other social science subjects are constituted by a series of debates, for example, the debate over skilled work and technical change in contemporary industrial society (Braverman, 1974). It is imperative that such debates are assessed critically. Second, it identifies what the researcher understands to be the key issues, the important questions and the glaring gaps in the current state of knowledge. Third, it offers signposts as to how previous research, theories and principles have informed the proposed research. In other words, the literature review provides the foundations for your own original research so, just like the academic researchers who wrote the classic texts we referred to at the start of the chapter, you too will need to draw on your literature review to show how this has informed the specific objectives of your dissertation.

Once you have completed your literature review, a good exercise is to try to operationalize specific research questions based on your evaluation of the existing knowledge (Box 7.3). The aim is to narrow down the scope of the work to a project that will be personally manageable within the time and resource constraints allowed. Once you have defined your research objectives, discuss and agree them with your dissertation supervisor.

Box 7.3 Devising Manageable Research Questions

Create three research questions for each of the three topic areas below:

1 a study of lone mothers' employment patterns;
2 the effectiveness of short breaks for people with learning disabilities and their parents;
3 the impact of the national telephone helpline NHS Direct.

Have you written the questions in the most specific terms that you can? Evaluate each question with a view to operationalizing it in an actual research study. Consider whether the focus of the research is clear. Is it still too general or too broad? If you have used words such as 'effectiveness' or 'impact', is their meaning clear to the reader, for instance, who should be the focus of the impact of NHS Direct: the telephone caller; the patient; the nurse handling the call; the nursing profession; the medical profession?

Before you can write a literature review, you have to conduct a literature search which involves a range of different activities. There is a particular sequence which must be followed to complete your literature review; this is set out in Box 7.4, and the activities involved are elaborated below. We know from our own experience the amount of time that a literature search takes, and we cannot stress too much how important it is for you to allow sufficient time to conduct the searches and gather the material together. Otherwise, you will find that you are running out of time, and you have to rush through the all important stage of analysing and synthesizing the material for the literature review chapter.

Box 7.4   Sequence for Doing a Literature Review

1   Decide on the research area.
2   Define the key words or search terms.
3   Implement search using a range of information sources, such as the university library, academic databases, national and local government publications, statistical surveys, and freely available Internet websites.
4   Save the search results to file.
5   Retrieve the full text documents.
6   Assess the retrieved material for relevance and quality.
7   Synthesize the literature included in the final review.
8   Position your own original research in relation to the existing body of knowledge.

How to Conduct a Literature Search

The first thing to say is that effective searching requires two things: (1) planning and (2) time. To this end, the first task in conducting a literature review is to develop a 'search strategy', which contains a list of key words – and some useful synonyms for them – to search for. You also need to state the date(s) that the search will cover and the types of material to be included. It is important to consider how to limit the search. This can be achieved by restricting the area covered: the publication years covered in the search; research set only in the UK (or your own country), publications only written in English, or other specified language; the type of document sought (for example, journal article, review, editorial). The search strategy should also identify all the relevant information sources that you intend to use.

Our second piece of advice is to be transparent about how you conduct the search, record exactly what sources you have used and the order in which you searched them. Keeping good records at this stage, including records of authors, website URLs and dates, will make writing up this part of the work all the easier. You should also be keeping a research log or diary, where you can make notes of significant events, successes and failures. This will be a useful basis for writing up a reflective commentary on the research process to be included in the dissertation.

The Library as a Resource

Your own institution's library is the place to start for general background information for a literature review. The reading material it holds will include books, newspapers, printed journal titles, government publications, statistical series, reference works, DVDs, videos and audio-tapes. Ask the library staff for assistance; many universities have subject librarians who provide seminars and workshops on information sources and research techniques, as well as giving individual assistance. Use the library catalogue which will include all the library materials to look for relevant publications. Check whether your institution's library is associated with other libraries in the local area that you could also use. Alternatively, UK Libraries Plus is a cooperative scheme among UK higher education libraries, and there may be a participating library you could access (either for borrowing or on a reference-only basis) which is closer to where you live than your home institution. Make use of any photocopying services that are available, either on a self-service or serviced basis, but remember that you must comply with current copyright regulations. Most libraries can supply items not in stock quickly and easily. Check with your library how their system works and if they make a charge.

Electronic Resources

A wide range of electronic resources to provide more detailed or specialist material for your literature review is available through university libraries. Electronic resources can make it easier and quicker to acquire relevant, up-to-date information. There are two different types:

1 **Electronic resources that retrieve general information available via the Internet, such as national and local government reports or statistical**

surveys, and which anyone can access either direct or via search engines such as Google.

2   Electronic resources that retrieve academic and more specialized litera-ture available via university libraries. Most of these will be free to students at the point of delivery; in fact, many of those that appear to be 'free' actu-ally require an institutional subscription, and access is likely to be restricted to current staff and students. Subscription-based databases vary from one university to another, which often means that students can only use what their particular institution provides for them. It is likely that UK students will need what is called an Athens username and password to access numerous web-based services throughout the UK and overseas, so make sure that you register beforehand (this may change after the end of July 2008 when the current contract arrangements run out).

There is a further useful distinction that can be made, which is between the 'tools' that help you to find the resources in the first place, and the resources themselves. By 'tools', we mean search engines and information gateways which are freely available via the Internet for anyone to use:

1   Search engines include Alta Vista (http://altavista.com), Google (http://www.google.co.uk) and Google Scholar (http://www.scholar.google.com/). Google Scholar is well worth using; it indexes journal articles, and is a quick and simple way to search across many discipline areas and sources for relevant literature. It now includes a link to the British Library's document delivery service. If search results match the Library's holdings, users have the option to buy full text papers via the Library's online document ordering interface.

2   Information gateways which provide free access to Internet resources. These include SOSIG (Social Science Information Gateway; http://www.sosig.ac.uk), BUBL LINK (http://www.bubl.ac.uk) and Pinakes (http://www.hw.ac.uk/libWWW/irn/pinakes/pinakes.html). BUBL LINK and Pinakes both cover a huge range of academic subject areas.

The list below indicates some of the different types of electronic resources, but remember that these will vary from one institution to another, so one of your first activities should be to find out exactly what databases and other electronic sources of information are available in your institution's library.

1   Bibliographic databases that index core journals, including research and scholarly articles, book and other reviews, editorials, letters and bibliographical items (author[s]; work; year). An example is the Social Sciences Citation Index, which is available through the ISI Web of Knowledge Service via **MIMAS** (http://wos.mimas.ac.uk/). The ISI Web of Knowledge Service is an electronic resource that allows you to search multiple databases at the same time. So, too, is ASSIA (Applied Social Sciences Index and Abstracts), and the Social Sciences section of CSA Illumina, which contains six separate databases; if you do not want to search all of them at once, then you use checkboxes to select which of the six to search.

2   Individual electronic journals, such as *Sociological Research Online* (http://www.socresonline.org.uk/) or the *Electronic Journal of Sociology* (http://www.sociology.org/).

3   Electronic journal suppliers, who supply 'packages' of journals, such as Science Direct, which makes available the full text of over 1,000 journals (http://www.sciencedirect.com), or Ingenta (http://www.ingenta connect. com/) indexes electronic journals in different research areas, and allows you to download journal articles direct. It is important when searching electronic journal packages to know which is the best subject area for your particular research interest.

4   Newspapers, such as *The Times* (www.the-times.co.uk) and the *Guardian* (http://www.guardian.co.uk/). Alternatively, NewsBank Newspapers is a full-text online database of articles from over 40 national and regional UK newspapers and journals to which your university might subscribe.

Searching

Broadly speaking, there are two means of searching bibliographic databases: 'free text' or uncontrolled searching, and 'key word' or 'controlled' searching using a thesaurus approach. Free text searching is when you yourself decide on significant vocabulary, terms and phrases that you want to search on. It facilitates less exact searches, and can generate large numbers of references. When searching free text, the first step is to identify the main key words or concepts related to the research questions you are addressing. Having identified these, then make a list of a few common synonyms or related terms or phrases to widen the search.

As well as thinking about synonyms, you need to consider different spelling and terminology. Many of the databases are American, so differences in words such as 'organisation' and 'organization', or 'programme' and 'program' need to be taken into account. Likewise, terminology can be different. Hilary's main area of research is informal care. In the UK, people who look after disabled, sick and older people are known as 'carers', but the equivalent terminology in North America is 'care-givers'. She has recently been involved in three literature reviews, and every time the database searches had to include both terms otherwise a lot of potentially relevant articles and reports would have been missed.

One way to quickly search for alternative spellings or plurals is called 'truncation' searching. This involves using a symbol (sometimes called a 'wild card') such as *, !, # or ? after the main part of the word. The search strategy in Hilary's studies, for example, included care-giv*, which retrieved care-giver and care-giving. Many databases will let you specify that you want to search for a phrase by enclosing your search terms in quotation marks, for example, 'dementia care'.

You may want to carry out an advanced search which enables you to build a more complex search strategy. This can be done by combining terms with the words AND, NOT or OR (Box 7.5). AND and NOT narrow a search. AND links two terms together and retrieves only records containing both terms, whereas NOT excludes articles containing the second search term. Take care using NOT as you might unintentionally exclude items that would have been useful. In contrast, OR expands a search by retrieving articles in which either of the two terms appears. An alternative way to execute an advanced search is to conduct two (or more) separate searches and then add the two together.

Box 7.5 Combining searches

Hilary used the following combinations to narrow down a search to carers of people over 65:

>   carer AND older people
>   carer NOT disabled children.

And this combination to help ensure she captured everyone over 65:

>   older people OR elderly.

The second way to search a database uses a thesaurus approach. This form of searching can be more precise because the terms you can search on are already prescribed or fixed in the vocabulary making up the index. Some databases have a thesaurus search option, but not all; Sociological Abstracts is one that has a thesaurus in English, Spanish and French. You can still combine searches from a thesaurus using combinations of AND, NOT or OR. It is important to note that thesaurus terms are database specific. This means that if you are implementing a single search on multiple databases that use different thesauri, you may not retrieve potentially relevant records from all the databases.

Be creative in the way you search. Dave had to learn the hard way that searching under 'gender' might produce better results than searching under 'feminism', and that a further search under 'identity' or 'queer theory' can turn up still more valuable sources. If you are interested in this area, you should also be using the names of some writers on the topic as search items – Aitchison, Butler, Deem, Fraser, Mulvey, and so on.

Finally, each database has its own search procedures and rules, so you are well advised to check the respective 'Help' screens. Alternatively, you might find that your library has prepared individual sets of guidelines that explain how to use the different databases.

Recording/Saving Results

There are different ways to deal with the results. We would always recommend that you save the results to file so that they are available for you at a later date. Other options include printing out all of them, or marking a selection for printing, there and then. If there are no immediately available printing facilities, then relevant information can be copied and pasted into a word processing programme. A fourth tactic is to e-mail the results of the search to yourself.

It might be worth learning how to use bibliographic software such as Endnote or Reference Manager, which enables references to be exported from databases directly to a personal 'library' or reference collection. Another valuable feature with this sort of software is that it is possible to create reference lists or bibliographies using the Harvard reference system, or alternative acceptable systems, more or less instantaneously in a Microsoft Word document.

Finding the Full Text and Assessing Its Quality

Once you have identified potentially relevant literature, you need to locate the full journal articles, books, research reports, conference proceedings and the like. Finding the full document is likely to take much longer than you anticipate, and it is one that you need to allow plenty of time for. Hopefully, many will be available either in paper form in the library or you can download electronic versions using your (Athens) password. For those that are not available, and which you think may be critically important to your work, then an inter-library loan may be the only solution. Remember that these could take yet more valuable time, and you may be restricted in the numbers you can use before you have to pay.

Once you have retrieved the full documents, the next task is to assess them for relevance to your topic area and quality. The likelihood is that you will be more confident about the quality and robustness of academic literature you have acquired from scholarly databases than the more general material you might have obtained via the Internet. This is because the academic community operates a system of quality control that is called 'peer review'. Peer review is a way to ensure high standards in terms of journal articles and other published work. It means that other experts in the field check articles for validity, significance and originality before they are published. Anonymous referees evaluate the work, and make recommendations to the editor of a journal about whether to accept, reject or ask for revisions. The aim is to ensure that flawed, incomplete or poor quality work is not published.

Synthesizing the Results

Chapter 5 was devoted to developing writing skills, critical analysis and academic argument. We are not going to repeat our comments here beyond emphasizing that it is important to appreciate that a literature review is not just a descriptive list or an article-by-article summary. When writing the review, you need to assess the material according to a guiding concept, namely, your own research interests or objectives. The review should demonstrate your depth of knowledge about the research field; identify the knowledge, theories and concepts that have already been established; evaluate the strengths and weaknesses of different arguments and points of view; point out any methodological flaws; and identify any gaps in the literature. In particular, the review provides the intellectual context for your original research and enables you to position your own work in relation to the established body of knowledge.

On a practical note, organize the literature review into sections that cover common themes, and use plenty of headings to help guide the reader through the work. Start by taking a wide view of the literature included in the review and gradually narrow down to focus on the specific area of your own research. In the conclusion, summarize major contributions to the body of knowledge under review, identify gaps in previous research, point the way forward for further research and link your own research to the existing knowledge base.

Getting the Best Out of Google!

While the Internet has dramatically increased potential sources of information, the bad news is that there are few restrictions on what is posted on the web, which in turn casts doubt upon the authority and quality of information derived from these general Internet sources (Denscombe, 2003). Key questions to ask yourself about freely available Internet resources are: has the material been written by a reliable source? Is it likely to have been scrutinized through the academic peer review process? Is it accurate and up to date? You can learn more about quality checks through 'Internet Detective' (website: http://sosig. ac.uk/desire/offline/1.html). Internet Detective is an interactive, online tutorial which provides an introduction to issues about information quality on the Internet and teaches the skills required to critically evaluate the quality of an Internet resource.

Space constraints mean that we have only been able to give a brief introduction to information retrieval for the literature review for your dissertation. The Resource Discovery Network (RDN), at the University of Bristol, aims to help students, lecturers and researchers develop their Internet information literary skills and IT skills. The site offers a subject-based approach to Internet skills training, and can be accessed at: http://www.vts.rdn.ac.uk/ (major changes to the current RDN service are planned, as well as a change of name to Intute – see www.intute.ac.uk). The specific hints given about assessing the credentials of the sources/material available are particularly useful, given that the quality of information on the Internet is extremely variable. Hart (2001) is another useful guide about how to conduct a search in the social sciences.

Chapter Summary

1 Undertaking a piece of small-scale research and writing it up in the form of a dissertation is challenging and time-consuming, but demonstrating the full range of skills acquired at university in this way can be rewarding.

2 It is important to have a dissertation supervisor whom you get on with, and who will give you good feedback and advice.

3 The selected topic area should be one that interests you, but must be kept within manageable proportions – do not be over-ambitious!

4 The first stage of a dissertation is the literature review, from which should emerge the research question(s) to be investigated. This involves devising and conducting a literature search using a range of information sources, including the university library and electronic resources.

8 Collecting the Data

CHAPTER OVERVIEW

- Different types of research strategies.
- Good practice when collecting data.
- Sampling and accessing study participants.
- Ethical considerations.

This chapter concentrates on practical issues related to designing good research. The topic areas that are covered include the range of research strategies that are available with advice about which strategies suit which particular research activities. We also tell you about the different approaches to collecting research evidence as well as how to go about finding people to take part in a study – never an easy task, as anyone who has stood on a shopping mall or high street corner with a clipboard in their hand can testify to! Research generally gives rise to ethical issues and dilemmas, and we give you some advice about how best to resolve them. And be warned – ethical questions are just as likely to arise in a piece of small-scale research as they are in a much larger study, in fact maybe more so.

Research Strategies

As we stressed in the last chapter, your research and dissertation must be do-able. This means that the empirical element must not be over-ambitious for the time available. For instance, just how feasible is it for you to administer and analyse a postal questionnaire distributed to a sample population of 800, or to conduct 50 qualitative interviews which are all going to be tape-recorded and then transcribed?

The chosen research strategy and data collection methods need to be fit for the research purpose (Arksey and Knight, 1999); essentially, they have to answer the specific research questions, or prove/disprove the hypothesis (Box 8.1). What are the most common types of research strategies?

1 *Social surveys*: surveys are one of the most widespread approaches to social research and can be used, for example, to find out factual information, or, alternatively, particular views, attitudes or beliefs. They offer the opportunity for wide coverage, and generally relate to the 'here and now'. The Office for National Statistics (www.statistics.gov.uk) conducts a number of annual national household surveys such as the General Household Survey (GHS), the Labour Force Survey and Social Trends. In the run-up to general elections, market research organisations such as MORI conduct opinion polls with a view to predicting how many seats the different political parties will win in the next parliament.

2 *Case studies*: case studies involve in-depth study in a 'natural' setting of just one 'case', which can be an individual, a group, a setting or an organization. The aim is to provide a detailed account of relationships and processes within the phenomenon in its own context. The emphasis is on the 'particular'. A classic sociological case study is Cavendish's ethnographic study (1982) of migrant and minority ethnic women employed in a motor components factory, which documents their daily experience and reflects on the relationship between class, gender and imperialism in a metropolitan setting.

3 *Action research*: action research is known for its practical orientation; it is geared to making a difference. The research findings are fed back into the action research process with a view to initiating changes in professional practice in the workplace or an organizational setting. Action research is participatory in that the research is driven and 'owned' by the practitioners who are the focus of the research as much as by the researcher. Today, action research is commonly used in the areas of education, health and social care, although Collier's study (1945) of developing farming methods in a North American Indian reservation is often cited as the first example of this sort of inquiry. Recently, Hilary worked with a primary care team on an action

research project of team members' understandings and expectations of their own, and colleagues' roles (Arksey et al, in press).

4 *Ethnographic studies*: ethnographic studies seek to gain in-depth knowledge about how specific cultures or groups of people understand and make sense of their lives from their own 'insider' point of view rather than from the researcher's or practitioner's analysis of the situation. Typically, the researcher will immerse him or herself in the setting under investigation in order to share in the lives and culture of the people being studied. Examples include Bourdieu's account (2000) of Algerian workers reacting to cultural colonization in the 1960s, and Stoller's study (2002) of African street traders in New York. If you remember, we advocated this approach at the start of the book in order to understand the social values and cultural practices of the university.

5 *Grounded theory studies*: grounded theory studies are closely associated with Glaser and Strauss (1967) and more recently Strauss and Corbin (1997, 1998). The main concern is to develop a theory which is 'grounded' in the data collected during the course of the study. The researcher is expected to adopt an iterative process, moving backwards and forwards between the field, where the data are collected, and the research base, where they are then analysed and interesting or unexpected findings fed into the next round of data collection. Data collection ceases when nothing new emerges. Examples include Elling et al.'s study (2003) of social integration according to sexual preference, and the formation of gay sports clubs in the Netherlands.

6 *Experimental studies*: experimental studies involve the manipulation of circumstances, and the comparison of one condition (the experimental condition) with another (the control condition). The researcher tries to identify all the variables (characteristics or properties of a person, an object or a situation) that are significant and then introduces, or excludes, one or more variable to try to determine the cause of any observed change in the behaviour of the subjects taking part in the experiment. Milgram's famous series of experimental studies (1974) on obedience to authority, despite disagreement over ethics and generalizability of findings, is one of the most important – and shocking. Other classics include the perennial issue of the effects of violent TV or video on behaviour (see Anderson and Dill, 2000).

Box 8.1   Designing Research Studies

Imagine you are studying the social impact of travel and tourism on the social life of a particular area. Think of one different study you could undertake using each of the above research strategies. Identify two advantages and disadvantages for each one.

Data Collection Methods

Certain data collection techniques are associated with particular research strategies, for instance, social surveys usually employ questionnaires. However, there is scope for choice about what methods to use. To repeat an earlier point, time and resource constraints are important factors that should be taken into consideration when developing the research design.

Before outlining different data collection methods, it is worth drawing attention to a key distinction between quantitative methods and qualitative methods. Quantitative methods produce results in the form of numbers. Examples of quantitative methods are structured questionnaires for large-scale surveys such as the Census undertaken in Britain in 2001. In contrast, qualitative methods produce results in the form of words. Examples here are in-depth or unstructured interviews and (participant) observation. Conventional wisdom would have us believe that quantitative research produces more objective or valid results in comparison with qualitative methods but that black and white distinction is hotly disputed within the social science community.

Questionnaires

Questionnaires comprise a list of written questions answered by the 'respondent', which is the technical name for the person answering the questions. They can be administered face-to-face – think back to how many times you have spotted, and possibly tried to avoid, someone with a clipboard who looked like they wanted to stop you in the street to ask your views on, say, animal cruelty or your eating and drinking habits. Alternatively, they are self-completed and the respondent is not in direct contact with the researcher – perhaps as part of a postal survey trying to evaluate, for example, customers' levels of satisfaction with their bank or building society. To facilitate consistency, the questions are standardized or structured so that all respondents read (or have read to them) an identical set of questions.

The key to a 'good' questionnaire is thorough planning and preparation, especially in relation to constructing the wording of questions. Even though this may sound time-consuming, it can save time in the long run if it later turns out that the questions do not make sense, they are vague or can be interpreted in different ways. Unclear, ill-thought-out questions tend to lead to incomplete or poorly completed answers. Data which are poor quality are likely to cause problems in the subsequent analysis stage of the research.

There are specific principles to follow when devising the wording and phrasing of questions (see Box 8.2 for examples of what not to do):

- **Use *vocabulary* that is simple, understandable and appropriate for the particular age, social or cultural group who will be completing the questionnaire. Avoid technical jargon and abstract concepts.**

- **Avoid *leading questions* that suggest or 'lead' the respondent towards a particular answer.**

- **Ensure that the wording is *unambiguous* and cannot be interpreted in different ways.**

- **Avoid *double-barrelled* questions that ask two questions in one.**

- **Do not ask questions in the *negative* as they can be difficult to understand.**

- **Make sure that the questions do not contain *assumptions* that may be ill-founded.**

- **Keep the questions *short*:**

- **Avoid *prejudicial* language or words/phrases that might cause *offence*.**

- **Questions must not assume that respondents' *levels of knowledge* about the topic area under investigation are sufficient to answer the question.**

Box 8.2   Devising Questions to Include on a Questionnaire

Look at the four questions below. What is wrong with them?

1   When you go to work, do you drive there in your own automobile?
2   Have you been on holiday to France or Greece recently?
3   Do you approve of the government's policy on nanotechnology?
4   Don't you agree that after a while scroungers who live off the state should be made to go back to work?

Rewrite the questions and improve their wording.

You might have noticed that the four questions in Box 8.2 are all structured so that there are only two main options for answers, namely yes or no. These sort of questions are called *'closed' questions*, and they have the advantage of being easily transferable into quantitative data and then entered into a computer software package specifically designed for statistical analysis. There can be disadvantages, in particular, there is little scope for the respondent to provide answers that do not fit the range of options included in the questionnaire. In the first question in Box 8.2, what if the respondent's mode of transport depended on whether it was fine weather or raining, or whether it was the school holidays? How easily could the questionnaire accommodate alternative answers to that particular question?

'Open' questions overcome these sorts of difficulties by allowing the respondent to answer in their own words, either by writing their response down themselves on blank lines in the questionnaire or by having the researcher writing it down for them. Whilst open questions facilitate the collection of fuller and more detailed data, the subsequent analysis will be more complicated and time- consuming because the researcher has to organize and try to make sense of what could be quite disparate data.

There is an issue about the order in which questions are asked; the general advice is to ask the more straightforward and easy-to-answer questions at the start of the questionnaire and the more complex, personal or sensitive questions at the end. This strategy should help overcome any thoughts the respondent might have about not persevering to complete the full questionnaire.

Just as we said earlier in the book that the appearance of your written work is important, even more critical is the presentation of a questionnaire. Essentially, it should be as attractive and user-friendly as possible to encourage respondents to complete it. In particular, do not cram it up to save paper or to make it look shorter. Enough space needs to be left for the 'tick box' answer column on the right-hand side, and/or for responses to any open questions. A large font will mean that the questions can be easily read. Include brief information about the purpose of the research, and a reassuring sentence about confidentiality (see section below on research ethics).

If the questionnaire is to be self-completed, it is very important to give clear instructions to the respondent about how they should set about answering the questions. Including an example of a completed question at the start of the questionnaire can be helpful here. And if it is a postal questionnaire, then make sure that full contact details of the person to whom it should be returned are very clear, together with a deadline. If expenses allow, then stamped addressed envelopes are one way to increase the response rate, which for postal questionnaires can be quite low – between 20 and 30 per cent.

As part of your preparation, for undertaking survey research, try to obtain examples of questionnaires and review them for usability and visual appearance. You can find question banks that contain the 'final product', as it were, via the Internet. Social Surveys Online (http://qb.soc.surrey.ac.uk) is a freely available online resource that contains complete social survey questionnaires from large-scale policy relevant UK studies. Alternatively, the National Statistics website includes a social capital question bank (www.statistics. gov.uk/about_ns/social_capital/default.asp). The Economic and Social Research Council is another source (http://www.esrcsocietytoday.ac.uk/ESRCInfo Centre/research/ResearchMethods/).

For any student considering a job in a market research company or an organization that might conduct customer satisfaction surveys, then here is an opportunity to critique existing survey instruments, before constructing, administering and analysing your own – an activity that has the potential to give you a head start over other competitors for the same job.

The next step is to prepare your own questionnaire, taking account of the strengths and weaknesses of those you have reviewed. And then you need to try it out, or pilot it. This activity is best done with two or three of the target population, but if that proves difficult, then ask some of your friends or family members. Here is the real test of how well it works or not, as the case may be. Are the instructions for completing the questionnaire clear? Is the wording of the questions straightforward and unambiguous? How long does it take to complete? Are the answers providing the sort of information that will help answer the original research questions? Can the data be easily analysed? You will be very fortunate indeed if you find that the first version of the questionnaire is satisfactory. It is far more likely that you will have to make changes to it in the light of the comments and feedback obtained at the piloting stage. But if this means that you will obtain better quality data when it comes to the 'real thing', then this is time well spent.

We will be discussing how to analyse the survey data in the next chapter. Take it from us, though, that it is important to start thinking about the analysis right at the very start of a survey. You might want to take a look at a website called StatPac (www.statpac.com) which contains a (free) tutorial on how to design a questionnaire and conduct a survey. There is also some survey software that can be downloaded.

Interviews

There are three basic types of interview for research purposes: structured interviews, semi-structured interviews and unstructured interviews. A structured interview, is very much akin to a standardized questionnaire, but the questions are read out by the researcher to the respondent. We referred to those in the section above about social surveys, and the remainder of this section focuses on semi-structured and unstructured interviews.

Semi-structured and unstructured interviews both aim to acquire in-depth accounts of what matters to people and why. They are about exploring and understanding the perspective of the interviewee or 'informant'. What is the difference between these two types of interview? Essentially, it is the extent to which the researcher exercises control during the interview; a semi-structured interview involves greater control in comparison to an unstructured interview. Accordingly, the informant has far more freedom to lead the flow of conversation, introduce new ideas and the like in an unstructured interview. How does this work in practice?

Semi-structured interviews are directed by what is often called a 'topic guide'. This contains a list of the questions or topic areas to be covered, but flexibility is built in to facilitate changes to the order in which questions are asked. In particular, there is scope for the interviewee to respond at length, to elaborate and to clarify points raised in an event that is rather like a discussion or conversation. Having said that, the interviewer must always remember that having asked the questions, they are there to listen to and follow up the answers. They are not there to lead, or impose their own views on the informant.

As their name suggests, unstructured interviews take this a stage further by placing more or less no structure whatsoever on the questions asked. The interviewer takes a back seat role, and having introduced the topic area to be discussed then encourages the informant to take the lead in the ensuing discussion.

Interviews are not necessarily conducted on a one-to-one basis. Sometimes, joint interviews (with a husband and wife, say) may be conducted, or group interviews which involve four or five people. Focus groups, initially commonplace in market research organisations but now increasingly used in social science research, generally comprise between six and ten people and are managed by a 'moderator' and an 'observer'. The main issue for the person leading interviews with more than one person is not to allow any one individual to dominate the discussion at the expense of hearing the views of quieter, less confident participants. See Grogan and Richards (2002) for a good example of focus group work.

Consideration needs to be given to practical matters related to organizing interviews. They have to be arranged at a time that is mutually convenient to both the researcher and the informant; the length of time that the interview is likely to take is best negotiated before. It is unlikely that the informant will be prepared to give up more than an hour or an hour-and-a-half, so bear this in mind when preparing the topic guide for semi-structured interviews. The venue is important, too; it must be easily accessible to both/all parties, as well as offering a degree of privacy.

There is very little time to waste in an interview, so right from the start it is important to build up trust, and what could be called a good working relationship with the informant. It goes without saying that effective interviewers are polite and friendly. If the interview is taking place in the informant's own home, then it is important to respect their property and private space. Remind informants of the purpose of the interview, give them the opportunity to ask questions, confirm that they still give consent to take part in the study and finally reassure them about issues relating to confidentiality and anonymity (see below). As with structured questionnaires, start with the easier, relatively straightforward questions before tackling those that are more complex and abstract. Once the interview is over, do not make an immediate rush for the door. Tell the informant what will happen next, as well as whether and when they are likely to hear from you again. Most importantly, thank them for the time and information they have given you; it is good practice to send a short 'thank you' letter or card afterwards.

What interview skills are needed to encourage informants to feel at ease and able to express their own views on the subject under discussion? It is especially important that the interviewer listens, pays attention and values what the informant has to say. They must show sensitivity and empathize, and give the informant space to reflect and think about what they want to say. In other words, interviewers must be able to handle silences. Hilary still remembers the three Ps which she was taught to use during her teacher training: *P*ose a question, *P*ause for thought, *P*rompt for a reply. This is as true for social science research interviews as for teaching. A fourth P could be added here, too: *P*robe and explore points raised more deeply.

A useful tactic that Hilary uses during an interview – often before she changes to a different topic area – is to occasionally stop to summarize what she thinks the informant has said to her. This is an opportunity for the interviewee to correct misunderstandings. If chronology is important to the research, then it is also helpful to summarize dates of when events happened as poor memory recall often means that times and dates can get confused. Doing this can help the informant identify more accurately when, or the order in which, things happened. Asking the informant to give concrete examples is another valuable tactic, especially if they are being vague about, say, why they think that something is good or bad. Not only will this give deeper insights into what matters to them, the examples might be useful illustrative material to include when writing up the dissertation. Again, it can be helpful to ask for examples if there appear to be contradictions or inconsistencies in what informants are saying.

Most professional researchers prefer to record their interviews, usually on cassette or mini-disc, with the consent of the individual taking part, so that they can concentrate on the discussion rather than on taking notes. Whatever type of audio-recording equipment is being used should be of good enough quality to provide clear sound reproduction so that it can either be fully transcribed or used to make comprehensive notes of key themes emerging from the data.

Observation and Participant Observation

Observation research is just as the name suggests: the researcher observes at first hand the activities, events or phenomena that form the data for the research study. There are two kinds of observation: direct or structured observation which has its roots in social psychology, and participant observation which is particularly related to the Chicago School of Sociology.

Direct or structured observation means that the researcher is collecting 'real-life' data on behaviours or events in their natural setting rather than in a contrived setting such as a laboratory or clinic. For example, many years ago, Hilary undertook an observation study of children in a swimming pool. She was part of a small team testing out the hypothesis that boys were rougher or more boisterous than girls in the swimming pool – a task which was fraught with difficulties as the first step was to try to define what was meant by the rather abstract concepts of 'rough' and 'boisterous' so that team members worked to the same definition or criteria consistently. To help them with this task, and to ensure that the work had a sound theoretical basis and was academically credible, the team undertook a literature review. This identified verbal, non-verbal and spatial behaviours consistent with an umbrella definition of 'boisterousness', and which talked about this in terms of variables such as gender differences and children's ages. The team then devised a rota and took it in turns to do a 45-minute shift at the pool side recording occurrences of identified behaviours by boys and girls.

This is where a study can get complicated, if people become aware that you are observing and recording their behaviour. Once they realize what you are doing, they may not like it and stop; alternatively, they may change how they are behaving. There are also ethical issues involved here: should you really be doing this without the consent of those you are observing?

The instrument or tool employed to collect data in a direct observation study is called an observation schedule. An example of one (Tall, no date) can be found on: http://www.edu.bham.ac.uk/edrt06/observation.htm. An observation schedule is a form which enables the researcher(s) to record data systematically and consistently. It is rather like a checklist, with instructions about what to observe and when. All the items (behaviours or events) being monitored are included, together with space for recording how many times a particular behaviour occurred. Depending on the research questions being addressed, you might also want to record the length of time the event continued.

Participant observation, in contrast, is where the researcher/observer seeks to immerse him or herself in the daily lives of the group being studied, to the point that they become a member of the observed group and do not tell others that their prime motivation is to conduct a piece of research. Concealing the true purpose of the research and not obtaining 'informed consent' raises ethical issues, and increasingly these days it is considered unacceptable to undertake covert research.

Not surprisingly, the full 'insider' experience can be very onerous, demanding and time-consuming for the researcher; we are talking here in terms of months and possibly even years. For practical reasons, many researchers are not able to make this sort of commitment so another possibility is for lower levels of involvement, in other words, adopting a role which is more on the margins of the group as opposed to one of total participation. In this sort of alternative 'participant-as-observer' role (Robson, 2002), the researcher would make it clear to the group right from the start that they are there as an observer for research purposes, and in this way neatly circumvent any ethical problems. One of Dave's undergraduate students undertook a study of fox-hunting, which involved both a questionnaire survey and participant observation (Baker, no date). An important finding was that the fox-hunters were very good at offering evasive and contradictory replies to questions about what the pleasures were; they were well aware of the need to maintain a public front and to avoid all suggestions that it was actually about killing.

The task of recording in participant observation can involve a wide range of data collection methods including on-the-spot notes, journals or diaries containing notes made after the event, photographs, video recordings and speech recordings. Researchers can quickly amass a huge disparate unstructured database, which somehow has to be organized and analysed. Some good researchers (such as Becker et al., 1995) make a particular point of noting whether responses were 'spontaneous' or made as the result of prompts and they also took care to record ambiguous or unusual statements or behaviours so they could test their explanations.

Documents and Other Media

Written documents, such as books, newspapers, magazines, letters and diaries, can all be used as data for research purposes. So, too, can non-written media such as films and television programmes, pictures, drawings, photographs or music.

Again, we can illustrate the sort of research that uses documents by outlining a small piece of research that Hilary worked on some time ago (see Warde, 1997, for fuller details). This study involved a detailed examination of a sample of women's magazines published in 1967–68 and 1991–92. Some 80 issues were examined in depth, and in each issue all the articles and columns relating to food were examined. The number of recipes included in the magazines, the amount of space given over to articles on food and to advertisements for food were calculated. Finally, a systematic sample of recipes was drawn, and subjected to content analysis. Other studies include Attwood's textual analysis (2002) of a British soft pornographic magazine, *Fiesta*.

Box 8.3 should help you assess the advantages and disadvantages of the different methods of data collection.

Box 8.3   Data Collection Methods

Identify at least three advantages and disadvantages for each of the four main methods of data collection. What do you think is the most appropriate research strategy, and type(s) of data collection, for the seven research studies detailed below? Why?

1   A study of older people's views about residential care.
2   A study to determine whether the incidence of arranged marriages has increased or decreased in the last 25 years.
3   A study into the types and levels of crime on the London Underground.
4   A study into the number of family doctor appointments missed per year in England.
5   A study examining press reports of mixed marriages in the UK.
6   A study of living with multiple sclerosis.
7   A study to improve how the different members of a primary health care team work.

Sampling Techniques

A sample is generally selected for study because it is impractical to investigate the population in its entirety: it is simply too large. Sampling is the term used to describe selecting just who or what (for example, people, places, events, times, written documents) from the whole population are to be studied. Sampling implies sampling variability, that is, that samples drawn from the same population have characteristics that vary.

Researchers, especially quantitative researchers, tend to want to make inferences about the whole population of interest and not just the sample. However, the way in which the sample is derived can affect the strength of the claims that can be made based on the findings and their significance for the whole of the population being investigated. A useful website with more detailed information is Questionnaire Design and Surveys Sampling which can be accessed on http://obelia. jde.aca.mmu.ac.uk/resdesgn/arsham/opre330Surveys.htm.

Researchers 'generalize' their findings from the study sample to the population at large. There are two basic kinds of sampling techniques used by social science researchers. A probability sample is one in which each member of the population has an equal chance of being selected, rather like drawing names out of a hat. Statistical inferences about the population can be made on the basis of the responses. The larger the sample is, then the lower any error in generalizing. In a non-probability sample, chances of selection are unknown and statistical inferences cannot be made.

Probability Sampling

The probability techniques that are most familiar include the following:

1 *Random sampling*, as its name suggests, is an approach where people or events are selected 'at random' from a previously drawn up sampling frame. The sampling frame is an up-to-date list of the complete eligible population from which the sample is to be drawn, the electoral role, for example, or a school class register. The required number of study participants is then selected using a table of random numbers or a computer.

2 *Systematic sampling* is similar to random sampling, but instead of selecting randomly you chose every *n*th name or case from the sampling frame.

If the frame consisted of 500 people and you wanted to identify 100, then systematic sampling means that you would select one in five: every fifth, tenth, fifteenth, twentieth case, and so on.

3 *Stratified sampling* is where all members of the population who share a particular characteristic (for example, age, gender, ethnicity) are divided into groups or 'strata'. Within each stratum, a simple random sample or systematic sample is selected. The final numbers included within each category should be directly in proportion to those in the population as a whole. For instance, if the population contains 60 per cent women and 40 per cent men and you want to reflect that in the sample, then there should be 1.5 times as many women in the sample as men.

4 *Cluster sampling* involves locating naturally occurring 'clusters' of subjects to study by drawing different samples following the principles of probability sampling. For example, residents living in the village of Coxwold in North Yorkshire may have been chosen for a survey as follows. Stage 1: within the UK, North Yorkshire (county) is selected at random. Stage 2: within North Yorkshire, York (city) is selected again at random. Stage 3: Coxwold (polling district) is selected at random. Stage 4: individuals selected at random from the electoral register.

Non-probability Sampling

Commonly used non-probability techniques are as follows:

1 *Purposive sampling* is a strategy where a 'hand-picked' sample is selected subjectively by the researcher to satisfy the needs of the study. The researcher will try to obtain a sample that appears to be representative of the population under scrutiny.

2 *Quota sampling* is often used in market research. Interviewers are given quota of particular types of people to interview (for example, in terms of gender, age, ethnicity, social class, marital status). It is rather similar to stratified sampling in that it tries to ensure the sample contains representatives of all the categories in the sample in proportion to their occurrence in the full population.

3 *Convenience sampling* is where the researcher stops and questions anyone who is nearby, or 'convenient', and is willing to stop and answer the

questions asked. The process continues until the full sample size is reached. Although this is a popular method, it is not satisfactory because it is not possible to know how representative the sample is or how reliable the results are. This negates the possibility of drawing any meaningful conclusions from the data collected.

4 *Snowball sampling* **is a way to access individuals or groups, especially those who might otherwise be difficult to locate. The researcher initially starts with just one or two people from the population of interest, and then asks each person to nominate one or two more individuals who are likewise part of the target study group. In this way, the sample 'snowballs' until sufficient participants have taken part in the data collection.**

A crucial question is, what sort of sample size is considered adequate for small-scale quantitative research? According to Denscombe (2003), sample sizes involving between 30 and 230 cases are considered adequate although it is important to pay attention to the issue of how representative the sample is. This is because it may be imprudent to generalize the research findings from the sample population to the population as a whole. If the number of cases are below 30, then statistical analysis which breaks the sample down into different sub-groups (according to, say, age, gender and ethnicity of respondents) can become inappropriate as there might only be three or four people in some of the groups.

Qualitative research tends to produce a huge wealth of material that takes different formats, is unwieldy and complex. It can be very daunting for a novice researcher to deal with. However, relatively small sample sizes are considered adequate for small-scale research projects. This is something to check out with the person supervising the research, but we consider that around 10 interviews would suffice for an undergraduate dissertation (especially if you do not make strong claims about the representativeness of the sample and comment on sampling theory to show you know the issues).

Accessing Research Subjects

Having got some idea of sampling and numbers of study participants, the next step is to try to access people to help with the research. Some people are easier to access than others; at the risk of stating the obvious, it is far easier to access university and college students than government ministers. There are more of the former, they are more accessible and they have more time. Many students have run into trouble hoping to get people to answer questions at the last minute – so try to test out the possibilities early.

Unless you are doing a survey and approaching individuals in the street or shopping mall, then it is more than likely that you will need to get clearance or permission from official channels. That means identifying a key person in the organization (or wherever the research is going to take place) who has the power to agree that (1) the research can go ahead, and (2) you can approach people to ask them if they will contribute to the data collection – which might mean taking part in an interview or a small group discussion, or alternatively completing a paper questionnaire or an e-mail questionnaire.

Individuals who have the power to grant or restrict access to research settings are often referred to as 'gatekeepers'. We cannot emphasize enough how important it is to gain their cooperation. One way to do this is to approach them formally, by letter, giving them full details of the study, in particular, the aims, research strategy, timescale and resource implications of participating. Emphasizing the ways in which the study could be of some value to the organization itself, as well as to the research, can also be an important persuading factor. You may be asked to supply a letter from your tutor guaranteeing that you are a registered student and you are being supervised responsibly.

Ethical Considerations

Social science research, whether a small-scale interview study or a large-scale survey, must always be carried out to high ethical standards. The research involves human subjects and it goes without saying that the dignity, rights, safety and well-being of the participants are of prime concern. To this end, it is important that anyone undertaking a research study is aware of his or her ethical obligations and responsibilities. Students who have completed any research methods training will already have been introduced to the issue of research ethics as it is becoming increasingly important, especially in relation to research conducted within the health and social care fields.

A pertinent question to ask yourself throughout your dissertation is: are you conducting your research in such a way that the individuals who have taken part would consider participating in a future research project? To help ensure that the answer is 'yes', the last part of this chapter is given over to ethical considerations. The principles about best practice are drawn from the ethical guidelines produced by the British Sociological Association (2002) and the Social Research Association (2003).

Informed Consent

Freely given informed consent is at the heart of ethical research. To this end, it is important to be open and honest about the proposed research. Covert research involves serious ethical and legal issues and should be resorted to only where it is impossible to use other methods to obtain essential data. We are assuming that your dissertation will not involve any form of deception or raise questions of legality.

When you are approaching people to take part in a study, you should give them full information about the study. We have set out a checklist of items to cover in Box 8.4. However, be sensible about how much you tell people, for instance, do not overwhelm them with unnecessary details about the background or scientific rationale to the study, but at the same time give them enough information for them to make a well- informed decision about whether or not to take part.

Box 8.4   What to Tell Potential Study Participants

The project title
Your name, the institution you belong to and your contact details
The names, positions and contact details of any others connected with the research
The specific purpose of the study
The background to, and justification for, the study
The research design
The extent of people's participation in the study in terms of time commitment and data collection settings or venues
Opportunities for commenting on transcripts of interviews, altering their content, or withdrawing statements
The procedures to safeguard the confidentiality of records
The arrangements for ensuring participants' anonymity
How the project will comply with the requirements of the current data protection legislation
Any potential risks (including emotional discomfort) that might be incurred
Any potential benefits or gains that might be incurred
How the research findings will be published
How you intend to offer feedback on findings, for instance, in the form of a summary report

---

Ideally, people who agree to take part in a research project should give their consent both orally and in writing. An example of an informed consent form is provided in Box 8.5. You should keep a signed copy of the form yourself, and leave a second copy with the study participant so they have a written reminder of what they have agreed to. Note that if there is any likelihood that you will be using quotations from interviewees or focus group participants, then you should ask people to agree to that explicitly. The reason for this is because copyright of the words, whether taken down verbatim or recorded, is owned by whoever said those words and therefore permission is needed before they can be quoted in a report, or used in a conference presentation.

Processes should be put in place to safeguard the rights of vulnerable participants who may not be able to fully assess the implications of the proposed work. For example, relatives, or professionals such as doctors or social workers, could be asked to give proxy consent on behalf of people with learning difficulties or older people with dementia. Where children under 16 years of age are concerned, written informed consent should be obtained from parents or guardians. Good practice suggests that children who have sufficient understanding should also be asked. If the parent refuses, and the child agrees, then the parent's decision stands; if the parent agrees, but the child does not, then common sense suggests there is little point in pursuing the matter because the child is unlikely to cooperate.

Individuals approached to take part in a research inquiry should be volunteers, and not led to believe that they are obliged to participate. Even if someone does agree, they should be told that they may withdraw their assistance and any data they have previously provided at any time without giving any reason and without penalty. Needless to say, they must not be put under any pressure to continue at a later date. In some situations, for instance, longitudinal research, it may be necessary for consent to be obtained not as a 'once and for all' prior event, but instead as a process which is subject to renegotiation over time.

Anonymity, Privacy and Confidentiality

The anonymity and privacy of everyone taking part in social research should be respected. Consequently, identities, accompanying personal information and any research records documenting research participant's details should be kept

Box 8.5   Example of Informed Consent Form

(For the purposes of this book, details of the institution and contact information have been removed.)

HELPING CARERS TO CARE

This consent form is to check that you are happy with the information you have received about the study, that you are aware of your rights as a participant and to confirm that you wish to take part in the study.

Please tick as appropriate

	YES	NO
1 Have you read the research information leaflet?		
2 Have you had the opportunity to discuss further questions with a member of the research team?		
3 Have you received enough information about the study to decide whether you want to take part?		
4 Do you understand that you are free to refuse to answer any questions?		
5 Do you understand that you may withdraw from the study at any time without giving your reasons, and that this will not affect future service provision in any way?		
6 Do you understand that members of the research team will treat all information as confidential?		
7 Do you agree to take part in the study?		

Signature ....   Date ....

Name in block letters, please ....

I confirm that quotations from the interview can be used in the final research report and other publications. I understand that these will be used anonymously.

Signature ....   Date ....

Name in block letters, please ....

Source: Arksey and Knight (1999: 131)

confidential. You need to specify procedures for how this can be achieved. One way is to give interviewees pseudonyms or identity numbers on material such as interview tapes, transcripts and any quotes used for illustrative material in a dissertation or research report. This means that there is no written record of the participant's real name 'side-by-side' with the data they have provided.

Keeping the identities of individuals taking part in any research study confidential is generally not a problem in large-scale survey work, or studies with a large sample. In contrast, it can develop into a real issue in qualitative studies with relatively small samples – and undergraduate dissertations are characteristically small scale. However, this was also an issue for Hilary in a recent piece of research involving interviews with 16 members of a primary care team (Arksey et al, in press). Despite not disclosing any names or job titles in the written report, it was nonetheless quite easy for staff to guess (correctly) who had expressed the comments in supposedly anonymous quotations. The lesson Hilary learned from this experience was that researchers should be careful not to give unrealistic guarantees of confidentiality!

Promises of confidentiality and anonymity given to research participants must be honoured, unless there are exceptional circumstances, for example, if someone discloses that they are at risk of sexual, physical or mental abuse, or involved in illegal activities. At this point in the interview, the researcher should explicitly state that they can no longer guarantee to keep the research data confidential and that they may feel obliged to pass the information on to the appropriate authorities. They should also ask whether or not the interviewee wishes to continue with the discussion, given its sensitivity.

Protecting the Interests of Participants

Some people may find the experience of taking part in research disturbing. While they may not suffer any actual physical harm, they may nonetheless feel some intrusion into their personal lives, or they may be upset by the content of the discussion especially if it touches on a sensitive area. For example, Hilary still vividly remembers a research interview conducted over eight years ago with a man in his seventies who became very distressed talking about his wife with dementia, who no longer lived at home because her care needs were now beyond what he (and social services) could accommodate. He found taking part in the research interview gave rise to a sense of failure and a loss of self-esteem. In other circumstances, research can result in false hopes or unnecessary anxiety/stress. It is therefore incumbent on the researcher to try to minimize any disturbance. As just implied, one way to protect participants' own interests is to give them full information about the consequences of participating at the 'informed consent' stage. However, there are no hard and fast rules as to whether you should include a warning that someone might get distressed and, of course, you cannot always anticipate whether this will happen – Hilary was taken by surprise in the interview just referred to.

There is further potential for harm to arise once the research findings are published, especially if they attract the attention of the media. Researchers should be aware of the possible consequences of their work, for instance, study participants may be upset or angry to read about the work in terms that they consider offensive or derogatory. Dave remembers a case, which was eventually settled out of court, that involved an educational researcher who was actually threatened with legal action by a woman who claimed she could be identified as one of three 'progressive' teachers in a small primary school. Wherever possible, researchers should try to anticipate, and guard against, any potentially harmful effects. It is hard for us to give foolproof advice about how to ensure that these situations do not arise; it is good practice, however, to provide unusually explicit information to the participants about what might occur and how they might still be identifiable if they take part in research work, and especially in studies that are (very) small scale.

We do not want you to think that taking part in research is invariably negative. That is not the case. Some people can benefit from taking part in research, and find the experience positive, and cathartic or therapeutic. Taking part can increase levels of confidence. People feel altruistic because they have contributed to a worthwhile endeavour, and/or valued because they have been singled out to express their own views and opinions on a one-to-one basis.

Ethical Approval

Recent years have seen a growth in research governance. It might be the case that undergraduate research at your university has to be approved by a research ethics committee before it can go ahead. In this case, it is important to find out as early as possible what procedures you have to follow. In addition, in the UK, any research on national health service staff or patients must be subject to local and/or regional committees for ethical approval. This means that you will also need permission from the local research ethics committee if you are keen to do research within a health centre or hospital setting, for example, a survey of patient satisfaction of waiting times for appointments.

Whilst the questions asked by an ethics panel might seem overly detailed and/or abstract, at the same time they do make researchers think long and hard about how to conduct the research in an ethically responsible way. Issues that are more or less certain to be covered in any application for ethical approval for research relate to: consent to take part; preserving confidentiality and anonymity; data collection instruments; protection from harm or distress; and adhering to data protection regulations. We know to our cost that obtaining ethical approval can be a time-consuming process, so make sure that you factor that into your timetable.

Data Protection

Along with North America and other European countries, the UK has strict data protection legislation. One of the responsibilities of the Information Commissioner's Office (http://www.informationcommissioner.gov.uk/eventual. aspx?id=250) is to oversee the Data Protection Act 1998. The new Act applies to personal data stored electronically and also to records stored on paper. What is most pertinent from the researcher's point of view is that all data must be kept secure, not only while the project is on-going but also once it has finished. This means that all the data (for example, audio or video recordings, interview transcripts or interview notes, completed question-naires, field notes) must be securely stored in lockable filing cabinets or cupboards and not left lying around on the tops of desks on view to anyone passing by.

For more detailed information about research ethics, read the codes or statements of ethical practice devised by professional organizations such as the British Sociological Association (www.britsoc.co.uk), the American Sociological Association (www.asanet.org) and the Social Research Association (www.the-sra. org.uk).

Chapter Summary

1 Research strategies include social surveys, case studies, action research, ethnographic studies, grounded theory studies and experimental studies. Different data collection methods, such as questionnaires or qualitative interviews, are appropriate for different sorts of research strategies.

2 There are a range of different approaches to sampling in order to select who or what to study from the population as a whole. Some approaches are more appropriate for quantitative research, and others are better suited to qualitative research.

3 Study participants can be difficult to access, especially if access has to be negotiated via gatekeepers.

4 All research should be conducted to the highest ethical standards.

9 Data Analysis and Writing Up a Dissertation

CHAPTER OVERVIEW

- Describing and presenting quantitative data.
- Analysing qualitative data.
- Writing up a dissertation.

This chapter completes our discussion of the research process and writing up. We pick up where the last chapter ended, and concentrate on data analysis and how to write up the dissertation. Following our earlier advice to take advantage of whatever help your dissertation tutor provides, we strongly recommend that you register for any short courses or specialist tuition in data analysis software that many universities and colleges offer. There is also much useful material online such as the large site maintained by Dr Arsham on http://home.ubalt.edu/ntsbarsh/Business-stat/opre504.htm. As well as learning about techniques for dealing with data, the skills learned will stand you in good stead in terms of future employability.

There are some issues that you need to seriously consider before plunging into the actual data management and analysis. In particular, how detailed or complex does the analysis need to be? Do you have to make comparisons between different sub-groups in the sample, for example, between different age groups or members of different ethnic communities, or can you take a broader approach? Of course, the answer to this lies partly in the research questions being addressed. It is something to think about in the early stages of the research process, especially when undertaking quantitative research as it might make a difference to the way in which the data are recorded. And at the risk of stating the obvious, this sort of detailed analysis is only possible if there are sufficient numbers in each of the various sub-groups.

Describing Quantitative Data

This section of the book is aimed at those students who have done a small research project with limited data that are quantitative in nature and which measure or count populations, volumes, distances and the like. It concentrates on how to describe quantitative data, rather than giving detailed information about undertaking complicated statistical analysis. This is because most under-graduate students will be unable to mount a quantitative survey of any signif-icant size that would be worth analysing statistically to any advanced extent because of the time and expense involved. Where there are exceptional cases, we would advise those students to complete a taught statistics course that cov-ers topic areas such as inferential statistics and hypothesis testing.

What we are concentrating on here is known as 'descriptive statistics'; this is the name given to numerical and graphical methods for organizing, presenting and analysing data. For example, suppose you were investigating swimming pool usage, you could observe or count how many individuals of different types used the pool and at what time each day over a period of four weeks. These 'observations' or values would allow you to work out: the average num-ber of people swimming in the pool each day; whether the pool was more pop-ular in a morning, afternoon or evening; the proportion of swimmers who were male or female, children or adults, on their own or with family/friends. These data, which would all be descriptive data, could then be presented in tables or pictorially, as we discuss below. The great advantage of descriptive statistics is that they condense what could be a very large data set into a relatively small number of statistics, or a picture such as a bar chart or a line graph. In this way, the results of the research are summarized and easier for readers to understand.

Percentage calculations are a form of descriptive statistics. Percentages are statis-tics that standardize the total number of cases to a base value of 100 (Argyrous, 1997). In other words, 5 per cent means '5 out of 100', 39 per cent means '39 out of 100', and so on. Percentage calculations are useful because they make it easy to compare and contrast different groups, as we show in Box 9.1.

Box 9.1 Women's Favourite Time to Swim

Suppose that on the first Monday morning in the month, 65 swimmers out of a total of 90 were women; in the afternoon there were 78 female swimmers out of a total of 130; and in the evening there were 21 females out of 52 swimmers. When the figures are presented like this, it is not very easy to spot whether women preferred to swim on a Monday morning, afternoon or evening. If you calculate the percentages for the different total number of women swimmers in the morning, afternoon and evening, you will see that women comprised 72 per cent of the swimmers in the morning. This figure compares with 60 per cent in the afternoon and 40 per cent in the evening. By using percentages, we know that women's favourite time to swim on a Monday is in the morning.

Average values, which are another type of descriptive statistics, are often useful for answering research questions. For example, you might have to report how well used the pool was to make a case for keeping it open in the face of closures because of financial cutbacks. There are three different ways to measure the typical or average value of a distribution, in this case of number of swimmers, and it is important to choose the most appropriate one. These are known as the *mean*, the *mode* and the *median*. Statistics such as the mean, mode and median are said to be measures of central tendency.

How do we use the three different kinds of averages? Suppose we wanted to find out the average number of people using the pool. Table 9.1 shows the number of people swimming in the pool every day during April 2006.

The mean is the most commonly used measure of the average, and can be used to answer the question how many people usually use the swimming pool. The mean is calculated by adding together all the numbers or values shown in Table 9.1 below, and dividing this total by the number of observations, i.e. 30:

396+412+380+400+421+390+395+408+422+386+366+404+367+380+401+417+
375+432+426+379+390+411+430+392+398+401+390+372+420+419 = 11980
  11980÷30 = 399.3.

Table 9.1 Daily number of swimmers, April 2006

Sun	Mon	Tues	Wed	Thurs	Fri	Sat
						396
412	380	400	421	390	395	408
422	386	366	404	367	380	401
417	375	432	426	379	390	411
430	392	398	401	390	372	420
419						

Source: Author's data

So the mean number of swimmers in April 2006 was 399.

Another way to do this same calculation would be to use a software package such as Microsoft Excel. After you had entered the data into the appropriate cells in the spreadsheet, all you would need to do then would be to enter the appropriate formula into the cell in which you wish to perform the calculation (this is the 'active' cell which has a heavy border round it). You want to perform the 'AVERAGE' function. To create the formula, type '=' followed by 'AVERAGE', open a bracket, highlight the relevant column, close the bracket and press 'Enter'. The formula will also appear on the input line above the spreadsheet, and the answer will appear in the 'active' cell where you just entered the formula.

The mode is the number or value that occurs most frequently. In the swimming pool dataset, there were 380 and 401 swimmers on two separate occasions. But there were 390 swimmers on three different days, so the modal number of swimmers is 390. As you can see, there is a difference of nine between the mode and the mean number of swimmers. Is this important? Well, yes, it could be. For example, it might help to find the mode because we would then know the commonest amount of use of the swimming pool, which would then help to manage the lifeguard shifts. If the dataset had not contained the three cases of 390 swimmers, then the two numbers that occurred most frequently were 380 and 401. This distribution is called bimodal because there are two modes.

The median is the third method to find an average. The median is the observation or value in the middle of a dataset. If all the observations are ranked from lowest to highest, then half will have values that are greater than the median and half will have values that are less. In the dataset, there are 30 observations. Because this is an even number, the median is the average of the two middle scores when they are ranked in order. If there had been an odd number of observations, the median would have been the middle score.

The first stage in working out the median is to rank or order the data:

366 367 372 375 379 380 380 386 390 390 390 392 395 396 **398 400** 401 401 404 408 411 412 417 419 420 421 422 426 430 432.

Because the dataset contains an even number of observations, then there are two in the middle, i.e. the 15th (398) and the 16th (400). Add these two observations together and divide by two to work out the median: 398 + 400 ÷ 2 = 399. If we omitted the first observation from the dataset to leave just 29 observations, then the median would be the 15th because there would be 14 on either side of it. In this case, the median would be 400. Again, you could use Microsoft Excel to calculate the median. Follow the instructions given earlier, but this time type in '=' followed by 'MEDIAN' in the active cell where you want the answer to appear, open a bracket, highlight the relevant column, close the bracket and press 'Enter'.

The swimming pool data were distributed reasonably symmetrically; we know this because the mean and median values were about the same. If the data were skewed, for instance, because there was an extreme score, or 'outlier', then the values of the mean and median will be different because the mean would be affected by the outlier. If data are distributed in a symmetrical 'bell-shaped' pattern, then they are described as following a normal distribution – the normal distribution is the most important statistical distribution. Most of the values occur in the middle of the curve, with some on either side. Data reporting the heights and weights of adults using the pool, for instance, would tend to follow a normal distribution, because most people are around the average height. An example of a dataset figure that follows a normal distribution is shown in Box 9.2.

However, the shape of the distribution would probably be different if the focus of interest was ages. If there were more observations or values at the lower end of the age range, for instance in the 5–16 age group because the swimming pool was running 'learn to swim' courses, then the data would not be symmetrical but instead would be said to be positively skewed. A positively skewed distribution has a longer tail to the right, and the mean is higher than the median. The shape of the distribution would look like the example in Box 9.3.

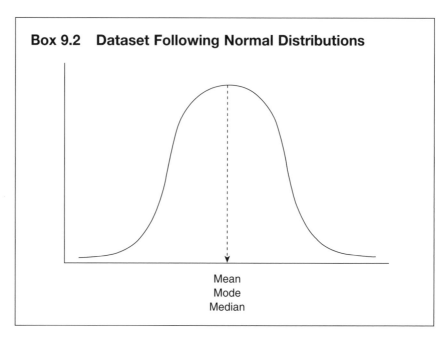

Box 9.2   Dataset Following Normal Distributions

Mean
Mode
Median

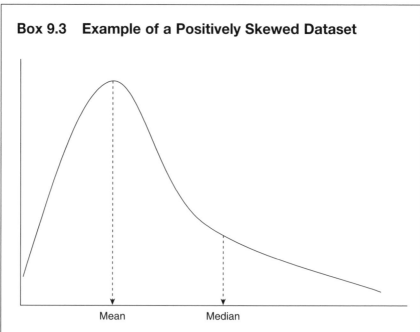

Box 9.3   Example of a Positively Skewed Dataset

Mean   Median

Suppose the swimming pool ran some sessions targeting the over-50s. In this case, the data on ages are likely to be concentrated at the top end of the range and there will be more observations with a high value. This means that the data set will be negatively skewed. A negatively skewed distribution has a longer tail to the left, as shown in Box 9.4, and the mean is less than the median because of the presence of a few small values at the negative end of the distribution.

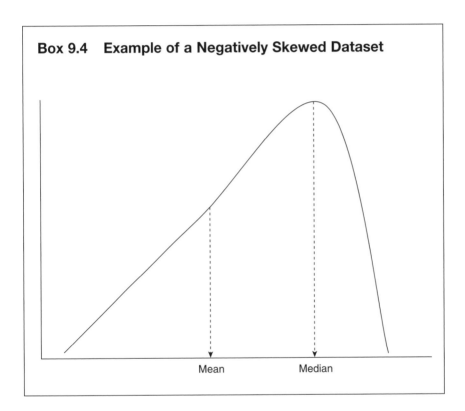

Box 9.4   Example of a Negatively Skewed Dataset

Mean   Median

To end this section of the chapter, you might find the points detailed in Box 9.5 useful when deciding which measure of central tendency to use, i.e. a mean, a mode or a median.

For introductory books about statistics to help understand basic concepts and underlying principles, and how to use them to think statistically, see Rowntree (1981), Clegg (1983), Marsh (1988), and Rose and Sullivan (1996).

Box 9.5 Guidelines for Choosing a Measure of the Average

1 Modes are not used very often, though they can be useful in certain circumstances. Avoid them in general.

2 The median is more intelligible to the general public because it is the 'middle' observation. The median is used to calculate whether people are living in poverty or not, for instance, the UK Government defines the poverty line as 60 per cent of median income level.

3 The mean uses all data, but the median does not. Therefore the mean is influenced more by unusual or extreme data. If the data are particularly subject to error, use the median.

4 The mean is more useful when the distribution is symmetrical or normal. The median is more useful when the distribution is positively or negatively skewed, because outliers do not affect the median.

5 The mean is best for minimizing sampling variability. If we take repeated samples from a population, each sample will give us a slightly different mean and median. However, the means will vary less than the medians. (For example, if we took 10 different samples of 20 students and calculated the average weight for each of the 10 groups, the mean weights would differ less between the 10 groups than the median weights.)

Source: Based on Diamond and Jefferies (2001: 56)

Presenting Descriptive Statistics

Calculations like the ones described above can be done manually using a calculator or using a software package like Microsoft Excel. Our advice would be to enter the data into a software package because it is then easy to display the results pictorially. Producing tables and charts can be done either using a statistical package (Microsoft Excel does marvellous ones), or, alternatively, using the 'chart' facility of a word processing package such as Microsoft Word. Whichever type of presentation is chosen, the aim is to present the information succinctly, in a way that is attractive to readers and which will make it easier for them to understand the meaning and significance of the results. This does not mean that there should be no accompanying explanatory text, though!

Table 9.2   Number of wedding guests, by age and sex

Age group	Sex	
	Male	Female
Under-10s	3	5
11–24	8	10
25–44	19	23
45–64	12	13
65 and over	15	18
Total number	57	69

Source: Author's data

Table 9.2 shows the number of guests at a large (and expensive!) wedding that one of the authors (HA) attended recently. You can see that the table is numbered and has a clear title describing what the data refer to. The columns are clearly named, and the source of data is included.

You might want to show the above data pictorially, which might make it easier to understand. For example, you could present the above raw data in a bar chart as we have done in Figure 9.1. A bar chart represents the frequency of cases in each category relative to each other, rather than (as with pie charts, see below) relative to the total number of cases. In a bar chart, the bars are always rectangular and the same width. The height of each bar is proportional to the number (or percentage) in each category. Common practice is to order the bars from the shortest to the tallest, or tallest to the shortest, although this is not a 'hard and fast' rule. There may be some occasions when the categories fall into a natural order, as is the case in our example of age range when there is a logical order from youngest to oldest.

We used Microsoft Excel to produce the bar chart in Figure 9.1. It was very easy; we just entered the data into the appropriate cells, highlighted them and clicked on the 'Chart Wizard' button. Next, we selected 'Column' in the 'Chart Type' list, and then we selected 'Clustered Column Chart' from the Chart sub-type area. We clicked 'Next' and the bar chart was displayed. Finally, we added headings, labels and a key (legend) to make clear what the data referred to. It is easy to see that the majority of both male and female guests were in the age group 25–44 years.

An alternative way to display the same data would be to use what is called a stacked bar chart. In a stacked bar chart, each bar is divided into layers, with

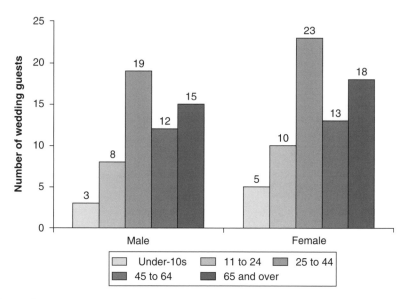

Figure 9.1   Number of wedding guests, by age and sex

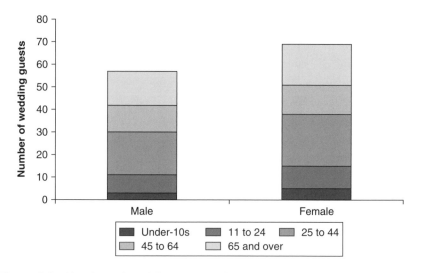

Figure 9.2   Number of wedding guests, by age and sex

the area of each layer proportional to the frequency of the category it represents. We can display the wedding guest data in a stacked bar chart, as shown in Figure 9.2. This shows quite clearly what proportion each of the five different age groups is for all the male and female guests respectively. We

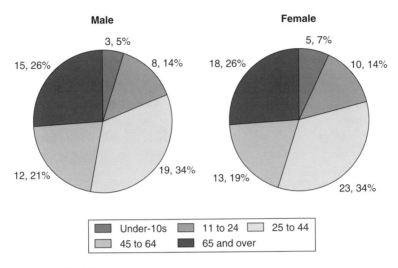

Figure 9.3 Wedding guests, by age and sex

produced the stacked bar chart by choosing the 'stacked' sub-type from the chart options offered by Excel and then added in the labels and the key.

Finally, we could use a pie chart to show how many guests attended the wedding according to age group (Figure 9.3). A pie chart shows the distribution of cases in the form of parts of a circle or 'slices of a pie'. If you are using Excel, all you need to do is enter the data into the relevant cells, highlight appropriately, click on the 'Chart Wizard, and choose the 'Pie' chart type. Do not forget to label it clearly.

Box 9.6   Working with Descriptive Statistics

Collect a dataset for yourself. You could ask 10 of your friends how long it takes them to walk 2 kilometres. Record responses according to people's real ages, and whether they are male or female. Work out the average age of respondents. Compare the average walking time between men and women. How much difference is there according to the three different types of average? Split the sample by age group, for example, group people's ages into two bands (15–21 years and 22–30 years), and compare average walking times according to age. Display the results using a range of differ-ent methods, such as tables, charts and graphs. When you are looking at the different displays, consider:

(Continued)

(Continued)

1   If the choice of table or chart is appropriate to the specific purpose of the data. Is it easy to read? Are the figures clearly titled and labelled?
2   If there is a better way to present the data. Try at least three other options from the Excel chart wizard menu.

Analysing Qualitative Data

Qualitative research, even small-scale projects, produces a wealth of data which can take a wide variety of formats, including interview transcripts or comprehensive notes, field notes, audio and/or video recordings, recordings/ descriptions of observations or documents. Because the data are so diverse, unwieldy and voluminous, it is far less straightforward to analyse qualitative data than quantitative data. Even though there is no one single set of conventions for researchers to follow, it is nonetheless important they conduct their analysis in a rigorous and systematic way. It is also necessary when writing up the dissertation to be able to comment reflectively on any 'threats to validity', findings that did not fit the general picture or that were difficult to understand, or areas where too many assumptions might have been made (see below).

It is worth noting that many qualitative researchers see data analysis as part of the data collection stage of the research process, thus early or preliminary findings may influence the subsequent direction of data collection. In practice, this might mean that further questions are added to a topic guide in order to follow up what are emerging as potentially important areas of (theoretical) interest. This is certainly the view taken by supporters of grounded theory, whose proponents argue that researchers should set aside any theoretical preconceptions when they first begin their research. Instead, the theory should be grounded in empirical reality and emerge as the data are collected.

A basic research skill is to impose some order and coherence on what is in effect a vast bulk of complex material without losing the original accounts/ observations from which it has been derived. For the initial analysis, it is best to start with the obvious, so look for fairly concrete concepts and then move on to the more abstract. Make a note of significant ideas, concepts and points of interest. And then look for what is more novel, theoretically interesting and/or surprising. Do not just look for evidence to confirm your expectations or initial hunches. In this way, that is by gathering together all the material that is relevant to one particular topic area, you are developing what could be regarded as a coding or indexing framework. The idea is that later on you can retrieve everything that has been 'filed' under that particular category.

Manual qualitative data analysis can involve 'charting', in other words writing down key themes and issues emerging from the data on to very large sheets of paper. If you are interested in manual data analysis methods, then see Maykut and Morehouse (2001) or Ritchie and Lewis (2003), which both provide practical guidance.

Word processing packages and spreadsheet software have simplified the task of storing and managing data. However, specialist software packages for qualitative data analysis are now available that can handle large amounts of data very quickly. Commonly used software packages for qualitative data analysis include Nvivo, ATLAS-ti and MAXqda. The CAQDAS Network Project (http://caqdas.soc.surrey.ac.uk/index.htm), which is funded by the UK's Economic and Social Research Council, is an excellent resource base for qualitative data analysis and a good place to start if you are thinking about software usage. It provides practical support, information and training (some of which is free of charge) on a range of software. This can be useful if you have the luxury of choosing which package to use (this decision might well be made for you, as more than likely it will depend on what software your institution provides/supports).

Different approaches or 'tools' have their respective costs and benefits, and which you choose might well come down to something basic like time constraints. Generally speaking, though, whichever method you select for this part of the analysis is likely to be time-consuming, although at the same time you will be developing skills to help you deal with the fascinating problem of trying to understand the views of others – skills which are likely to be transferable into the workplace and thus valuable for your future career. You will get points for doing the analysis well, though, and you might find it worthwhile to keep a log or record to help write the reflective element of the dissertation. This also applies to quantitative work too. There are lots of options and decisions to reflect about, such as sample size, leading or inadequate questions and their effects, or the distortions from poor response rates.

When the data are coded up or organized in some way, then is the time to move on to a further stage of the analysis and piece together the whole thing – this is where creativity comes in, which is quite difficult to describe. Essentially, you are going to ask further questions of the data. This may involve comparing and contrasting evidence in the same category; identifying sub-categories; exploring links and connections (between people's experiences and attitudes, circumstances, motivations). You might want to explore what informants say in relation to particular sociological variables, such as gender, age, ethnicity, levels of income, or you could create typologies. You could look for (implicit/explicit) explanations to account for, say, people's behaviour. What you need to beware of is imposing too many of your own views; the whole point is to try to make sense of the study participants' views.

What guides creativity? These are the things that we think help direct researchers when it comes to analysing qualitative data:

- **existing body of literature;**

- **analytical themes emerging from the data;**

- **recurrent views/experiences;**

- **prior issues behind the research questions;**

- **emerging issues (identified during the fieldwork);**

- **important policy issues;**

- **survey data (which provides different types of answers);**

- **theoretical concepts.**

Every specialist qualitative data analysis computer package adopts a slightly different approach, but the underlying purpose is to use the software as a tool to reduce the data down to manageable proportions, to display the data, and to make it easy to retrieve the data through the search facilities of the particular software package used. From here, the researcher looks for the patterns, emerging themes, associations, commonalities and differences that we have just been describing. The process is undertaken more than once. This is so that researchers can refine their understanding or explanation of the phenomenon under investigation, or test out assumptions and check hypotheses in a wider context. In other words, there is an 'iterative' process in operation; research activities are repeated as new themes emerge, and new knowledge is gained and extended through cycles of research.

The conclusions reached, and the way in which the research questions are answered, need to be justified by the evidence – as much as, if not more so, than quantitative research. This is because qualitative research has been criticized for the degree of subjectivity and lack of rigour in the techniques used. The iterative process described above can be viewed as a verification process of the findings. 'Triangulation' is another technique designed to improve the reliability and validity of qualitative research. Triangulation involves using two or more alternative data collection methods to study the same phenomena, for example, using interviews in conjunction with observational techniques, and/or documentary sources. Ideally, the different methods will reveal similar findings about the topic under investigation, thereby boosting confidence in their validity. Another way to check for validity is to feed back the research findings to the study participants and/or 'experts' in the field and ask them for their opinion on the conclusions arrived at. There would only be cause for concern if people had problems identifying with the work, and did not feel that it was consistent with their experiences, opinions or behaviours. See Miles and Huberman (1994) for a more comprehensive list of tactics to assess the quality of qualitative data analysis.

The following website includes detailed information about qualitative data analysis, which people who are new to research might find useful: http://onlineqda.hud.ac.uk/Introduction/index.php. Another useful website for qualitative (and quantitative) research is SOSIG, the Social Science Information Gateway, which can be accessed via http://sosig.ac.uk/. See the 'Research Tools and Methods' subsection.

Writing the Dissertation

Once you have collected all the data and completed the analysis, the next stage is to start the writing up. A good way to tackle writing a dissertation is to think of it initially as several shorter sections, of about 2,000–3,000 words. The benefit of this is that it makes the task more manageable. You might find it better to write up the empirical research section first, or the literature review section, or whatever, regardless of the order in which it appears in the final version.

The majority of dissertations and research reports follow a similar structure: title page; abstract; contents page; introduction; literature review; research methods; findings; discussion; conclusion; references; appendices. You might also choose to include acknowledgements to those who helped or supported you. Depending on the content matter, an alphabetical glossary explaining technical or any other special terminology (e.g. policy terms, acronyms) might also be useful.

1   *Title page*: the title page should be short and an accurate indication of the contents of the research. One approach is to have a two-part title. The first part is the main title, and the second part or sub-title qualifies the nature of the study by adding more detail. This is sometimes helpful if you have to register your title early on, before you have really decided what to do in detail. Check out good quality journal articles for examples of titles.

2   *Abstract*: the abstract is a succinct synopsis of the dissertation. It is normally no more than 300 words in length and should include the aim or purpose of the study, the research methods and important findings. Some abstracts might include summaries of each chapter or section.

3   *Contents page*: the contents page helps the reader to find their way around. At the very minimum, it should contain chapter headings and page numbers. A more detailed contents page may also include sub-sections of chapters. References, tables, graphs and appendices are listed separately.

4   *Introduction*: this is the first chapter in the main body of the dissertation. It should contain information about the background or context to the work, the research questions under investigation or hypotheses being tested, explanations of key definitions, theoretical approaches and concepts to be used, and a short summary of the structure of the report. In other words, by the time the reader has finished the chapter, they should know what you are doing and why.

5   *Literature review*: this chapter contains a review of the existing body of knowledge about the field of study, as well as anything else that may be relevant to the investigation. As we indicated in Chapter 7, a literature review should discuss relevant research findings, comment on research methods used, critically discuss any perceived weaknesses and suggest how the studies could be improved. It is important to write up the literature review in such a way that it demonstrates how the new research being reported relates to, and further develops, previous research.

6   *Research methods*: this chapter describes and justifies the methods used for data collection and analysis. Consideration should be given to both the strengths and the weaknesses of the specific research methods adopted. The chapter should contain precise details of the sample and sampling techniques used, data collection instruments, how access to study participants was obtained and how ethical issues were addressed. Information about how the data were analysed should also be included.

7   *Findings*: in this chapter, the data are presented and analysed or interpreted in terms of what they have to say in the context of the original research questions or hypothesis being tested. Sub-headings to separate out different sections of the findings greatly improve readability.

8   *Discussion*: the discussion chapter relates the findings to the theoretical or policy discussion, and any other relevant issues, that were referred to in the literature review chapter. In principle, this chapter should be the most interesting one of the whole dissertation as it is where you place the findings in the broader context identified in an earlier chapter. It is the place to consider how your findings relate to the findings of others, for instance, does your analysis confirm or refute other people's hypotheses? How useful are the findings in shedding light on the research questions? What do the results say in terms of different perspectives or different stakeholders with an interest in the topic area?

9   *Conclusion*: the concluding chapter draws together what has gone before. Typically, it will contain an overall assessment of what the research found, if and how it contributes to existing knowledge, recommendations for

improvements or change and suggestions for future research. This is also the place to be self-critical about matters like samples, coding, interviewing glitches, and so on, which is where the research log can be useful. It is conventional not to introduce any new data at this late stage; nor should you introduce ideas relating to evidence that have not already been presented. In any event, this is where you try to meet the usual criteria of critical discussion, coverage, analysis, insight, 'original-ity', and so on. The aim is to show you are now able to undertake some independent work of your own, fully aware of the pitfalls and possibilities.

The final version of the dissertation is likely to be around 10,000 words – and that does not include all the words you have discarded in previous draft versions! And this is the first thing to realize: generally, dissertations go through a number of re-writes before they are ready to be handed in for marking. It is usually much easier to do this on a word processor, but you must be careful to organize/save your files so you do not confuse the different drafts. Make sure you back up your work, and, ideally, keep a printed version as well. One of the roles of a dissertation supervisor is to read through and comment on draft chapters so make sure that you act on whatever (expert) advice you are given. Do not waste their time either – they are skilled advisers, so consult them about the best literature in the field, the dilemmas of research, how to structure an argument, and so on, but do not ask them to proofread or check the spelling – you must do that yourself.

We are not going into any further detail here about how to write a dissertation. Chapter 5 focused on writing skills, and the principles and points made in relation to essays and examination questions are equally valid when it comes to producing a dissertation. We do have a few specific hints, though, which you might find useful:

- **Break down the task of writing into small and manageable sections; this can be helpful to sustain motivation levels.**

- **Leave the abstract until the end.**

- **Review the introductory chapter once the dissertation is completed, and consider revising it to take account of the new findings and your conclusions.**

- **Make sure that the order of the chapters is logical and coherent, and will make sense to the reader. Add an overview at the beginning of each chapter, and a summary at the end, if you think that would help the reader.**

- **Read through your dissertation as a whole to make sure the argument flows logically; it makes sense and demonstrates your understanding of the issues; it does not repeat itself; the points made are not contradictory; it includes analysis and not just description.**

- **Check that you have provided evidence of reading around the subject.**

- **Provide evidence of reflection, e.g. treat any theories you write about objectively and critically.**

- **Make sure that the conclusion is justified by the preceding evidence. In particular, focus on the argument you have developed.**

- **Assess the dissertation against the marking criteria.**

Chapter Summary

1   Specialist software packages are available for both quantitative and qualitative data analysis. Websites on the Internet offer freely available resource material including online tutorials and downloadable software.

2   Data analysis must always be conducted systematically and rigorously; it is helpful to keep a research log documenting the range of activities undertaken, and any problems encountered.

3   Descriptive statistics are numerical and graphical ways to describe data. They can be used to summarize a large amount of numerical information so that the data are concise and easier to understand.

4   Quantitative data can be presented in a number of different ways. Sometimes, graphical or pictorial displays can be more accessible and easier to read than tables.

(Continued)

(Continued)

5   Qualitative research can produce a mass of data that can be complex and unwieldy. Looking for patterns, relationships, similarities and anomalies are the basic techniques for making sense of the evidence. Comparing and contrasting accounts of study participants from different sub-groups have the potential to shed light on differences in people's opinions, behaviours, priorities and trade-offs.

6   There is a fairly standard format to follow when writing up the dissertation. It is important to be organized in terms of word processing, and knowing which is the most recent version on your USB memory stick. Writing might seem less daunting if different sections are tackled one at a time.

10 Pulling It All Together

CHAPTER OVERVIEW

- Managing university life.
- Knowing your tutors.
- Transferable skills and employability.
- Study skills.

As the authors, we cannot be sure how you will have read this book. It is common these days for students to read selectively, dipping in and out of relevant chapters. Indeed, we recommend this technique ourselves. We have provided some guidance to the contents of the book if you want to do this. However, we cannot assume that you will have seen any general themes or issues emerging unless you have been looking for them. There are some overall points that seem to be worth making.

You will have seen from the Introduction that we have assumed that you will already know some of the conventional study skills involved in keeping accurate records, taking lecture notes, and recording some of your social and leisure activities so that you can build an effective CV. The conventional study skills themselves are not particularly difficult to learn, and you will encounter some additional techniques while you are at university. It is a matter of selecting those routines and techniques that you find effective. For some, it will be mind-mapping, while for others more conventional ways to structure your notes might seem easier. We have included some recent work on structuring academic arguments (in Chapter 6 particularly), and this work seems likely to become more popular in the future, and perhaps will involve electronic forms.

Our approach towards conventional study skills is slightly different in that we want to try to get you to think about the underlying principles rather than the techniques as such. For example, what you are doing when you take notes, we suggest, is trying to reproduce academic argument. We try to explain what this might actually involve, and how it might differ from ordinary common-sense arguments. We suggest that you try to read academic materials, or student dissertations and reports, with a view to trying to get to the underlying arguments. We advise you to think in terms of a basic structure of summary and comment, perhaps with particular attention given to the requirement to comment, which might be different from academic approaches encountered before you came to university. We further suggest that you investigate assessment criteria and learning outcomes, and go even further to try to examine characteristic values that academics express when they discuss their own work.

This research orientation is particularly useful if you are coming to university from one of the 'unconventional' social backgrounds – if you are the first in your family to be an undergraduate, for example, or if you are from a currently under-represented minority, or if you are one of the growing band of mature students. You will need to research your new environment because, as a number of studies have found, it will not be totally transparent to you right away. Researching your environment can also help you develop a way of coping with what might seem to be a challenging situation. We suggest that you think of yourself as an anthropologist or an ethnographic researcher, and spend some time trying 'to play your way in'. At the same time, we do not suggest or imply that you see any need to apologize for your presence. Universities are committed to welcoming diversity in the student body, but you may simply have to help them realize on occasion that 'different' does not mean 'inferior'.

As your confidence develops, apparently daunting tasks, such as doing a presentation or speaking in a seminar, should look more straightforward. Similarly, picking up what is required in academic writing should appear as a technical task that can be learned and practised, not an occasion for making social judgements. What looks like the most daunting task to an undergraduate – writing a dissertation – can also be researched and the requirements understood. All these things may have to be (re)learned. We hope that our book will help, but it is also up to you to work towards an understanding in your own circumstances. You will need to develop your own resources, and also to draw upon the social support of specialist support staff and tutors, both personal and academic, fellow-students and family members.

Part 1: University Life and Employability (Chapters 1–4)

If there is one major theme in the first part of this book, it is that you will need to adjust your activities at university in order to relate to the aims and wants of others. It is not a matter of simply finding out what other people want and then giving it to them, but rather negotiating your way so that your own particular aims and wants are maximized as well. You certainly do not have to pretend to be something like an ideal student, nor decide to cut off all your past friends and family, and abandon the leisure and recreational activities that you once enjoyed. You may feel you want to 'pass' as an ideal student at first, but no one can live like that for very long. At the other extreme, you do not want to retreat into a shell, denying yourself all new contacts, pleasures and interests, desperately clinging to the past. It is really a matter of managing new situations in ways that you feel comfortable with, not forgetting that a challenge can be very interesting and life-enhancing.

Students

We have suggested that you might consider finding out how other students have managed this important negotiation when they faced their challenges. We have summarized our own research on students, but also discussed some of the famous studies done by professional researchers. We are certainly not recommending that you simply follow the activities of the students we are discussing. Some of them will be pursuing activities that are ethically dubious if not positively illegal, ranging from trying to get away with plagiarism to consuming recreational drugs. What is more interesting, perhaps, is that many of the students studied seemed to have approached university life with certain fears and reservations that seem common, and which may be shared by you.

A central anxiety, experienced by many newcomers, including ourselves when we were starting out, seems to involve doubt about their own abilities to cope. In some cases this can become quite a serious question of whether people feel they belong at university at all. Many students seem to think that they are really impostors who will be found out and humiliated. This feeling seems to be particularly common among those who have come to university from social backgrounds which are usually seen as 'unconventional'. We think this experience is tapping into a lingering influence from the old social origins of the university. Until very recently universities were designed mostly for students from elite backgrounds, and, although they are changing, there is still much of the atmosphere which remains unchanged. It is important for unconventional students to recognize this and not to see the occasional social discomfort which results as a problem with themselves necessarily.

Students react to the atmosphere of 'the university' in a number of ways, it seems. Some realize that universities leave you rather a lot of freedom in areas such as how you actually do your work and write your assignments. As a result, all kinds of short cuts, 'rules of the game' and downright cheating become possible. We do not wish to simply condemn this activity as immoral, but to try and understand it first, as one response to a challenging environment. We also feel the need to point out to you, quite frequently in this book, that universities may be very liberal about many things, but that there is a substantial consensus that plagiarism is such a sin that those convicted of it should be expelled from the academy altogether.

Other students react by dividing their lives into academic work and 'normal' life outside. Normal life might involve youthful recreation in a range of activities from extreme sports to binge drinking. For other students, normal life will be a return to home and family, their families of origin or the families they have established themselves. Many students will have to take on paid work as a normal part of their life. Although there may be some slight reservation about these activities in university circles, we think that, on occasion, they can provide excellent resources to cope with the unusual world of the academy. We suggest that maintaining both normal and academic lives is an important coping strategy, although there is also sometimes a tendency for students to see it in terms of completely contradictory and opposing spheres. As usual, people who can 'juggle' different aspects of their lives and enjoy all of them seem to be more successful.

Tutors

We have also tried in Part 1 to investigate the wants, needs and values of some of the important people you will be encountering. We have a chapter on tutors (lecturers, academics or staff), for example. Our views here are based on our own research and experience, published studies, and some documents which can express official values for the teaching profession. We take a particular interest in the specific activities which best express these beliefs and values in a concrete form – assessment. We are not suggesting that you merely need to find out what tutors want and then give it to them. Usually, your knowledge of tutors will not be that detailed, and it may still be influenced by all sorts of stereotypes based on your past experience or on media representations.

When you do investigate afresh the professional world of the tutor, we anticipate that you will find it more complex than these media representations and experiences might suggest. For example, you do not have to simply agree with tutors in order to get good grades. The university is one of the few areas left in life where you are encouraged to challenge and criticize received wisdom. Of course, you have to do this in a particular way: a university does not offer simply a free-for-all when it comes to the expression of opinions, but values particular kinds of views, expressed in a suitably impersonal way and supported by agreed evidence and argument. Here, there is a link with a later chapter, where we try to give you some specific examples of academic argument to make some of this more concrete.

We hope you are also able to see what lies behind standard university practices such as course design. You do not need to investigate the technicalities, but these practices represent and embody important sources of academic values. In particular, once you know how to read course documents and assessment criteria, you can detect all sorts of expectations implicit in them. Academics expect students to be embarked upon a journey, from immediate and fairly simple forms of understanding to more complex and abstract forms, for example. Once you understand these goals, university life makes far more sense, and you can also assess your own progress in terms of developing forms of understanding. At the time of writing, for example, we can already detect some changes among our first-year students: at first, they thought they would be learning lots of facts, dates, names and detail, but now they realize that they are required to do something rather different and get to grips with underlying principles and arguments.

For an academic, it would be possible to describe these changes in terms of a shift from 'surface' to 'deep' learning. These terms are based on some highly influential work which is very widespread among tutors in higher education. Whatever the merits of this work as educational psychology, we certainly feel that it describes central and important values at the heart of university life. We think it is important to tell students about it as well as new lecturers. Even the most cynical students might be able to see some benefit here: we do not recommend that students simulate a 'deep' approach, but if they are going to do so, they might at least know what it is they are supposed to be simulating. We are confident that the 'deep' approach does deliver genuine pleasure and a sense of achievement such that even cynical simulators can find themselves drawn into the real thing.

Employers

Finally, in the first part, we examine what is known about employers. University life was once seen as a welcome escape from the world of work, but now gaining a good degree tends to be valued primarily as a passport to a good occupation. Once more, we attempt to describe and explain rather than discuss whether this is a good or bad thing. Your Careers Service and local student support networks will help you to undertake the necessary practical steps to prepare for work. You will certainly be urged to think of and prepare a CV as soon as possible. As we shall see below, this is by no means a tedious chore.

It seems clear, for example, that specific skills that can be directly used right away are possibly less important now, especially in the social sciences. The successful expansion of universities has produced a 'glut' of graduates with sufficient technical skills, Williams et al. (2006) suggest, and employers are turning more and more to other qualities to select the best ones. Employers appear to want more general skills, for example. These are usually known as transferable skills, and, increasingly, they turn on interpersonal skills – being able to communicate effectively, understand others, deal with people confidently, analyse tasks, apply a certain critical thinking, and so on. We think that this sort of skill shows a considerable overlap between academic and subsequent tasks in employment: as you learn the one, so you will also prepare for the other. There happens to be a fairly extensive academic debate about whether these terms are helpful, whether 'skill' is the right term to describe capabilities, and whether or not it is the skill that is valuable or the motivation and understanding that lie behind it, and you can follow this up yourself in Williams et al. (2006).

However, the main implication in practice seems to be that the whole area is still rather vague and controversial, and so it is up to you to define what you have done in suitable terms. If job applications require a list of skills and competencies, you should be practising the ability to describe what you have done in terms of those skills and competencies. We give some examples in the book showing how even leisure and recreational activities can be described like this. Again, this could be seen as advice to be cynical, but there is some evidence to suggest that employers really do expect you to have engaged in active and creative leisure pursuits, as long as you can justify doing so in their terms: it is almost the old belief that activity on the games field reveals 'character', perhaps. We think that raising a family, running a household and managing the family budget are also valuable 'skills' that can be used to support job applications.

Another increasing area of interest concerns the role of 'social capital'. Again, academics themselves may disagree about definitions and implications, but our point here is that you may possess some assets that employers can be persuaded to see as valuable capital. We think that students of social sciences can make a strong claim that they have investigated the difficulties and problems of understanding others, and that they understand better than most the dynamics of social solidarity. It does not require much rephrasing to see these abilities as important assets for developing 'bridging', and 'bonding', types of social capital (to use currently fashionable terms). Social sciences can give you an additional technical vocabulary to help you develop your account of what you have studied.

What these discussions reveal for us is that getting a good job does not require you to completely reshape your personality and interests, any more than surviving at university does. Surviving at work will require negotiation, reflection, and an ability to see if there is room for the values and activities that you want to hold to. You can try this out with work placements or familiarization visits, and by talking to company representatives at careers fairs. In this sense, there are many more aspects of university life that can help you get – and sustain – a good job than might appear to be the case at first. It is not just the immediately vocational aspects of your courses that count.

Part 2: Maximizing Your Performance (Chapters 5–9)

Part 2 of the book considers the practical matters of producing academic work. You will be expected to produce a variety of written pieces for assessment, including essays, reports and examination scripts. The dissertation is special and important enough (for UK students) to deserve a substantial account to guide you towards effective performance in this peculiar form. You will also be expected to demonstrate the ability to present your work in a variety of formats, and to contribute to a number of discussions in seminars and tutorials. It is increasingly common to expect students to undertake placements or practical elements as well.

Perhaps we should deal with the last one first, because we have not discussed it as much in the actual book. We think we have given sufficient general hints on how to approach academic work which can easily be applied to placements and fieldwork, however. We suggest that you consider yourselves as ethnographic researchers in the professional field as well as in the university teaching rooms. You need to play your way in, to observe how things are done, to be prepared to investigate and reflect upon ways of behaviour that may not seem natural or obvious to you. Working on a placement is an unusual experience because you do not yet have the full powers, rights, or duties of the fully qualified professional. Some students find it best to take advantage of their relatively marginal status to try things out. They often consider themselves as playing a role, as teacher, social worker, community worker or whatever, and we would support that approach. Later, as confidence and experience increase, it is possible to introduce more of your own preferences and professional knowledge. As usual, it is a matter of judging and balancing: you need to learn from others, but you also need to try out your own ideas.

We suggest, in fact, that this stance should be applied to academic work as well. There is no point going to university if you are not prepared to learn from others, but there is also a need to develop your own personal thinking and powers of reflection. We think that demonstrating a balance of these two qualities is what really lies behind academic success in the broadest sense. You can find qualities like this disguised in the specific assessment criteria that will govern the grade that you get, and also in the implicit values and expectations of tutors that we described in the first section. Obviously, you will need to find out the specific requirements of your particular institution, make sure you understand them, and gain experience and help in applying them to your own work.

Summary and Comment

We give some detailed advice in the relevant chapters, but we want to stress the general principles here. Applied to academic tasks this time, you need to demonstrate that you have made a real effort to understand arguments and theoretical work that will not seem obvious or natural to you. This requires some effort and motivation, but, above all, an open-mindedness and willingness to try to grasp new perspectives on the social world. Because that world is familiar to us all as participants, academic work in social science can often be seen as particularly challenging, strange or clearly wrong.

To take a very recent example, we have been exploring Freudian discussions of desire and how it might manifest itself in pleasure in sport or cinema. Our students have reacted with frank incredulity, in some cases, because this is such an unfamiliar approach, and it is also rather unsettling. The idea that support for a football team might be driven by some homoerotic mechanism of desire can be really difficult to take seriously at first. Yet we do expect students to take it seriously, at least seriously enough to try to understand why anyone would want to develop such a theory. We expect a technical discussion to ensue, based on arguments, their internal consistency, and the evidence that might be used to defend or criticize such a view, alternative explanations for passionate commitment, and so on. It is still possible to see students almost pinching themselves as they attempt to discuss what must seem like an evidently dubious and crackpot theory.

To put it in terms of a student task, the first and challenging step for any student tackling an assignment on Freudian discussions would be to summarize the argument effectively, not be distracted by any of the more lurid claims or implications, and not to give up in despair or sheer disbelief. However, to get maximum grades, students would also be expected to comment on their own summaries. We have argued in the text that despite the enormous knowledge displayed in arguments by experienced academics, it is still possible for beginners to make critical comments. Indeed, it is expected that they will. Comments that can always be made include challenges to consistency, a demand for more recent applications or research findings, and a comparison with other academic work, for example. This can seem like it is heading nowhere, that nothing can be taken for granted, that there is no secure and final knowledge in the social sciences – but this is the basis of a mature academic understanding, and a feature of the professional life of the social science academic. It does not rule out the option that, having considered all the arguments, you can choose one that seems to be the best available, in full and mature awareness that there are still problems. However, it does rule out naïve belief in the complete supremacy of any one approach.

This basic structure of effective summary followed by critical comment is at the heart of what is required in essays, reports and examinations, although there may be different combinations of the two elements that are required. There are also limits imposed by matters such as time constraints and the precise nature of the question to be addressed. However, the basic structure is useful from the very beginning in tackling an academic task. For example, a good way to organize your note-taking or revision is to think of these twin tasks at that stage. Most students will realize that they need some kind of effective summary, but they also need to note down their reflections, remind themselves to do so, revise those critical reflections as well as their summaries, and work to expand their abilities to reflect and criticize as well as just to summarize and memorize.

We are aware that for many students, presentations and seminars are unpopular and even stressful, but they take on a much more positive role once you remember that discussion, argument and criticism are a required and valuable part of academic life. In this sense, we are doing something different from ordinary life again: discussion and criticism in ordinary life can be seen as unwelcome, aggressive, confrontational, competitive and personal. The trick is to insist that academic discussion is technical rather than any of these other things. Your tutor can be expected to insist on technical rather than personal criticism, and you can do so too as a presenter or a participant. Generating critical discussion is to be welcomed, not dreaded. We think it helps if you deliberately detach yourself to some extent at first, and try to consider issues and topics abstractly. Later, you can develop the skills of shaping discussion so that it does reflect more of your personal agendas and interests, although personal agendas should never dominate academic work.

You have a responsibility as a participant to try to generate a suitable atmosphere which will make your own contributions and presentations less personal and therefore less stressful. You should avoid rudeness and aggression or personal remarks in questions or challenges to others. You should try to think of technical or substantive questions to ask – some of those suggested here can be useful in providing you with some ideas for making your own critical comments and reflections in your assignments. You should also respond positively to any efforts from tutors to focus on the issues as such.

We are not suggesting that technical seminars are necessarily the most fun-filled, but it is a matter of building up expertise again. Once people feel comfortable about talking to each other without risking personal attack, the whole group can relax and move towards more open kinds of conversation. You can feel more confident and expansive as a presenter or contributor, more willing to take risks, not so concerned about keeping control or dominating the discussion, more prepared to consider the audience and their interests. This is exactly the kind of advice commonly given these days to new lecturers, but students can also benefit from it.

We have left discussion of the student dissertation to the end of the book, because we think that it is probably the most specialized academic task, and perhaps the one that is furthest away for you if you are a beginner. Being able to complete one is the defining characteristic of 'graduateness'. Having served your apprenticeship by being able to summarize and comment upon professional academic work, with an increasing degree of sophistication and familiarity with academic conventions, the final hurdle is to produce a longer piece of writing that classically shows that you are able to practise as an academic yourself, even if this is not actually your intended destination. In recognition of the special value of the dissertation, it often receives particular weight in the assessment process. In one of our local universities, for example, it counts as two whole modules, out of a total of 12: those 12 determine your final class of degree. In our experience, the dissertation often carries even more weight informally in discussions of academic worth and grades and commentaries can be decisive in borderline decisions.

Writing a dissertation is actually not that different from writing an essay, and the basic structure of being able to summarize other people's work and to add comments of your own will guide your efforts here too. At the same time, there may be additional conventions to follow, particular stages which you must indicate you have achieved, or particular requirements which you must take into account, and we list some in the relevant chapters. You may be required to undertake some research of your own, for example, and even if you are not, you will often be advised to do so. This can add certain refinements to the tasks of summarizing and commenting.

If you are undertaking some research of your own, you will have some additional problems to solve. You will be required to discuss research methods, and also to practise the craft of the professional researcher. As you will discover from reading Chapter 8, there is a wide variety of research methods to choose from, and each has a characteristic set of advantages and disadvantages. There are also theoretical and philosophical issues attached to the choice of research methods, and you may well be expected to comment on those as well. Actually doing the research can take up a lot of time, and it will require a good deal of planning. When you have the data, further issues arise, and you will have to decide how to analyse and display your results.

However, there will be one major advantage in doing this extra work. You will be able to demonstrate that you can actually do some research in practice. There is an important practical element to research. It does not just involve choosing a suitable method after some reading and philosophical reflection. Any researcher has to work within a budget, for example, and you will need to decide the most effective way to spend limited time and resources at your disposal. If you are thinking of some questionnaire-based research, you will have to think of designing your questionnaires so as to achieve the maximum amount of relevant data for a given budget. These practical problems need to be solved alongside the more theoretical issues of choosing a relevant sample or deciding whether to run self-administered questionnaires or structured interviews.

As a practising researcher, you will also be able to comment from the inside on important matters usually described as 'threats to validity'. You will doubtless encounter a theoretical argument suggesting that the presence of observers can have an effect on action itself, but this argument becomes much more vivid and relevant when you are attempting to do an observational study yourself. Similarly, there is some general advice on interviewing which warns students against asking leading questions or trying to affect the answers of the interviewee in some way – but there is nothing to match actually trying to do an interview and noticing how subtle and complex such interaction can be.

The same kinds of considerations apply when you attempt to analyse your raw data. There are theoretical debates about matters such as coding, or, indeed, on the difficulties of interpreting other people more generally, but when you actually try to do this, the problems become much more concrete: it is very tempting to try to tidy up your data, ignore cases that do not fit conveniently with your coding categories, or take a rather simplistic line in interpreting what others have said.

Students undertaking research sometimes think that they need to try to cover up any problems of this kind that they have encountered. Our advice is almost the opposite, and we would recommend instead that you keep the research diary or log, and note down precisely these sorts of issues and practical dilemmas. The reason for this is that the experience will provide you with a rich source of potential comment on the research process itself. It is not a matter of undermining your own efforts, and, as usual, you should check carefully with your local conventions first. If you get the balance right, however, you will demonstrate that you have learned a great deal about the professional business of academic research, both the theory and the actual practice of the craft.

Over to You

We hope that we leave you overall with a view that taking a social science degree at university is a challenge, but that finding out what is required is the essential step to meeting that challenge. We do not believe that possessing a few conventional study skills and practising them will guarantee success. Taking a degree is much more complex than that, despite public views and stereotypes that suggest that almost anyone can do well in social sciences. At the same time, we also think that there are unnecessary obstacles put in the way of many students, especially if they come from an unconventional background. They will have cultural and social problems to negotiate as well. The best thing about universities is that they offer a largely tolerant social life, one that is probably more open than anything you will encounter afterwards, providing a very valuable opportunity to gain real insights into the lives of others and of yourself.

We are sure you will enjoy your time at university, and we wish you the best of luck with your studies. We hope you will continue your momentum into a successful career afterwards.

Afterword

This is a section of the book addressed primarily to academic colleagues. Everything else has been written with student readers in mind, but we need to clear some initial ground. We have taken a slightly unusual approach to study advice in this book. There are several reasons for this, which we would like to discuss.

There is a massive amount of material on conventional study skills already available, for example, general overviews like Burns and Sinfield (2003), McIlroy (2003), Williams (2004) and more specific ones like Oliver (2004) on writing a thesis, or Tracy (2002) on taking examinations. As the dates of the above indicate, there seems to have been a recent publishing boom in the genre. Many students will have already received advice on these conventional skills at schools, colleges, or while taking access courses. Any who have managed to arrive at university without contact with a study skills course are likely to encounter one on campus, and to be able to gain advice in much more detail. There are many excellent online discussions too. It is probably not necessary to add to this material, although some of it is surprisingly dated (much of it barely mentions electronic forms of delivery and seems to think that taking lecture notes and reading books are still the dominant forms). Although there are some honourable exceptions, the move towards conventional study skills, in the form of handbooks or conventional study skills courses on campus, still seems to make a number of crucial assumptions that we would want to question.

Much of it is surprisingly abstract, for example. An early clue is often provided by books which claim to provide study skills for a wide range of students, and often assume that the same skills will be relevant across all sectors. This is true, but only at a very basic level, and we are particularly worried that students will not see the need to adjust to the particular requirements of higher education. It is a worry shared by many students themselves, of course. This is not to make an elitist point, or to deny the significance of the importance of education at other levels, but simply to point out that there may be special requirements for university modules and courses. It may be a matter of requiring more 'independence' in learning, for example. Yorke (2000) identifies the failure to adjust to more independent study as a major reason for dissatisfaction and non-completion, in certain subjects especially, while Bonnett (2001) sees the ability to argue as the crucial differentiator.

Much of the advice is also clearly exhortatory or rhetorical. The frequently cited SQR3 technique (survey, question, read, review, revisit), for example, simply insists, in effect, that students work a lot harder than before. Of course, the survey and question sections invite students to impose their own interests on the material, but after that they simply have to read it several times. Some study skills texts insist that students should spend their time memorizing a variety of information, ranging from key facts to module handouts and assessment regulations. There is a constant theme of regulation, both in the ordinary sense of urging students to manage their time effectively, and in the more specialized Foucaldian sense, of learning to be a well-disciplined subject.

This sort of approach might be more acceptable if there were clear evidence that the pursuit of study skills like this brings tangible benefits. Of course, we have met students who claimed that following study skills regimes have delivered success, in the sense of keeping them in the system and helping them survive long enough to get a good degree. This is an important kind of success, but there is little evidence that we could find which suggests that study skills are specifically responsible, and we suspect that the 'Hawthorne effect', arising from receiving skilled and dedicated interest from support staff, is just as likely to deliver the result. We also feel that success at university should be defined rather more broadly and generally than just struggling through – indeed, we think that going to university should even be pleasurable. There is precious little evidence of any interest in pleasure in much conventional study skills literature. At best, students are allowed to reward themselves for unrelenting and rather tedious hard work by planning for short periods of escape.

Without discussing pleasures, it is hard to see why anyone would want to apply the demanding conventional study skills that are often recommended, and we think that actually very few students do. This is the point made by Halliday (2000), that merely providing a list of skills fails to address the issue of motivation altogether. There is usually just a simple admonition to apply the skills. Other forms of persuasion include trying to develop some particular form of argument from authority – the authors are experienced lecturers and tutors, and their books sometimes contain all sorts of enthusiastic reviews from users. But this can contradict the very independence that university students are supposed to develop, even if the appeal to authority works. The only other area that might be seen as addressing motivation is the claim that pursuing conventional study skills will deliver mastery of the subject, or, more crudely, a good degree at the end. We find that this claim also is facing diminishing appeal among students. Many are only too aware that a fully instrumental or strategic approach can also produce good grades.

There is a lot of information around these days about how to study at university, and, for that matter, a lot of information offered to tutors about how to teach effectively. However, the strange thing about this material is that it is not based on any particularly deep understanding of students, what they want from a university, and how they communicate and study already. The conventional material features one-way and one-sided communication, and its aim is to explain the main characteristics of universities and academic subjects to students. We believe it is time that an approach was developed that attempted to explain some of the characteristics of modern students to people who work in universities.

This is an ambitious task, and it would be nice to be able to point to an extensive body of research and literature that has been undertaken already. There are some excellent studies of students, and a few critical studies of universities, and we refer to them, but there is still much to be done. We have drawn upon our own personal experience, both as students from rather unconventional background ourselves, and as people who have been attempting to establish two-way communications with students for some years.

We are not claiming that our experience is typical, but we have met students who have approached their university studies with a very interesting mixture of anxiety and reluctance. Our intention is to understand and not immediately condemn this sort of approach. We want to understand it in order to communicate more effectively, even if this means being critical about some of the more established practices in university teaching. The alternative seems to be to prolong non-communication, and we have seen rather a lot of this in universities as it is – lecturers desperately trying to engage students and pass on their enthusiasm for academic subjects; lecturers who have become disillusioned and are now simply teaching their subjects mechanically or giving up and trying merely to entertain; students who are bored, unhappy and disengaged; students who are cynical about their whole university experience and who are quite prepared to bend the rules and even cheat as a result.

Given the large amounts of state finance flowing into the sector, shouldn't universities be producing more students who find university pleasurable, challenging and stimulating? There is quite a bit of comment suggesting what might be wrong with modern students, but is there anything wrong with modern universities as well? It is not that long ago that universities were catering primarily for students who had pursued standard A-level courses in selective grammar schools or public schools. It would be wrong to think of even these students as exclusively middle class, since a famous study (Halsey et al. 1980) pointed out that a third of university entrants in the post-war period came from working-class backgrounds originally. Gender barriers were high, however. Nevertheless, there was a certain continuity between academic study in schools, especially in post-compulsory 'sixth forms' as they were then called, and academic study at universities.

What about the modern era of much expanded higher education? There is still a substantial group of recruits from grammar and public schools, of course, but now there are students from quite different backgrounds as well.

One group consists of relatively young people who have not attended grammar or public school, and who may not have taken A-level qualifications. Alternative qualifications are now more and more common as well, including new vocational qualifications of various types and levels. Although there is still some choice in the system, there is more of a vocational emphasis in these award-bearing courses, and a correspondingly smaller emphasis on the classic academic skills. This may be a good thing, of course, but it is easy to see that such courses might lead to some problems of adjustment encountered by those going on to study the academic curricula valued by conventional universities.

Many young people come to university without particular enthusiasm for conventional academic subjects either. A recent discussion at a conference in 2006 suggested that 'student' is now predominantly a 'leisure identity'. We are not blaming students, or wishing to rant about lower standards or the moral laxity of youth, but it is important to point out any changes. Otherwise, we might find ourselves in the position of many lecturers of our acquaintance who simply assume that students will be as enthusiastic as they are about their subject, talk to them accordingly, and then get disillusioned when they realize that enthusiasm is not shared to the same extent. In our view, the point is to understand that enthusiasm may now have to be cultivated and developed and can no longer simply be assumed. At the same time, we are not suggesting that young people will never develop an enthusiasm for academic subjects, and certainly not that they are incapable of grasping academic work and should be 'warehoused' or entertained instead.

Unfortunately, this is often a view embraced by young students themselves. Many of them seem to experience a mixture of guilt and anxiety about their university attendance. They describe themselves as 'not really very academic', and apologize for their inability to understand academic argument. Sometimes the guilt and anxiety produce resentment and even hostility towards lecturers or towards other students who do seem to be adjusting more readily. There is a strong temptation to disengage from the academic activities of university and to spend time doing something much more immediately interesting and rewarding instead – enjoying a full social life, playing sport, or even spending lots of time keeping contact with reassuringly 'normal' life outside the university.

It is also the case that such students must have developed some academic skill to get sufficient qualifications in the first place. Here, however, a second layer of guilt and anxiety is sometimes revealed. Students can feel that their qualifications have been obtained under false pretences. They have been coached by their school or college tutors. They have been helped by their parents with course work. They have bent the rules in various ways, including finding material on the Web and using it to make their own work look more impressive. Even those who have not gone that far can feel that they have been pretending: they have scrambled together work at the last minute, and they have incorporated material which have never really understood or learned. They are afraid they will be found out at university. Obviously, they cannot really discuss this sort of guilt and anxiety with their tutors, because they are afraid their tutors will start preaching at them, condemning them, or suspecting them. Again, avoiding the threat of exposure by disengaging from academic work and by avoiding genuine communication with their tutors seems the only alternative.

'Mature' students are another group with similar problems. It is worth pointing out that about one-third of students in the UK currently are 'mature' students. Some of them will have taken conventional qualifications at a further education college. Others will have taken special access courses to give them the equivalent. Many mature students will be attending their local universities or colleges, and many of them will have families. The students may well be more established financially, but often will have left full-time paid employment to enter the university and face short-term adjustments.

There may be special features which apply to mature students. They may want to gain a university degree to get a better job, but that is not the only source of motivation. They may have more 'personal' motives too. They may want to overcome some perceived lack of education in their lives as well, possibly because they felt they left school too early, or that they have never properly developed their talents, or that they feel that family life is 'making their brains rust'. They might be seeking some personal change in their lives as well – changes of partners and domestic circumstances are relatively common.

They will also often display a sense that they have made considerable sacrifices to get to university. They sometimes feel acutely that they have asked their family to make sacrifices too. They may have reduced the family income by giving up a job. They may have asked their partners to take on more of the work of running the household. They may feel guilty about spending less time with their partners or children. Given this sort of pressure, they may feel they have to do particularly well at university, not to waste their time, to try to read everything on the booklist and to attend all the lectures and seminars, and to get a first-class degree. They are 'overmotivated' (Hopper and Osborn, 1975): as we all know, excessive motivation can itself lead to underperformance.

It has been impossible to describe these groups without using terms that might imply that we disapprove of them, or see them as offering nothing but problems. That is certainly not our intention. We want to understand the situation that students like this find themselves in. It is very easy to blame poor attendance among younger students on some lack of discipline. It is easy to see married female students as people who demand too much time of us, and who can never attend a seminar late in the afternoon because they are too disorganized to arrange proper childcare. Nor are we saying that students are always blameless. Our intention is to understand first before leaping to any conclusions about blame or responsibility.

The intention to understand should also be pointed in the other direction. It is very often the case in our experience that students do not understand where lecturers are coming from, or what the point of a university education might be. As before, the absence of understanding leaves room for simple and often stereotyped judgements. Lecturers are hopelessly 'other-worldly', shy boffins only happy when they are in the library, completely unaware of the realities of having to work or run a family. Only rather strange and inadequate people would want to read academic work for pleasure, this stereotype insists. We may have to make special efforts ourselves to weaken this stereotype (without trying to be 'down with the kids', of course).

The practices of a university are often equally misunderstood as well. A lecture can look like an occasion where someone just talks about something because they have been overcome by a particular enthusiasm. Seminars can look like the sort of rather contrived polite social chat with authority figures, or as terrifying interrogations aimed at catching people out. University teaching can look like preaching, especially if it is about matters such as social inequality.

We have certainly met students who are really rather surprised by the idea that a lecture can be actually designed to try to teach somebody something, or get them to think about something. The craft aspects of lecturing, where material is chosen deliberately, and arguments assembled carefully, are all too easily disguised under a casual and sometimes even naïve presentation style. We have met students who do not take notes in lectures because they do not see that there is any connection at all with assignments that have to be written. Attending a lecture seems a bit like attending a compulsory sermon which delivers a sense that duty has been done, but can be conveniently forgotten as soon as one leaves. It can be equally surprising to discover that lecturers are not necessarily personally enthusiastic about a topic, nor personally committed to a particular approach. Critical analysis need not express personal feelings either, and this extends to the critical remarks that are sometimes made on student essays. Criticism from fellow-students may not always be personal. People may disagree quite vigorously about particular topics and yet still have high personal regard for each other.

As some of the literature suggests, the whole enterprise of seeing education as a matter of developing 'skills' simply sidelines these important issues. Taylor (2005) identifies a strong underlying moral discourse in Australian discussions aimed at correcting the perceived absence of a work ethic among the young. Payne (2000) argues that the debate about skills in the UK is probably driven, ironically, by the realization that fewer skills are actually required by employers. Halliday (2000) suggests that getting employers to predict employable skills in any specific sense has been abandoned, leading to a general plea for 'flexibility', but that such a quality is probably not a 'skill' in the usual sense: to call it one is to blur quite different competencies and thus risk unintended consequences (he has in mind the specific argument that 'critical thinking' is a core transferable skill). Finally, there is a substantial literature on the occupational strategies of semi-professions, such as teaching, which suggests that 'skill' is really a political term anyway, used to gain market advantages, rather than any agreed abstract quality of the actual work – see Lawn and Ozga, in Ozga (1988).

Many of these points come together in the recent study by Williams et al. (2006), based on research undertaken on the actual selection processes used by British employers (in elite occupations). Briefly, the emphasis on skills and competencies, even when expressed in psychometric testing at specialized Assessment Centres, is not actually that relevant. In the current 'graduate glut', possessing sufficient skills and competencies is common to most applicants, and other forms of selection and sifting are employed in practice. Unsurprisingly, these forms often depend on social and cultural judgements, above all the requirement that applicants 'fit in' and appear to have the same social, personal and cultural qualities as those in post already.

Turning to the educational context itself, providing conventional study skills so widely for undergraduates probably began in the UK as a supposed technical fix to solve the problems of expanding higher education to include unconventional students at minimum cost (Harris, 1994). It was accompanied by a corresponding move toward a 'new pedagogy' of activity and involvement, rather paradoxically based on clear outcomes or objectives and a new audit culture.

It is unlikely that the requirement to engage with academic argument in social sciences can ever be reduced to the application of a few basic skills or a few exercises designed to 'involve' students. Instead, such engagement probably resembles something more like a craft or apprenticeship, aimed at acquiring a number of tacit competencies sufficient to be able to deal with specific material. Acquiring those depends on successful social and cultural rapprochement with the destabilizing tendencies of work in social science. It is only that sort of engagement that can bring a real pleasure of feeling confident at handling the material, a sense of adventure as new concepts and ways of thinking are encountered, an acceptable balance of risk and security, which delivers both some of the pleasures of risk, and a feeling that some personal development has taken place.

The approach we find useful is developing in another area of expertise, one which seems quite separate from the usual work on study skills. This work addresses matters raised by considering widening access, student drop-out (and sometimes 'adding value'). Studies of the problems faced by 'unconventional' students tend to point precisely to the sorts of issues we think are deeply connected to study skills in the usual sense. Such students face social and cultural problems in entering institutions that are still dominated by the residues of an elite culture. Merrill (2001: 7), for example, argues in terms similar to our own that 'Adult students must learn to present the self in lectures and seminars, and quickly learn the student role.' We know best the work rediscovering the classic sociological concerns with social class, 'race' and gender and how these continue to affect students arriving at university. Archer et al. (2001), Plummer (2000) or Reay (2002) offer some powerful analyses which explore the important social dimensions of debates about participation. To make an old point again that once was so well known, merely granting access to students without either changing the organizational culture or at least warning those students of the cultural and social challenges they will face, as well as the intellectual ones, will lead to high levels of drop-out, eventual disillusionment and reduced uptake.

Having sketched out some of the background, we hope that the focus of this book might be seen as making more sense. We want to confine it to university students taking social science courses, for example, rather than claiming that there are some universal skills independent of level or academic subject. We want to address a wide audience, but we have tried to address two categories of undergraduate students in particular – younger students from 'unconventional' social backgrounds and mature students returning to study.

These are the classic 'problem' groups addressed explicitly or implicitly in conventional study skills materials, but our view is that they need to be addressed rather differently. For one thing, their experience and interests need to be discussed with respect. It is simply no good condemning on moralistic grounds their apparent marginality, nor decrying instrumental interests in getting a good degree which leads to a suitable job – as Plummer (2000) points out, getting a good degree is often the only way that such students could possibly justify the sacrifices they have to make to themselves and their families. They need to be understood, and we summarize some academic research on matters such as the effects of social class backgrounds on confidence – Norman and Hyland (2003) point to the crucial role played by cultural or 'dispositional' factors here.

We even want to resist the strong pressures towards joining the moral panic over plagiarism, by trying to understand the factors that lead to it. We have no illusions about plagiarists, but nor do we want to thrust them for ever from the Academy, as moral outsiders. Often, however, academics cannot summon sufficient objectivity in this matter. The moral agenda takes over, and the need for exemplary punishment overrides all other considerations. We have even found ourselves accused of supporting plagiarism by not criticizing it with the same fervour. In fact, we are simply insisting that strong condemnation alone will not solve the problem and that some other way to tackle it should be investigated. One alternative might involve a policy of 'informed choice', for example, as in some strategies to regulate other illegal activities such as drug-taking, where students are fully apprised of the risks and invited to reconsider the best course forward for themselves. Understanding the circumstances which can lead to a temptation to plagiarize is also important in our view.

This stance continues in our discussion of matters such as the use of electronic materials as well: colleagues may wish the Web had never been invented, but we want to work towards an educationally effective way of using it, while withholding personal aesthetic judgements.

What we want to offer student readers in addition is some explanation of how we think universities operate. We cannot just assume that the way we do things is natural or simply 'good', and expect people to adjust to our ways or face the consequences of social rejection and personal failure. We encourage students to adopt an attitude of ethnographic distance towards the requirements of their lecturers and of their educational programmes, and we attempt some self-reflection to guide them. We do not expect students to embrace the values that we are describing, but it is important to try and explain them, if only to break some of the expectations and impressions that unconventional students bring with them when they enter the Academy.

We see this kind of work as operating in two directions. First, we hope to explain to students that universities are not as bad as they might think, not as stuffy and 'serious', not as other-worldly. The attempt is to 'normalize' the experience, to see the university as an organization with familiar dynamics of compromise, idealism, micropolitics, internal and external constraints. The second ambition takes what might seem to be the opposite view that university life is actually rather special and has some unusual conventions, which are probably rather unlike those of school or work. Students are encouraged to understand those conventions, in their full combination of strangeness and familiarity.

This provides another match with the material on widening access, associated with arguments in the professional literature that, for example, assessment criteria must be made far more transparent, for staff and students (see Rust et al., 2003). There seems to be no point in trying to maintain a secret garden to nourish our ineffable skills: a modern sceptical student audience is more likely to be impressed by an open discussion of professional dilemmas and new procedures and processes designed to solve them.

The effects of these twin efforts should be to encourage a broader but more complex understanding of university life. We happen to think it is a reasonably valid one, based not only on our own limited experience, but on the published views of others. We suggest that this complex understanding is required for adequate motivation and successful social action on the part of students.

Certainly, the alternatives seem unattractive. Withdrawal, of a temporary or permanent kind, seems likely to grow, including a possible middle-class disillusionment. A narrow instrumentalism is also growing, where students reduce their efforts to merely coping with the immediate demands of the assessment system, and see no value in university life as such, except in terms of gaining a qualification for the job market, the precise value of which can vary alarmingly anyway. Instrumental attachments are only weak attachments. University academics should look to their own interests here: there may be future developments where instrumental students can be accommodated by 'distance' systems, possibly at lower cost, or where marketable qualifications are offered by companies themselves.

We hope that colleagues will therefore see the need to rethink the issues in terms of a wider agenda, not only in an attempt to deliver full value to students, including the values of leisurely thought and speculation, but in a bid to retain a role for the conventional university sector itself.

References

Aldridge, S. (2004) 'Life chances and social mobility: an overview of the evidence', [online] http://www.strategy.gov.uk/downloads/files/lifechances_socialmobility.pdf.

Allen, T. et al. (no date) 'The taxonomy of educational objectives', [online] www.humboldt.edu/~tha1/bloomtax.html (accessed 24 July 2005).

Anderson, C.A. and Dill, K.E. (2000) 'Video games and aggressive thoughts, feelings and behaviour in the laboratory and in life', *Journal of Personality and Social Psychology*, 87: 722–90.

Archer, L., Pratt, S. and Phillips, D. (2001) 'Working-class men's constructions of masculinity and negotiations of (non) participation in higher education', *Gender and Education*, 13(4): 431–49.

Argyrous, G. (1997) *Statistics for Social Research*. Basingstoke: Macmillan.

Arksey, H. (1992) *How to Get a First Class Degree*. Lancaster: Lancaster Unit for Innovation in Higher Education, School of Independent Studies, Lancaster University.

Arksey, H. and Harris, D. (2005) 'The neutralisation of risk by students in higher education', [online] http://www.arasite.org/bsa05.html.

Arksey, H. and Knight, P. (1999) *Interviewing for Social Scientists*. London: Sage Publications.

Arksey, H., Marchant, I. and Simmill, C. (1994) *Juggling for a Degree: Mature Students' Experience of University Life*. Lancaster: Lancaster Unit for Innovation in Higher Education, Lancaster University.

Arksey, H., Snape, C. and Watt, I. (in press) 'Roles and expectations of a primary care team', *Journal of Interprofessional Care*.

Attwood, F. (2002) 'A very British carnival: women, sex and transgression in *Fiesta* magazine', *European Journal of Cultural Studies*, 5(1): 91–105.

Baker, N. (no date) 'Foxhunting in the UK', [online] http://www.arasite.org/guests.html (accessed 18 September 2005).

Barker, E. (1984) *The Making of a Moonie: Brainwashing or Choice?* New York: Basil Blackwell.

Becher, T. (1989) *Academic Tribes and their Territories*. Buckingham: Society for Research Into Higher Education and Open University Press.

Becker, H., Geer, B. and Hughes, E. ([1968]1995) *Making the Grade: The Academic Side of College Life*, with a new introduction by Howard S. Becker. London: Transaction Publishers.

Belenky, M., Clinchy, B., Goldberger, N. and Tarule, J. (1986) *Women's Ways of Knowing: The Development of Self, Voice, and Mind*. New York: Basic Books.

Bonnett, A. (2001) *How to Argue: A Students' Guide*. London: Pearson Education.

Bourdieu, P. (1984) *Distinction: A Social Critique of the Judgement of Taste*. London: Routledge and Kegan Paul.

Bourdieu, P. (1988) *Homo Academicus*, trans. P. Collier. Oxford: Polity Press.

Bourdieu, P. (2000) 'Making the economic habitus: Algerian workers revisited', *Ethnography*, 1(1): 17–41.

Boyer Commission (1998) 'On educating undergraduates in the research university', [online] http://naples.cc.sunysb.edu/Pres/boyer.nsf/.

Braverman, H. (1974) *Labor and Monopoly Capital: The Degradation of Work in the Twentieth Century*. New York: Monthly Review Press.

Brennan, J. and Jary, D. (2004) 'What is really learned at university? The SOMUL Project: conceptualisation and design', [online] http://www.tlrp.org.dspace/handle/123456789/102

British Sociological Association (2002) *Statement of Ethical Practice for the British Sociological Association*, [online] http://www.britsoc.co.uk/user_doc/Statement %20of%20Ethical%20 Practice.pdf (accessed 6 May 2006).

Burns, T. and Sinfield, S. (2003) *Essential Study Skills: The Complete Guide to Success @ University*. London: Sage.

Careers Research and Advisory Centre (CRAC) (2003) *Hobsons Directory 2004*. London: Careers Research and Advisory Centre.

Casey, N., Sutton, P., Casey, B., Dawson, C. and Warren, D. (2002) 'Comparing seminars and workshops: student views on learning in Sociology', [online] http://www.c-sap.bham.ac.uk/resources/project_reports/admin/extras/16_S_ 01.pdf.

Cavendish, R. (1982) *Women on the Line*. London: Routledge.

Chryssafidou, E. (2000) 'DIALECTIC: enhancing essay-writing skills with computer-supported formulation of argumentation', [online] http://citeseer.ist.psu.edu/409053.html.

Cioffi, F. (2005) 'Argumentation in a culture of discord', *Chronicle of Higher Education*, 51(37): 86–9.

Clegg, F. (1983) *Simple Statistics: A Course Book for the Social Sciences*. Cambridge: Cambridge University Press.

Collier, J. (1945) 'United States Indian administration of a laboratory of ethnic relations', *Social Research*, 12: 275–86.

Critcher, C. (2000) '"Still raving": social reaction to Ecstasy', *Leisure Studies*, 19: 145–62.

Crow, G. (2005) *The Art of Sociological Argument*. London: Palgrave Macmillan.

Denscombe, M. (2003) *The Good Research Guide for Small-Scale Social Research Projects*, 2nd edn. Buckingham: Open University Press.

Diamond, I. and Jefferies, L. (2001) *Beginning Statistics: An Introduction for Social Scientists*. London: Sage.

Douglas, J. (1967) *The Home and the School: A Study of Ability and Attainment in the Primary School.* St Albans: Panther Books Ltd.

Du Gay, P., Hall, S., James, L., Mackay, H. and Negus, K. (1997) *Doing Cultural Studies: The Story of the Sony Walkman.* London: Sage Publications in association with the Open University Press.

Dunleavy, P. (1986) *Studying for a Degree in the Humanities and Social Sciences.* London: The Macmillan Press Ltd.

Elling, A., De Knop, P. and Knoppers, A. (2003) 'Gay/lesbian sport clubs and events: places of homo-social bonding and cultural resistance?', *International Review for the Sociology of Sport*, 38(4): 441–56.

Entwistle, N. (2000) 'Promoting deep learning through teaching and assessment: conceptual frameworks and educational contexts', [online] http://www.ed.ac.uk/etl/docs/entwistle2000.pdf.

Fink, A. (2005) *Conducting Research Literature Reviews: From the Internet to Paper*, 2nd edn. London: Sage.

Franklyn-Stoakes, A. and Newstead, S. (1995) 'Undergraduate cheating: who does what and why?', *Studies in Higher Education*, 20(2): 159–72.

Gibbs, G. (1998) *Practice Guide 2 Lecturing.* Oxford: Alden Group.

Glaser, B.G. and Strauss, A.L. (1967) *The Discovery of Grounded Theory: Strategies for Qualitative Research.* New York: Aldine de Gruyter.

Goffman, E. (1963) *Stigma.* London: Penguin.

Goffman, E. (1969) *The Presentation of Self in Everyday Life.* London: Penguin.

Goffman, E. (1975) *Frame Analysis.* London: Penguin.

Goldman, R. and Papson, S. (1998) *Nike Culture.* London: Sage Publications.

Goldthorpe, J., Llewellyn, C. and Payne, C. (1980) *Social Mobility and Class Structure in Modern Britain.* Oxford: Clarendon Press.

Grogan, S. and Richards, H. (2002) 'Body image: focus groups with boys and men', *Men and Masculinities*, 4(3): 219–32.

Halliday, J. (2000) 'Critical thinking and the academic vocational divide', *The Curriculum Journal*, 11(2): 159–75.

Halsey, A., Heath, A., and Ridge, J. (1980) *Origins and Destinations Family Class and Education in Modern Britain.* Oxford: Clarendon Press.

Hammersley, M. and Woods, P. (eds) (1976) *The Process of Schooling: A Sociological Reader.* London: Routledge and Kegan Paul.

Hampson, L. (1994) *How's Your Dissertation Going?* Lancaster: School of Independent Studies, Lancaster University.

Harris, D. (1994) '"Active learning" and "study skills", the return of the technical fix?', in T. Evans and D. Murphy (eds), *Research in Distance Education* 3. Geelong: Deakin University Press.

Harris, D. (2005) 'Critical notes on deep and surface approaches', [online] http://www.arasite.org/critdeepsurf.htm (accessed 5 August 2005).

Hart, C. (2001) *Doing a Literature Search: A Comprehensive Guide for the Social Sciences.* London: Sage.

Harvey, L., Locke, W. and Money, A. (2002) *Enhancing Employability, Recognising Diversity: Making Links Between Higher Education and the World of Work.* Manchester: Careers Service Unit (CSU).

Hawkins, P. and the Graduates into Employment Unit (GIEU) (1999) *The Art of Building Windmills: Career Tactics for the 21st Century,* [online] http://www.gieu.co.uk/Windmills_programme/intro.asp#graduates.

Henderson, E. and Nathenson, M. (eds) (1984) *Independent Learning in Higher Education.* Englewood Cliffs, NJ: Educational Technology Publications Inc.

Higher Education Quality Council (1995) 'What are graduates? Clarifying the attributes of "graduateness"', [online] http://www.city.londonmet.ac.uk/deliberations/graduates/starter.html.

Hirsch, L., Saeedi, M., Corillon, J. and Litosseliti, L. (2004) 'A structured dialogue tool for argumentative learning', *Journal of Computer Assisted Learning,* 20: 72–80.

Hopper, E. and Osborn, M. (1975) *Adult Students: Education, Selection, and Social Control.* London: Frances Pinter Ltd.

Humphreys, L. (1970) *Tearoom Trade: A Study of Homosexual Encounters in Public Places.* London: Gerald Duckworth.

Jackson, M. (2001) 'Meritocracy, education and occupational attainment: what do employers really see as merit?', [online] http://www.sociology.ox.ac.uk/swps/2001-03.html.

Jary, D. and Lebeau, Y. (2006) 'What students say they learn; the personal and subject identities of sociology students', paper presented at the BSA Annual Conference, Harrogate, April 2006.

Keller, S. (no date) [online] http://www.arasite.org/guests.html (accessed 18 September 2005).

Knight, P. and Yorke, M. (2003) *Assessment, Learning and Employability.* Maidenhead: Society for Research into Higher Education and Open University Press.

Knight, P. and Yorke, M. (2004) *Learning, Curriculum and Employability in Higher Education.* London: Routledge Falmer.

Levin, P. (2004) 'Beat the witch-hunt! Peter Levin's guide to avoiding and rebutting accusations of plagiarism, for conscientious students', [online] http://www.study-skills.net/plagiarism.pdf (accessed 10 December 2004).

Marsh, C. (1988) *Exploring Data: An Introduction to Data Analysis for Social Scientists.* Cambridge: Polity Press.

Marton, F., Hounsell, D. and Entwistle, N. (1984). *The Experience of Learning.* Edinburgh: Scottish Academic Press.

Maykut, P. and Morehouse, R. (2001) *Beginning Qualitative Research: A Philosophical and Practical Guide.* London: Routledge Falmer.

McIlroy, D. (2003) *Studying @ University.* London: Sage Publications.

Merrill, B. (2001) 'Learning and teaching in Universities; perspectives from adult students and lecturers', *Teaching in Higher Education,* 6(1): 5–13.

Miles, M.B. and Huberman, A.M. (1994) *Qualitative Data Analysis,* 2nd edn. London: Sage.

Milgram, S. (1974) *Obedience to Authority: An Experimental View.* New York: Harper and Row.

Morgan, A. (1993) *Improving Your Students' Learning: Reflections on the Experience of Study.* London: Kogan Page.

Norman, M. and Hyland, T. (2003) 'The role of confidence in lifelong learning', *Educational Studies*, 29(2/3): 261–72.

Northedge, A. (1990) *The Good Study Guide.* Milton Keynes: Open University Press.

Norton, L., Tilley, A., Newstead, S. and Franklyn-Stoakes, A. (2001) 'The pressures of assessment in undergraduate courses and their effect on student behaviours', *Assessment and Evaluation in Higher Education*, 26(3): 269–84.

Nussbaum, N. (2002) 'Scaffolding argumentation in the social studies classroom', *The Social Studies*, March–April: 79–83.

Oliver, P. (2004) *Writing Your Thesis.* London: Sage.

Online Writing Lab (Purdue University) (no date) [online] http://owl.english. purdue.edu/handouts/grammar/.

Open University (no date) 'Study strategies', [online] http://www.open.ac.uk/study-strategies/index.htm.

OU help with writing http://www.open.ac.uk/study-strategies/english/pages/further_7.asp.

Ozga, J. (ed.) (1988) *Schoolwork. Approaches to the Labour Process of Teaching.* Milton Keynes: The Open University Press.

Payne, J. (2000) 'The unbearable lightness of skill: the changing meaning of skill in UK policy discourse and some implications for education and training', *Journal of Educational Policy*, 15(3): 353–69.

Performance and Innovation Unit (2002) 'Social capital a discussion paper', [online] http://www.number-10.gov.uk/su/social%20capital/socialcapital.pdf.

Plummer, G. (2000) *Failing Working-class Girls.* London: Trentham Books Ltd.

Putnam, R. (2000) *Bowling Alone: The Collapse and Revival of American Community.* New York: Simon and Schuster.

Ramsden, P. (1992) *Learning to Teach in Higher Education.* London: Routledge.

Rapaport, W. (2004) 'William Perry's scheme of intellectual and ethical development', [online] http://www.cs.buffalo.edu/~rapaport/perry.positions.html (accessed 24 July 2005).

Reay, D. (2002) 'Class, authenticity and the transition to higher education for mature students', *The Sociological Review*, 50(3): 398–418.

Ritchie, J. and Lewis, J. (eds) (2003) *Qualitative Research Practice: A Guide for Social Science Students and Researchers.* London: Sage.

Robson, C. (2002) *Real World Research*, 2nd edn. Oxford: Blackwell Publishers.

Rose, D. and Sullivan, O. (1996) *Introducing Data Analysis for Social Scientists.* Buckingham: Open University Press.

Rowntree, D. (1981) *Statistics Without Tears: A Primer for Non-Mathematicians.* Harmondsworth: Penguin.

Rust, C., Price, M. and O'Donovan, B. (2003) 'Improving students' learning by developing their understanding of assessment criteria and processes', *Assessment and Evaluation in Higher Education*, 28(2): 147–64.

Schutz, A. (1971) *Collected Papers I. The Problem of Social Reality.* The Hague: Martinus Nijhoff.

Skinner, C. (2005) *Guide to Rules on Referencing: Quick Guide to Improving Practice.* York: Department of Social Policy and Social Work, University of York.

Social Research Association (2003) *Ethical Guidelines*, [online] http://www.thesra.org.uk/documents/pdfs/ethics03.pdf (accessed 6 May 2006).

Stoller, P. (2002) 'Crossroads: tracing African paths on New York City streets', *Ethnography*, 3(1): 35–62.

Strauss, A. and Corbin, J. (eds) (1997) *Grounded Theory in Practice.* Thousand Oaks, CA: Sage.

Strauss, A. and Corbin, J. (1998) *Basics of Qualitative Research: Techniques and Procedures for Developing Grounded Theory.* Thousand Oaks, CA: Sage.

Tackey, N. and Perryman, S. (1999) 'Graduates mean business, IES Report 357 (summary)', [online] http://www.employment-studies.co.uk/summary/summary.php?id=357.

Tall, G. (no date) 'Observation', [online] http://www.edu.bham.ac.uk/edrt06/observation.htm (accessed 18 September 2005).

Taylor, A. (2005) 'What employers look for: the skills debate and the fit with youth perceptions', *Journal of Education and Work*, 18(2): 210–18.

Taylor, E., Morgan, A. and Gibbs, G. (1981) 'Students' understandings of the concept of social class' Study Methods Group Report 10, unpublished, Open University.

The World Bank Group (no date) 'Social capital for development', [online] http://www1.worldbank.org/prem/poverty/scapital/index.htm.

Thinking Writing (2005a) [online] http://www.thinkingwriting.qmul.ac.uk/.

Thinking Writing (2005b) Exercise Using Short Writing Tasks, [online] http://www.thinkingwriting.qmul.ac.uk/shortwrite2.htm.

Tolmie, P. (2000) *How I Got My First Class Degree*, 3rd edn. Lancaster: School of Independent Studies, Lancaster University.

Tracy, E. (2002) *The Student's Guide to Exam Success.* Buckingham: The Open University Press.

Universities.net (no date) [online] http://www.universitiesnet.com/careers.htm.

University of Cambridge Education Section (2005) [online] http://www.admin.cam.ac.uk/offices/education/skills/.

University of Minnesota Duluth (2002) 'Transferable skills survey', [online] http://www.d.umn.edu/student/loon/car/self/career_transfer_survey.html.

University of Toronto (no date) 'Advice on academic writing', [online] http://www.utoronto.ca/writing/advise.html.

Wacquant, L. (1995) 'Pugs at work: bodily capital and bodily labour among professional boxers', *Body and Society*, 1(1): 65–93.

Warde, A. (1997) *Consumption, Food and Taste: Culinary Antinomies and Commodity Culture.* London: Sage.

Williams, D., Brown, P. and Hesketh, A. (2006) *How to Get the Best Graduate Job: Insider Strategies for Success in the Graduate Job Market.* London: Pearson Education Limited.

Williams, N. (2004) *How to Get a 2:1 in Media, Communication + Cultural Studies*. London: Sage.

Willis, P. (1977) *Learning to Labour: Why Working Class Kids get Working Class Jobs*. Famborough: Saxon House.

Willis, P. and Trondman, M. (2000) 'Manifesto for *Ethnography*', *Ethnography*, 1(1): 5–16.

Wisdom, J. (1996) 'What is a graduate? A consultation exercise with students', [online] http:www.city.londonmet.ac.uk/deliberations/graduates/consult.html.

Wolcott, H. (1999) *Ethnography as a Way of Seeing*. London: Sage.

Yorke, M. (2000) 'The quality of the student experience: what can institutions learn from data relating to non-completion?', *Quality in Higher Education*, 6(1): 61–75.

Young, J. (1971) *The Drugtakers: The Social Meaning of Drug Abuse*. London: McGibbon and Kee.

Young, M. (ed.) (1971) *New Directions for the Sociology of Education*. London: Collier Macmillan.

Index